Praise for C. James Jensen's
Expand the Power of Your Subconscious Mind

"Success is always an inside job. When you unlock the keys to the subconscious, you exponentially expand the powers of your mind. The result? The inner creates the outer, so that success becomes your default. A merging of wisdom from two leaders, this book offers invaluable tools for anyone who seeks to master their mind—and their destiny."

—**Sara Wiseman**, author of *Messages from the Divine* and *The Intuitive Path*

"Drawing upon knowledge from both the wisdom traditions and contemporary research, *Expand the Power of Your Subconscious Mind* shows us ways to advance the exploration of our soul's further reaches. Every one of us can participate in this adventure, on the greatest of all human frontiers."

—**Michael Murphy**, founder of the Esalen Institute and author of *The Future of the Body*

"An excellent take on how the rational mind can get in our way and how we can train the subconscious mind to work for us rather than against us. C. James Jensen's *Expand the Power of Your Subconscious Mind* is filled with living, breathing wisdom that we can infuse into every part of our lives to create more success, more love, more peace, and more joy."

—**John J. Murphy**, author of *Miracle Minded Manager*

"The root cause of human suffering is often thought to lie outside us. And yet, as Murphy and Jensen point out, it really lies within our subconscious mind. So too, we are so clearly reminded, lies the source of great joy and possibility. This book is essential reading for anyone who wants to wake up to their fullest capacities. As the authors note, consciousness 'brings guidance, freedom, and peace of mind.' The adventure of our unfolding potentials awaits us all."

—**Marilyn Mandala Schlitz, PhD**, former president/CEO,
Institute of Noetic Sciences

"This book is uniquely written and formatted in such a way that one could read this once and begin to take charge of one's life in ways to manifest unbelievable positive improvements. I know it will enhance your life as it already has mine."

—**Lyle Anderson**, chairman,
The Lyle Anderson Companies, LLC

"The greatest compliment I can give this book is that I want each of my kids to read it and internalize the concepts presented. I know what a powerful impact it can have if we take its principles and apply them to how we live our lives."

—**Mark Geist**, former CEO,
Montgomery Asset Management

"I was first exposed to these teachings when I was only nineteen. I had attended the same course, with the same teacher where Jim Jensen first learned this material. I'm amazed at Jim's ability to take a week's worth of learnings, countless years of implementation and refine all of it into this very powerful book."

—**Mark Dickison**, founder, Trifilm Productions, Inc.

"The greatest frontier is not the skies or the ocean. It is understanding the power of our miraculous selves. Herein is the primer to get started. Jensen's book is perfect for the action-oriented twenty-first century. The central themes of Dr. Murphy's landmark work set the stage. Excerpts from many of the finest thinkers of the last generation clarify and reinforce the salient points. Then the closer: Jim's specific steps of how to implement the most powerful principles of anyone's life. Get ready to be energized!"

—**Stan Freimuth**, retired chairman & CEO,
Ragen MacKenzie, Inc.

"Jim's outlook on life choices, business, and existence is far from traditional. It is inspiring. Bottom line, what I've learned from Jim is this: We all have a choice—fear and scarcity or love and abundance. When it comes down to it that is it. You have a choice, so do what's right."

—**breAnne O. Reeves**, consultant and coauthor of
The Nordstrom Way

"Sometimes a book comes along that offers the reader a life-changing opportunity. Murphy and Jensen have written one that does just that. I know from firsthand experience how you can improve your life by putting to work the principles and concepts contained in *Expand the Power of Your Subconscious Mind*. If you are going to read one book this year, make it this one."

—**Howard Behar**, president,
Starbucks Coffee International, retired

"*Expand the Power of Your Subconscious Mind* is permeated with words like *magic* and *miracles*. Such terms might seem quaint and out of place in the modern world, but as Jim Jensen's commentaries remind us, Joseph Murphy's classic book does not use these words lightly. There is a rapidly growing body of rigorous scientific evidence indicating that the mind can significantly influence matter, both within the body and beyond. The powers that Murphy describes might seem like miracles, but as science progresses we are slowly but surely unraveling its mysteries. Thus, this book is not a regression to a superstitious past, but a forecast of the future, where magic and miracles rest on sound scientific principles and are transformed into everyday marvels."

—**Dean Radin**, PhD, chief scientist, Institute of Noetic Sciences, and associated distinguished professor, California Institute of Integral Studies

"I have seldom read a book that so clearly leaves the reader to better understand the incredible relationship between the conscious and subconscious areas of the mind. I highly recommend it."

—**Jack Canfield**, coauthor of the *Chicken Soup for the Soul* series and a featured teacher in *The Secret*

EXPAND
the
POWER
of Your
SUBCONSCIOUS
MIND

DR. JOSEPH MURPHY

EXPAND
the
POWER
of Your
SUBCONSCIOUS
MIND

with commentary and teachings by
C. James Jensen
Foreword by Dr. Lee Pulos, PhD, ABPP

ATRIA PAPERBACK
New York London Toronto Sydney New Delhi

BEYOND WORDS
Portland, Oregon

ATRIA PAPERBACK
A Division of Simon & Schuster, Inc.
1230 Avenue of the Americas
New York, NY 10020

BEYOND WORDS
1750 S.W. Skyline Blvd, Suite 20
Portland, Oregon 97221-2543
503-531-8700 / 503-531-8773 fax
www.beyondword.com

Managing Editor: Lindsay S. Easterbrooks-Brown
Editor: Emily Han
Copyeditor: Jenefer Angell
Proofreader: Ashley Van Winkle
Interior design: Devon Smith

First Beyond Words/Atria Paperback edition September 2020

ATRIA PAPERBACK and colophon are trademarks of Simon & Schuster, Inc.
BEYOND WORDS PUBLISHING and colophon are registered trademarks of Beyond Words Publishing, Inc. Beyond Words is an imprint of Simon & Schuster, Inc.

For information about special discounts for bulk purchases, please contact Simon & Schuster Special Sales at 1-866-506-1949 or business@simonandschuster.com.

Manufactured in the United States of America

10 9 8 7 6 5 4 3 2

Library of Congress Cataloging-in-Publication Data

Names: Murphy, Joseph, 1898-1981, author. | Jensen, C. James, author of
  added commentary.
Title: Expand the power of your subconscious mind / Dr. Joseph Murphy ;
  with commentary and teachings by C. James Jensen ; foreword by Dr. Lee
  Pulos, PhD, ABPP.
Other titles: Power of your subconscious mind
Description: Hillsboro, Oregon : Beyond Words, 2020. | Includes
  bibliographical references.
Identifiers: LCCN 2019035669 (print) | LCCN 2019035670 (ebook) | ISBN
  9781582707181 (trade paperback) | ISBN 9781582707389 (ebook)
Subjects: LCSH: Mental discipline. | Subconsciousness.
Classification: LCC BF145 .M8 2020 (print) | LCC BF145 (ebook) | DDC
  154.2—dc23
LC record available at https://lccn.loc.gov/2019035669
LC ebook record available at https://lccn.loc.gov/2019035670

The corporate mission of Beyond Words Publishing, Inc.: *Inspire to Integrity*

This book is dedicated to my grandchildren, Maya, Tucker, Cole, and Reese, and to all the children of planet Earth. The future of our civilization rests in your hands. Only through the evolution of the consciousness of the human species can we fully live in a world of peace, love, and harmony.

We, collectively, do create our own reality.

CONTENTS

Part I: The Power of Your Subconscious Mind
Original, Unabridged Text by Dr. Joseph Murphy

Part II: Commentary and Teachings

by C. James Jensen

Foreword
by Dr. Lee Pulos

It is indeed an honor to be invited to write the foreword to *Expand the Power of Your Subconscious Mind*. These current and timely teachings from Jim Jensen—based on Dr. Joseph Murphy's work—vividly remind me of the visionary and psychological excitement I experienced when I read Murphy's original book over forty years ago.

This is not the same book I first read. Jim's Part 2: Commentary and Teachings bridges fifty-seven years of corporate and social evolution. He has also judiciously and wisely edited and reframed some of the concepts that were valid in 1963, redefining and upgrading them so they are consistent with current neuroscience, psychological theory, and research. However, the essence of Dr. Murphy's book has not changed: Our ego or conscious mind skims just the topmost surface of reality and awareness and focuses on the limited confines of our five senses. But the unrecognized and heroic portions of our psyche lie beneath the prosaic life.

The rational mind can be a barrier to the full use of our potential. It limits our capabilities with such a tight focus and has philosophically cut us off from the experimental theatre of our subconscious, the true source of our power. The older-growth forests of the mind contain the true potential—our intuition, our non-ordinary awareness, our dreams, our connection to the cosmic information field, our psychological, our spiritual landscapes, and, yes, our mysticism.

Most scientists today believe that mind somehow emerges from a mysterious but unprovable interaction of molecules in the brain. That matter creates mind. This leads to reductionistic, limiting explanations of who we are—a cosmic cynicism about human potential and our deeper beingness. But Joseph Murphy's brilliant insights—about the depth and richness of our many thresholds of intelligence and corridors of consciousness—have helped millions of men and women rediscover the deepest regions of our hearts and minds that we had forgotten. That we are much, much more than our rational minds.

Expand the Power of Your Subconscious Mind is a reminder of some of the oldest wisdom such as that of the Buddha, who said, "A man is the product of his thoughts." And from an even older tradition, the *Bhagavad Gita*, "Man is made by his belief—as he believes, so he is." Dr. Murphy himself most often explicitly examines this material through the lens of Christian scripture, though, like the dated social roles, the concepts transcend the religious and social dogma of any culture or era.

This is a book for every generation. An evolutionary adventure that can be comprehended and utilized by every age, from a twelve-year-old to his or her grandparents. It also follows and embraces one of Albert Einstein's favorite sayings, "Make everything as simple as possible—but not simpler."

I experienced great joy following the bold sweep of Joseph Murphy's and Jim Jensen's thoughts on the potential for creating miracles, awakening our deeper mind for physical and mental healing, overcoming limiting beliefs and fear-driven behavior, developing an inner sense for deserving, wealth consciousness, creating healing dreams, and overcoming roadblocks to success and leadership.

Jensen offers timely tools and lessons on how to reeducate and reprogram our subconscious to attain goals and to create and step into the most optimal, loving, successful, and healthiest possible future. And there's even more.

What resonates most for me is how our life is a printout of our beliefs. We create what we focus or concentrate on. Our life experiences then will follow our focus, beliefs, expectations, and intention. If we don't deal with our limiting beliefs, they will deal with us: in our health, work, relationships, financial prosperity, or other aspect of living. Fortunately, Jensen provides techniques to overcome the psychological antibodies we sometimes set up against ourselves that impede change and to help us develop self-esteem.

Of the thousands of patients I have seen over the years for a variety of issues, I estimate that at least 95 percent had an issue with self-esteem. Self-esteem is a sense of worthiness or unworthiness that influences the inner sense of deserving love, success, health, or prosperity. It is at the very root of every success or failure. It is the official and most important base of operations that determines what kind of experiences we attract into our lives. It is the hub of the wheel of life, containing and holding together the spokes necessary for creating and living our dreams easily, effortlessly, and without struggle.

This book describes various ways to access the three most important tools for manifestation, or giving voice to the subconscious.

Desire is the first tool for creating change. All change begins with desire: the purest of potential seeking manifestation or change. It is the fire in the belly of the beast. Plato recognized the importance of desire, which, as he said, "must drive the soul with a reigned-in craziness."

The second tool is expectation, which follows desire. Expectation awakens our slumbering giant, the subconscious, which then leads to our behavior becoming a self-fulfilling prophecy. Expectation is at the root of, and responsible for, all placebo responses in double-blind studies. Lowering expectations, of course, ensures you won't succeed.

You can use the third tool of manifestation, imagination, to create the visualizations and mental movies of your desired future successes. Imagination breathes life into your goals and supplies the mental energy for creating your most optimal and brilliant future.

This book offers a complete mental toolbox, and the implications of Murphy's and Jensen's insights are unlimited. They have taken wisdom of the ages and legitimized it with vocabulary that we can easily understand and embrace as we learn to release the past and become more than we ever thought possible. It connects us with the heroics of our strong inner self, the magic within that is yearning to find expression.

—**Lee Pulos, PhD**,
ABPP Clinical Psychologist,
author of *The Biology of Empowerment*
and *The Power of Visualization*

Introduction
by C. James Jenson

If you give a person a fish, you feed him for a day.
If you teach a person to fish, you feed him for life.

This book is all about the work of Dr. Joseph Murphy. I had the good fortune to be introduced to his profound teachings in my twenties, and I am happy to share with you some events that led to my serendipitous discovery of his book *The Power of Your Subconscious Mind.*

In my senior year of college, I started working for the worldwide publishing company Encyclopædia Britannica. I soon became one of their top salespeople, and when I was twenty-five, my wife and I were sent to Sydney, Australia, to be placed in charge of sales for all of Australia and New Zealand. Two years later, I was placed in charge of worldwide sales. That same month I was featured in the cover story of *Fortune* magazine entitled, "A Gallery of Business Wonders."

At that time, I was often asked, "To what do you attribute your success?" I had some stock answers—"I have very good work habits,"

"I have a lot of enthusiasm," "I am very positive," and so on—but nothing that would really benefit the person asking the question. Then I attended a four-day seminar entitled Omega, which was owned and taught by its founder, the late John Boyle, and for the first time I understood the principles of performance. It gave me a new vocabulary that let me describe in practical terms how to achieve success. Not only in one's work, but also in relationships, parenting, health, and all the essential elements of one's life. It was an incredibly profound experience. In fact, at the conclusion of the seminar, I went up to Mr. Boyle, affectionately poked him in the chest, and said, "Someday I am going to teach your seminars and someday I am going to own your company!" At the time, his only response was "Yeah, *right*," a look of pure disbelief on his face. But I decided to take what I had learned working at Omega and the subsequent companies where I became the CEO and president and incorporate everything into my own company. And fourteen years after attending my first seminar, I fulfilled my intention and acquired Omega from Mr. Boyle.

For eleven years, I was one of four instructors, and I also managed the business.

I often asked Mr. Boyle where he had learned all the Omega material, and his response was simply, "I have studied with Dr. Joseph Murphy." At that time of no personal computers or internet, I couldn't google Joseph Murphy. But as I gained fluency and understanding of the principles of Omega, I began to look beyond it, to every book and seminar I could experience, to help deepen my understanding of the subconscious and the power of our thoughts. Experiences that would always lead me back to the mysterious Dr. Murphy.

In 2005 one of my coworkers came into my office and handed me *The Power of Your Subconscious Mind* by Dr. Joseph Murphy, saying, "Jim, I heard you speak and I thought you might enjoy this book." I thought, could this be the very same Joseph Murphy?

In fact it was.

As I read the book, I realized that the content of the Omega seminar had come largely from this book, with Mr. Boyle brilliantly distilling Dr. Murphy's teachings into a four-day seminar format. Participants emerged with a tool kit that enabled them to bring about whatever life changes they desired.

During my own involvement with Omega, I personally witnessed hundreds, perhaps thousands, of people's transformational experiences after attending the four-day Omega seminar. The transformations were not limited to work, but helped with growth in relationships, parenting, teaching, coaching, personal health, and virtually any area of life.

● ● ●

One of the most personally rewarding things in introducing Dr. Murphy's work to others is observing how they apply what they have learned. I have seen countless examples where people in senior management positions purchase copies of Dr. Murphy's book and share it with their employees. I have had dozens of people reveal how Dr. Murphy's teachings have saved relationships and enhanced family involvement and participation.

The way we talk to ourselves constantly provides instructions to the subconscious, to ensure how we "behave," but these instructions may not align with what we desire. How many times have you heard people say things like this?

"I can never remember names."

"I always get nervous when speaking to large groups."

Or to their children:

"Why is your room always such a mess?"

"Why can't you do things right?"

Once we realize what we say to ourselves (positive or negative) affects employees, children, and others we love, we can begin to change that data, transforming it into the positive outcome we truly desire. Dr. Murphy provides these specific tools in the book you are about to read.

Why We Need the Power of Our Subconscious Mind

Although Dr. Murphy's writings are so full of treasures, if I had to accentuate one key lesson it would be discovering the incredible relationship between the conscious and subconscious areas of the mind: how to harness the incredible power of our own "self-talk."

These are not two different minds, but rather two spheres of our one mind. The conscious area is the part doing all the thinking. As you read these words, you are also talking to yourself about how you feel about what you are reading—along with what you are having for dinner tonight, and multiple other thoughts. This is self-talk.

Most people are unaware that we talk to ourselves all day long at a rate of 150 to 300 words a minute, or over fifty thousand thoughts a day. And what most of us have *not* learned is that our self-talk becomes instructions to our subconscious, which acts like a *servo-mechanism* (control system) carrying out the instructions given to it by the conscious area of the mind.

Most of us have been taught that our subconscious handles all of our bodily functions. It heals wounds, grows our hair and nails, digests our food, and so on. But most of us are unaware that the subconscious is continuously carrying out the instructions given to it by the conscious area of the mind with our own self-talk, 24/7. The subconscious is totally *nonjudgmental*. It will work just as hard to carry out negative instructions from your self-talk as it does to carry out positive instructions. Dr. Murphy's work teaches us to harness the incredible power of our own self-talk, and that what we say to others is not nearly as important as what we say to ourselves.

In his book, Dr. Murphy wonderfully illustrates how the relationship between the conscious and the subconscious works. The way I explain it today is to think of an ocean liner crossing the sea. The conscious mind would be like the captain barking out orders to the crew (subconscious). The "crew" doesn't argue with the "captain," but simply replies, "aye, aye, sir," and carries out the instructions given to it, not minding whether the ship runs into the rocks, hits another vessel, or safely reaches its destination.[1]

Our subconscious mind serves the conscious mind. That is its purpose.

Therefore, whatever instruction or order we give it, the subconscious follows without question, even to our own detriment. The analogy above presents a fundamental question to each of us: Are you the captain of your ship? In other words, are you captain of your crew, your subconscious mind? If you are, you have a powerful tool in your hands—a tool to steer your ship of life and consciously direct it to achieve what you truly desire. Dr. Murphy describes it as a . . .

> . . . miracle-working power that will lift you up from confusion, misery, melancholy, and failure, and guide you to your true place, solve your difficulties, sever you from emotional and physical bondage, and place you on the royal road to freedom, happiness, and peace of mind. This miracle-working power of your subconscious mind can heal you of your sickness; make you vital and strong again.

Who Was Dr. Joseph Murphy?

Joseph Murphy was born in a small town in the County of Cork, Ireland, on May 20, 1898. He was brought up in a devout Catholic household with a younger brother and sister. His father was a deacon and professor at the National School of Ireland, while his mother was a homemaker. Although his father had a steady income, Ireland at that time was suffering from a great economic depression, and like many other Irish families, Murphy's family was poor and struggled to keep food on the table.

Young Murphy eventually attended the National School and was an exceptional student. At one point, he considered the priesthood as a vocation and was accepted as a Jesuit seminarian. However, at age twenty-four he withdrew, deciding instead to leave Ireland and go to America.

A New Life

Arriving in New York in 1922, he eventually became a pharmacist, earning a degree in chemistry. During his studies, he began to explore and take classes on various Eastern religions and philosophies. He became so enamored with Hinduism that he eventually traveled to India to study more extensively under the tutelage of Indian sages. These early and profound experiences of Eastern thought and other world religions would eventually lead him to a whole new life and career path.

In the 1940s, Dr. Murphy moved to Los Angeles and became involved in the New Thought movement, which had started in the late 1800s and continued to develop in the early twentieth century. He was ordained a minister of the Church of Divine Science and would build one of its largest congregations in Los Angeles. As his church and fame grew, he supplemented his Sunday sermons with a weekly radio show, plus books and audio recordings. Dr. Murphy wrote over thirty books in his lifetime, but his most well-known is *The Power of Your Subconscious Mind*, which was first published in 1963 and became an instant bestseller. Over fifty-seven years later, with millions of copies sold, it's an international classic, and Dr. Murphy's legacy continues to thrive today.

How to Use This Book

The first half of the book is Dr. Murphy's original *The Power of Your Subconscious Mind* text. The publisher and I felt it was important to first present Dr. Murphy's unabridged text, so you can have an immediate and personal experience of his teachings written in his own words. As you will see, given his strong background in Christian doctrine, many of his ideas tie to truths he identified in scripture. But the concepts themselves are nondenominational. Likewise, while some of the examples and language reflect the social assumptions of the time the book was written, you will find that Dr. Murphy's writing style remains accessible and engaging, over fifty-seven years later.

The second half of the book comprises my writings: commentaries and lessons that update and expand on Dr. Murphy's teachings to demonstrate how transformative and relevant his teachings are today through real-life stories, examples, and simple practices that anyone can implement with tangible results. After decades of using and teaching Dr. Murphy's work, I am happy to share what I've learned—lessons I believe can be of value in achieving the life of your dreams.

So, to get the most out of this book, look over the whole thing first and get a feel for it, taking in what leaps off the page. Then read

Dr. Murphy's original text—in a linear fashion, jumping around, or in parts—letting your intuition guide you. Then read the second half. In time, I hope this book will be a valuable guide, your very own tool kit to help you unlock your full potential and live the life you deserve.

Enjoy the journey.

Part I

THE POWER OF YOUR SUBCONSCIOUS MIND

Original, unabridged text by
Dr. Joseph Murphy

How This Book Can Work Miracles in Your Life

I have seen miracles happen to men and women in all walks of life all over the world. Miracles will happen to you, too, when you begin using the magic power of your subconscious mind. This book is designed to teach you that your habitual thinking and imagery mold, fashion, and create your destiny; for as a man [or woman] thinketh in his subconscious mind, so is he.

Do You Know the Answers?

Why is one man sad and another man happy? Why is one man joyous and prosperous and another man poor and miserable? Why is one man fearful and anxious and another full of faith and confidence? Why does one man have a beautiful, luxurious home while another man lives out a meager existence in a slum? Why is one man a great success and another an abject failure? Why is one speaker outstanding and another immensely popular and another mediocre and unpopular? Why is one man a genius in his work or profession while the other man toils and moils all his life without doing or accomplishing anything worthwhile? Why is one man healed of a so-called incurable disease and another isn't? Why is it so many good, kind, religious people suffer the tortures of the damned in their mind and body? Why is it many immoral and irreligious people succeed and prosper and enjoy radiant health? Why is one woman happily married and her sister very unhappy and frustrated? Is there an answer to these questions in the workings of your conscious and subconscious minds? There most certainly is.

Reason for Writing This Book

It is for the express purpose of answering and clarifying the above questions and many others of a similar nature that motivated me to write this book. I have endeavored to explain the great fundamental truths of your mind in the simplest language possible. I believe that it is perfectly possible to explain the basic, foundational, and fundamental laws of life and of your mind in ordinary everyday language. You will find that the language of this book is that used in your daily papers, current periodicals, in your business offices, in your home, and in your daily workshop. I urge you to study this book and apply the techniques outlined therein; and as you do, I feel absolutely convinced that you will lay hold of a miracle-working power that will lift you up from confusion, misery, melancholy, and failure, and guide you to your truer place, solve your difficulties, sever you from emotional and physical bondage, and place you on the royal road to freedom, happiness, and peace of mind. This miracle-working power of your subconscious mind can heal you of your sickness; make you vital and strong again. In learning how to use your inner powers, you will open the prison door of fear and enter into a life described by Paul as the glorious liberty of the sons of God.

Releasing the Miracle-Working Power

A personal healing will ever be the most convincing evidence of our subconscious powers. Over forty-two years ago I resolved a malignancy—in medical terminology it was called a sarcoma—by using the healing power of my subconscious mind, which created me and still maintains and governs all my vital functions. The technique I applied is elaborated on in this book, and I feel sure that it will help others to trust the same Infinite Healing Presence lodged in the subconscious depths of all men. Through the kindly offices of my doctor friend, I suddenly realized that it was natural to assume that the Creative Intelligence, which made all my organs, fashioned my body, and started my heart, could heal its own handiwork. The ancient proverb says, "The doctor dresses the wound and God heals it."

Wonders Happen When You Pray Effectively

Scientific prayer is the harmonious interaction of the conscious and subconscious levels of mind scientifically directed for a specific purpose. This book will teach you the scientific way to tap the realm of infinite power within you, enabling you to get what you really want in life. You desire a happier, fuller, and richer life. Begin to use this miracle-working power and smooth your way in daily affairs, solve business problems, and bring harmony in family relationships. Be sure that you read this book several times. The many chapters will show you how this wonderful power works, and how you can draw out of the hidden inspiration and wisdom that is within you. Learn the simple techniques of impressing the subconscious mind. Follow the new scientific way in tapping the infinite storehouse.

Read this book carefully, earnestly, and lovingly. Prove to yourself the amazing way it can help you. It could be, and I believe it will be, the turning point of your life.

Everybody Prays

Do you know how to pray effectively? How long is it since you prayed as part of your everyday activities? In an emergency, in time of danger or trouble, in illness and when death lurks, prayers pour forth—your own and friends'. Just read your daily newspaper. It is reported that prayers are being offered up all over the nation for a child stricken with a so-called incurable ailment, for peace among nations, for a group of miners trapped in a flooded mine. Later it is reported that, when rescued, the miners said that they prayed while waiting for rescue; an airplane pilot says that he prayed as he made a successful emergency landing. Certainly, prayer is an ever-present help in time of trouble, but you do not have to wait for trouble to make prayer an integral and constructive part of your life. The dramatic answers to prayer make headlines and are the subject of testimonies to the effectiveness of prayer. What of the many humble prayers of children, the simple thanksgiving of grace at the table daily, the faithful devotions wherein the individual seeks only communion with God? My work with people has made it necessary for me to study the various approaches to prayer. I have experienced the power of prayer in my own life, and I have talked and worked with many people who also have enjoyed the help of prayer. The problem usually is how to tell others how to pray. People who are in trouble have difficulty in thinking and acting reasonably. They need an easy formula to follow, an obviously workable pattern that is simple and specific. Often they must be led to approach the emergency.

Unique Feature of This Book

The unique feature of this book is its down-to-earth practicality. Here you are presented with simple, usable techniques and formulas, which you can easily apply in your workaday world. I have taught these simple processes to men and women all over the world; and recently over a thousand men and women of all religious affiliations attended a special class in Los Angeles where I presented the highlights of what is offered in the pages of this book. Many came from distances of two hundred miles for each lesson. The special features of this book will appeal to you because they show you why oftentimes you get the opposite of what you prayed for and reveal to you the reasons why. People have asked me in all parts of the world and thousands of times, "Why is it I have prayed and prayed and got no answer?"

In this book you will find the reasons for this common complaint. The many ways of impressing the subconscious mind and getting the right answers make this an extraordinarily valuable book and an ever-present help in time of trouble.

What Do You Believe?

It is not the thing believed in that brings an answer to man's prayer; the answer to prayer results when the individual's subconscious mind responds to the mental picture or thought in his mind. This law of belief is operating in all religions of the world and is the reason why they are psychologically true. The Buddhist, the Christian, the Muslim, and the Hebrew all may get answers to their prayers, not because of the particular creed, religion, affiliation, ritual, ceremony, formula, liturgy, incantation, sacrifices, or offerings, but solely because of belief or mental acceptance and receptivity about that for which they pray. The law of life is the law of belief, and belief could be summed up briefly as a thought in your mind. As a man thinks, feels, and believes, so is the condition of his mind, body, and circumstances. A technique, a methodology based on an understanding of what you are doing and why you are doing it will help you to bring about a subconscious embodiment of all the good things of life. Essentially, answered prayer is the realization of your heart's desire.

Desire Is Prayer

Everyone desires health, happiness, security, peace of mind, true expression but many fail to achieve clearly defined results. A university professor admitted to me recently, "I know that if I changed my mental pattern and redirected my emotional life, my ulcers would not recur, but I do not have any technique, process, or modus operandi! My mind wanders back and forth on my many problems and I feel frustrated, defeated, and unhappy."

This professor had a desire for perfect health; he needed a knowledge of the way his mind worked, which would enable him to fulfill his desire. By practicing the healing methods outlined in this book, he became whole and perfect.

There Is One Mind Common to All Individual Men (Emerson)

The miracle-working powers of your subconscious mind existed before you and I were born, before any church or world existed. The great eternal truths and principles of life antedate all religions. It is with these thoughts in mind that I urge you in the following chapters to lay hold of this wonderful, magical, transforming power, which will bind up mental and physical wounds, proclaim liberty to the fear-ridden mind, and liberate you completely from the limitations of poverty, failure, misery, lack, and frustration. All you have to do is unite mentally and emotionally with the good you wish to embody, and the creative powers of your subconscious will respond accordingly. Begin now, today. Let wonders happen in your life! Keep on keeping on *until the day breaks and the shadows flee away.*

1

The Treasure House within You

Infinite riches are all around you if you will open your mental eyes and behold the treasure house of infinity within you. There is a gold mine within you from which you can extract everything you need to live life gloriously, joyously, and abundantly. Many are sound asleep because they do not know about this gold mine of Infinite Intelligence and boundless love within themselves. Whatever you want, you can draw forth. A magnetized piece of steel will lift about twelve times its own weight, and if you demagnetize this same piece of steel, it will not even lift a feather. Similarly, there are two types of men. There is the magnetized man who is full of confidence and faith. He knows that he is born to win and to succeed. Then, there is the type of man who is demagnetized. He is full of fears and doubts. Opportunities come, and he says, "I might fail; I might lose money; people will laugh at me." This type of man will not get very far in life because, if he is afraid to go forward, he will simply stay where he is. Become a magnetized man and discover the master secret of the ages.

The Master Secret of the Ages

What, in your opinion, is the master secret of the ages? The secret of atomic energy? Thermonuclear energy? The neutron bomb? Interplanetary travel? No, not any of these. Then, what is this master secret? Where can one find it, and how can it be contacted and brought into action? The answer is extraordinarily simple. This secret is the marvelous, miracle-working power found in your own subconscious mind, the last place that most people would seek it.

The Marvelous Power of Your Subconscious Mind

You can bring into your life more power, more wealth, more health, more happiness, and more joy by learning to contact and release the hidden power of your subconscious mind.

You need not acquire this power; you already possess it. But you want to learn how to use it; you want to understand it so that you can apply it in all departments of your life.

As you follow the simple techniques and processes set forth in this book, you can gain the necessary knowledge and understanding. You can be inspired by a new light, and you can generate a new force enabling you to realize your hopes and make all your dreams come true. Decide now to make your life grander, greater, richer, and nobler than ever before.

Within your subconscious depths lies infinite wisdom, infinite power, and infinite supply of all that is necessary, which is waiting for development and expression. Begin now to recognize these potentialities of your deeper mind and they will take form in the world without.

The Infinite Intelligence within your subconscious mind can reveal to you everything you need to know at every moment of time and point of space, provided you are open-minded and receptive. You can receive new thoughts and ideas enabling you to bring forth new inventions, make new discoveries, or write books and plays. Moreover, the Infinite Intelligence in your subconscious can impart to you wonderful kinds of knowledge of an original nature. It can reveal to you and open the way for perfect expression and true place in your life.

Through the wisdom of your subconscious mind you can attract the ideal companion, as well as the right business associate or partner. It can find the right buyer for your home and provide you with all the money you need and the financial freedom to be, to do, and to go as your heart desires.

It is your right to discover this inner world of thought, feeling, and power, of light, love, and beauty. Though invisible, its forces are mighty. Within your subconscious mind you will find the solution for every problem and the cause for every effect. You can draw out the hidden powers; you come into actual possession of the power and wisdom necessary to move forward in abundance, security, joy, and dominion.

I have seen the power of the subconscious lift people up out of crippled states, making them whole, vital, and strong once more, free to go out into the world to experience happiness, health, and joyous expression. There is a miraculous healing power in your subconscious that can heal the troubled mind and the broken heart. It can open the prison door of the mind and liberate you. It can free you from all kinds of material and physical bondage.

Necessity of a Working Basis

Substantial progress in any field of endeavor is impossible in the absence of a working basis, which is universal in its application. You can become skilled in the operation of your subconscious mind. You can practice its powers with a certainty of results in exact proportion to your knowledge of its principles and to your application of them for definite, specific purposes and goals you wish to achieve.

Being a former chemist, I would like to point out that if you combine hydrogen and oxygen in the proportions of two atoms of the former to one of the latter, water will be the result. You are very familiar with the fact that one atom of oxygen and one atom of carbon will produce carbon monoxide, a poisonous gas. But, if you add another atom of oxygen, you will get carbon dioxide, a harmless gas, and so on, throughout the vast realm of chemical compounds.

You must not think that the principles of chemistry, physics, and mathematics differ from the principles of your subconscious mind. Let us consider a generally accepted principle: "Water seeks its own level." This is a universal principle which is applicable to water everywhere.

Consider another principle: "Matter expands when heated." This is true everywhere, at any time, and under all circumstances. You can heat a piece of steel and it will expand regardless whether the steel is found in China, England, or India. It is a universal truth that matter expands when heated. It is also a universal truth that whatever you impress on your subconscious mind is expressed on the screen of space as condition, experience, and event.

Your prayer is answered because your subconscious mind is principle, and by principle I mean the way a thing works. For example, the principle of electricity is that it works from a higher to a lower potential. You do not change the principle of electricity when you use it, but by cooperating with nature, you can bring forth marvelous inventions and discoveries which bless humanity in countless ways.

Your subconscious mind is principle and works according to the law of belief. You must know what belief is, why it works, and how it works. Your Bible says in a simple, clear and beautiful way: *Whosoever shall say unto this mountain, be thou removed, and be thou cast into the sea; and shall not doubt in his heart, but shall believe that those things which he saith shall come to pass; he shall have whatsoever he saith* (Mark 11:23).

The law of your mind is the law of belief. This means to believe in the way your mind works, to believe in belief itself. The belief of your mind is the thought of your mind—that is simple—just that and nothing else.

All your experiences, events, conditions, and acts are the reactions of your subconscious mind to your thoughts. Remember, it is not the thing believed in, but the belief in your own mind, which brings about the result. Cease believing in the false beliefs, opinions, superstitions, and fears of mankind. Begin to believe in the eternal verities and truths of life, which never change. Then, you will move onward, upward, and Godward.

Whoever reads this book and applies the principles of the subconscious mind herein set forth, will be able to pray scientifically and effectively for himself and for others. Your prayer is answered according to the universal law of action and reaction. Thought is incipient action. The reaction is the response from your subconscious mind, which corresponds with the nature of your thought. Busy your mind with the concepts of harmony, health, peace, and good will, and wonders will happen in your life.

The Duality of Mind

You have only one mind, but your mind possesses two distinctive characteristics. The line of demarcation between the two is well-known to all thinking men and women today. The two functions of your mind are essentially unlike. Each is endowed with separate and distinct attributes and powers. The nomenclature generally used to distinguish the two functions of your mind is as follows: the objective and subjective mind, the conscious and subconscious mind, the waking and sleeping mind, the surface self and the deep self, the voluntary mind and the involuntary mind, the male and the female, and many other terms. You will find the terms "conscious" and "subconscious" used to represent the dual nature of your mind throughout this book.

The Conscious and Subconscious Minds

An excellent way to get acquainted with the two functions of your mind is to look upon your own mind as a garden. You are a gardener, and you are planting seeds (thoughts) in your subconscious mind all day long, based on your habitual thinking. As you sow in your subconscious mind, so shall you reap in your body and environment.

Begin now to sow thoughts of peace, happiness, right action, good will, and prosperity. Think quietly and with interest on these qualities and accept them fully in your conscious, reasoning mind. Continue to plant these wonderful seeds (thoughts) in the garden of your mind and you will reap a glorious harvest. Your subconscious mind may be likened to soil, which will grow all kinds of seeds, good or bad. Do men gather grapes or thorns, figs or thistles? Every thought is, therefore, a cause, and every condition is an effect. For this reason, it is essential that you take charge of your thoughts so as to bring forth only desirable conditions.

When your mind thinks correctly, when you understand the truth, when the thoughts deposited in your subconscious mind are constructive, harmonious, and peaceful, the magic working power of your subconscious will respond and bring about harmonious conditions, agreeable surroundings, and the best of everything. When you begin to control your thought processes, you can apply the powers of your subconscious to any problem or difficulty. In other words, you will actually be consciously cooperating with the infinite power and omnipotent law, which governs all things.

Look around you wherever you live and you will notice that the vast majority of mankind lives in the world without and the more enlightened men are intensely interested in the world within. Remember, it is the world within, namely, your thoughts, feelings, and imagery, that makes your world without. It is, therefore, the only creative power and everything that you find in your world of expression has been created by you in the inner world of your mind, consciously or unconsciously.

A knowledge of the interaction of your conscious and subconscious minds will enable you to transform your whole life. In order to change external conditions, you must change the cause. Most men try to change conditions and circumstances by working with conditions and circumstances. To remove discord, confusion, lack, and limitation, you must remove the cause, and the cause is the way you are using your conscious mind. In other words, the way you are thinking and picturing in your mind.

You are living in a fathomless sea of infinite riches. Your subconscious is very sensitive to your thoughts. Your thoughts form the mold or matrix through which the Infinite Intelligence, wisdom, vital forces, and energies of your subconscious flow. The practical application of the laws of your mind as illustrated in each chapter in this book will cause you to exchange abundance for poverty, wisdom for superstition and ignorance, peace for pain, joy for sadness, light for darkness, harmony for discord, faith and confidence for fear, success for failure and freedom from the law of averages. Certainly, there can be no more wonderful blessing than these from a mental, emotional, and material standpoint.

Most of the great scientists, artists, poets, singers, writers, and inventors have a deep understanding of the workings of the conscious and subconscious minds.

One time, Caruso, the great operatic tenor, was struck with stage fright. He said his throat was paralyzed due to spasms caused by intense fear, which constricted the muscles in his throat.

Perspiration poured copiously down his face. He was ashamed because in a few minutes he had to go out on the stage, yet he was shaking with fear and trepidation. He said, "They will laugh at me. I can't sing." Then he shouted in the presence of those behind the stage, "The Little Me wants to strangle the Big Me within."

He said to the Little Me, "Get out of here, the Big Me wants to sing through me."

By the Big Me, he meant the limitless power and wisdom of his subconscious mind. He began to shout, "Get out, get out, the Big Me is going to sing!"

His subconscious mind responded, releasing the vital forces within him. When the call came, he walked out on the stage and sang gloriously and majestically, enthralling the audience.

It is obvious to you now that Caruso must have understood the two levels of mind—the conscious or rational, and the subconscious or irrational level. Your subconscious mind is reactive and responds to the nature of your thoughts. When your conscious mind (the Little Me) is full of fear, worry, and anxiety, the negative emotions engendered in your subconscious mind (the Big Me) are released and flood the conscious mind with a sense of panic, foreboding, and despair. When this happens, you can, like Caruso, speak affirmatively and with a deep sense of authority to the irrational emotions generated in your deeper mind as follows: "Be still, be quiet, I am in control, you must obey me, you are subject to my command, you cannot intrude where you do not belong."

It is fascinating and intensely interesting to observe how you can speak authoritatively and with conviction to the irrational movement of your deeper self, bringing silence, harmony, and peace to your mind. The subconscious is subject to the conscious mind, and that is why it is called subconscious or subjective.

Outstanding Differences and Modes of Operation

You will perceive the main differences by the following illustration: The conscious mind is like the navigator or captain at the bridge of a ship. He directs the ship and signals orders to men in the engine room, who in turn control all the boilers, instruments, gauges, etc. The men in the engine room do not know where they are going; they follow orders. They would go on the rocks if the man in the bridge issued faulty or wrong instructions based on his findings with the compass, sextant, or other instruments. The men in the engine room obey him because he is in charge and issues orders, which are automatically obeyed. Members of the crew do not talk back to the captain, they simply carry out orders.

The captain is the master of his ship and his decrees are carried out. Likewise, your conscious mind is the captain and the master of your ship, which represents your body, environment, and all your affairs. Your subconscious mind takes the orders you give it based upon what your conscious mind believes and accepts as true.

When you repeatedly say to people, "I can't afford it," then your subconscious mind takes you at your word and sees to it that you will not be in a position to purchase what you want. As long as you persist in saying, "I can't afford that car, that trip to Europe, that home, that fur coat or ermine wrap," you can rest assured that your subconscious mind will follow your orders and you will go through life experiencing the lack of all these things.

Last Christmas Eve a beautiful young university student looked at an attractive and rather expensive traveling bag in a store window. She was going home to Buffalo, New York, for the holidays. She was about to say, "I can't afford that bag," when she recalled something she had heard at one of my lectures, which was, "Never finish a negative statement, reverse it immediately, and wonders will happen in your life."

She said, "That bag is mine. It is for sale. I accept it mentally and my subconscious sees to it that I receive it."

At eight o'clock Christmas Eve her fiancé presented her with a bag exactly the same as the one she had mentally identified herself with at ten o'clock the same morning. She had filled her mind with the thought of expectancy and released the whole thing to her deeper mind, which has the "know-how" of accomplishment.

This young girl, a student at the University of Southern California, said to me, "I didn't have the money to buy that bag, but now I know where to find money and all the things I need, and that is in the treasure house of eternity within me."

Another simple illustration is this: When you say, "I do not like mushrooms," and the occasion subsequently comes that you are served mushrooms in sauces or salads, you will get indigestion because your subconscious mind says to you, "The boss (your conscious mind) does not like mushrooms." This is an amusing example of the outstanding differences and modes of operation of your conscious and subconscious minds.

A woman may say, "I wake up at three o'clock if I drink coffee at night." Whenever she drinks coffee at night, her subconscious mind nudges her, as if to say, "The boss wants you to stay awake tonight."

Your subconscious mind works twenty-four hours a day and makes provisions for your benefit, pouring all the fruit of your habitual thinking into your lap.

How Her Subconscious Responded

A woman wrote me a few months ago as follows: "I am seventy-five years old, a widow with a grown family. I was living alone and on a pension. I heard your lectures on the powers of the subconscious mind wherein you said that ideas could be conveyed to the subconscious mind by repetition, faith, and expectancy.

"I began to repeat frequently, with feeling, 'I am wanted. I am happily married to a kind, loving, and spiritually minded man. I am secure!'

"I kept on doing this many times a day for about two weeks, and one day at the corner drugstore, I was introduced to a retired pharmacist. I found him to be kind, understanding, and very religious. He was a perfect answer to my prayer. Within a week he proposed to me and now we are on our honeymoon in Europe. I know that the intelligence within my subconscious mind brought both of us together in divine order."

This woman discovered that the treasure house was within her. Her prayer was felt as true in her heart and her affirmation sank down by osmosis into her subconscious mind, which is the creative medium. The moment she succeeded in bringing about a subjective embodiment, her subconscious mind brought about the answer through the law of attraction. Her deeper mind, full of wisdom and intelligence, brought both of them together in divine order.

Be sure that you think on *Whatsoever things are true, whatsoever things are honest, whatsoever things are just, whatsoever things are pure, whatsoever things are lovely, whatsoever things are of good report; if there be any virtue, and if there be any praise, think on these things* (Philippians 4:8).

Brief Summary of Ideas Worth Remembering

1. The treasure house is within you. Look within for the answer to your heart's desire.

2. The great secret possessed by the great men of all ages was their ability to contact and release the powers of their subconscious mind. You can do the same.

3. Your subconscious has the answer to all problems. If you suggest to your subconscious prior to sleep, "I want to get up at 6 AM," it will awaken you at that exact time.

4. Your subconscious mind is the builder of your body and can heal you. Lull yourself to sleep every night with the idea of perfect health, and your subconscious, being your faithful servant, will obey you.

5. Every thought is a cause and every condition is an effect.

6. If you want to write a book, write a wonderful play, give a better talk to your audience, then convey the idea lovingly and feelingly to your subconscious mind, and it will respond accordingly.

7. You are like a captain navigating a ship. He must give the right orders, and likewise, you must give the right orders (thoughts and images) to your subconscious mind, which controls and governs all your experiences.

8. Never use the terms "I can't afford it" or "I can't do this." Your subconscious mind takes you at your word and sees to it that you do not have the money or the ability to do what you want to do. Affirm, "I can do all things through the power of my subconscious mind."

9. The law of life is the law of belief. A belief is a thought in your mind. Do not believe in things to harm or hurt you. Believe in the power of your subconscious to heal, inspire, strengthen, and prosper you. According to your belief is it done unto you.

10. Change your thoughts and you change your destiny.

2

How Your Own Mind Works

You have a mind, and you should learn how to use it. There are two levels of your mind—the conscious, or rational, level and the subconscious, or irrational, level. You think with your conscious mind, and whatever you habitually think sinks down into your subconscious mind, which creates according to the nature of your thoughts. Your subconscious mind is the seat of your emotions and is the creative mind. If you think good, good will follow, if you think evil, evil will follow. This is the way your mind works.

The main point to remember is once the subconscious mind accepts an idea, it begins to execute it. It is an interesting and subtle truth that the law of the subconscious mind works for good and bad ideas alike. This law, when applied in a negative way, is the cause of failure, frustration, and unhappiness. However, when your habitual thinking is harmonious and constructive, you experience perfect health, success, and prosperity.

Peace of mind and a healthy body are inevitable when you begin to think and feel in the right way. Whatever you claim mentally and feel as true, your subconscious mind will accept and bring forth into your experience.

The only thing necessary for you to do is to get your conscious mind to accept your idea, and the law of your own subconscious mind will bring forth the health, peace, or position you desire. You give the command, or decree, and your subconscious will faithfully reproduce the idea impressed upon it. The law of your mind is this: You will get a reaction or response from your subconscious mind according to the nature of the thought or idea you hold in your conscious mind.

Psychologists and psychiatrists point out that when thoughts are conveyed to your subconscious mind, impressions are made in the brain cells. As soon as your subconscious accepts any idea, it proceeds to put it into effect immediately. It works by association of ideas and uses every bit of knowledge that you have gathered in your lifetime to bring about its purpose. It draws on the infinite power, energy, and wisdom within you. It lines up all the laws of nature to get its way. Sometimes it seems to bring about an immediate solution to your difficulties, but at other times it may take days, weeks, or longer. "His ways are past finding out" (Romans 11:33).

Conscious and Subconscious Terms Differentiated

You must remember that these are not two minds. They are merely two spheres of activity within one mind. Your conscious mind is the reasoning mind. It is that phase of mind which chooses. For example, you choose your books, your home, and your partner in life. You make all your decisions with your conscious mind. On the other hand, without any conscious choice on your part, your heart is kept functioning automatically, and the processes of digestion, circulation, and breathing are carried on by your subconscious mind through processes independent of your conscious control.

Your subconscious mind accepts what is impressed upon it or what you consciously believe. It does not reason things out like your conscious mind, and it does not argue with you controversially. Your subconscious mind is like the soil, which accepts any kind of seed, good or bad. Your thoughts are active and might be likened unto seeds. Negative, destructive thoughts continue to work negatively in your subconscious mind and in due time will come forth into outer experience, which corresponds with them.

Remember, your subconscious mind does not engage in proving whether your thoughts are good or bad, true or false, but it responds according to the nature of your thoughts or suggestions. For example, if you consciously assume something as true, even though it may be false, your subconscious mind will accept it as true and proceed to bring about results, which must necessarily follow, because you consciously assumed it to be true.

Experiments by Psychologists

Innumerable experiments by psychologists and others on persons in the hypnotic state have shown that the subconscious mind is incapable of making selections and comparisons, which are necessary for a reasoning process. They have shown repeatedly that your subconscious mind will accept any suggestions, however false. Having once accepted any suggestion, it responds according to the nature of the suggestion given.

To illustrate the amenability of your subconscious mind to suggestion, if a practiced hypnotist suggests to one of his subjects that he is Napoleon Bonaparte, or even a cat or a dog, he will act out the part with inimitable accuracy. His personality becomes changed for the time being. He believes himself to be whatever the operator tells him he is.

A skilled hypnotist may suggest to one of his students in the hypnotic state that his back itches, to another that his nose is bleeding, to another that he is a marble statue, to another that he is freezing and the temperature is below zero. Each one will follow out the line of his particular suggestion, totally oblivious to all his surroundings, which do not pertain to his idea.

These simple illustrations portray clearly the difference between your conscious reasoning mind and your subconscious mind, which is impersonal, nonselective, and accepts as true whatever your conscious mind believes to be true. Hence, the importance of selecting thoughts, ideas, and premises which bless, heal, inspire, and fill your soul with joy.

The Terms Objective and Subjective Mind Clarified

Your conscious mind is sometimes referred to as your objective mind because it deals with outward objects. The objective mind takes cognizance of the objective world. Its media of observation are your five physical senses. Your objective mind is your guide and director in your contact with your environment. You gain knowledge through your five senses. Your objective mind learns through observation, experience, and education. As previously pointed out, the greatest function of the objective mind is that of reasoning.

Suppose you are one of the thousands of tourists who come to Los Angeles annually. You would come to the conclusion that it is a beautiful city based upon your observation of the parks, pretty gardens, majestic buildings, and lovely homes. This is the working of your objective mind.

Your subconscious mind is oftentimes referred to as your subjective mind. Your subjective mind takes cognizance of its environment by means independent of the five senses. Your subjective mind perceives by intuition. It is the seat of your emotion and the storehouse of memory. Your subjective mind performs its highest functions when your objective senses are in abeyance. In a word, it is that intelligence, which makes itself manifest when the objective mind is suspended or in a sleepy, drowsy state.

Your subjective mind sees without the use of the natural organs of vision. It has the capacity of clairvoyance and clairaudience. Your subjective mind can leave your body, travel to distant lands, and bring back information, oftentimes of the most exact and truthful character. Through your subjective mind, you can read the thoughts of others, read the contents of sealed envelopes and closed safes. Your subjective mind has the ability to apprehend the thoughts of others without the use of the ordinary objective means of communication. It is of the greatest importance that we understand the interaction of the objective and subjective mind in order to learn the true art of prayer.

The Subconscious Cannot Reason Like Your Conscious Mind

Your subconscious mind cannot argue controversially. Hence, if you give it wrong suggestions, it will accept them as true and will proceed to bring them to pass as conditions, experiences, and events. All things that have happened to you are based on thoughts impressed on your subconscious mind through belief. If you have conveyed erroneous thoughts to your subconscious mind, the sure method of overcoming them is by the repetition of constructive, harmonious thoughts frequently repeated, which your subconscious mind accepts, thus forming new and healthy habits of thought and life, for your subconscious mind is the seat of habit.

The habitual thinking of your conscious mind establishes deep grooves in your subconscious mind. This is very favorable for you if your habitual thoughts are harmonious, peaceful, and constructive.

If you have indulged in fear, worry, and other destructive forms of thinking, the remedy is to recognize the omnipotence of your subconscious mind and decree freedom, happiness, and perfect health. Your subconscious mind, being creative and one with your divine source, will proceed to create the freedom and happiness, which you have earnestly decreed.

The Tremendous Power of Suggestion

You must realize by now that your conscious mind is the "watchman at the gate," and its chief function is to protect your subconscious mind from false impressions. You are now aware of one of the basic laws of mind: Your subconscious mind is amenable to suggestion. As you know, your subconscious mind does not make comparisons or contrasts, neither does it reason and think things out for itself. This latter function belongs to your conscious mind. It simply reacts to the impressions given to it by your conscious mind. It does not show a preference for one course of action over another.

The following is a classic example of the tremendous power of suggestion. Suppose you approach a timid-looking passenger on board ship and say to him something like this: "You look very ill. How pale you are! I feel certain you are going to be seasick. Let me help you to your cabin." The passenger turns pale. Your suggestion of seasickness associates itself with his own fears and forebodings. He accepts your aid down to the berth, and there your negative suggestion, which was accepted by him, is realized.

Different Reactions to the Same Suggestion

It is true that different people will react in different ways to the same suggestion because of their subconscious conditioning or belief. For example, if you go to a sailor on the ship and say to him sympathetically, "My dear fellow, you're looking very ill. Aren't you feeling sick? You look to me as if you are going to be seasick."

According to his temperament he either laughs at your "joke," or expresses mild irritation. Your suggestion fell on deaf ears in this instance because your suggestion of seasickness was associated in his mind with his own immunity from it. Therefore, it called up not fear or worry, but self-confidence.

The dictionary says that a suggestion is the act or instance of putting something into one's mind, the mental process by which the thought or idea suggested is entertained, accepted, or put into effect. You must remember that a suggestion cannot impose something on the subconscious mind against the will of the conscious mind. In other words, your conscious mind has the power to reject the suggestion given. In the case of the sailor, he had no fear of seasickness. He had convinced himself of his immunity and the negative suggestion had absolutely no power to evoke fear.

The suggestion of seasickness to the other passenger called forth his indwelling fear of seasickness. Each of us has his own inner fears, beliefs, and opinions. These inner assumptions rule and govern our lives. A suggestion has no power in and of itself except it is accepted mentally by you. This causes your subconscious powers to flow in a limited and restricted way according to the nature of the suggestion.

How He Lost His Arm

Every two or three years I give a series of lectures at the London Truth Forum in Caxton Hall. This is a forum I founded a number of years ago. Dr. Evelyn Fleet, the director, told me about an article which appeared in the English newspapers dealing with the power of suggestion. This is the suggestion a man gave to his subconscious mind over a period of about two years. "I would give my right arm to see my daughter cured." It appeared that his daughter had a crippling form of arthritis, together with a so-called incurable form of skin disease. Medical treatment had failed to alleviate the condition, and the father had an intense longing for his daughter's healing, and expressed his desire in the words just quoted.

Dr. Evelyn Fleet said that the newspaper article pointed out that one day the family was out riding when their car collided with another. The father's right arm was torn off at the shoulder and immediately the daughter's arthritis and skin condition vanished.

You must make certain to give your subconscious only suggestions which heal, bless, elevate, and inspire you in all ways. Remember that your subconscious mind cannot take a joke. It takes you at your word.

How Autosuggestion Banishes Fear

Illustrations of autosuggestion: Autosuggestion means suggesting something definite and specific to oneself. Herbert Parkyn, in his excellent manual of autosuggestion, records the following incident. It has its amusing side, so that one remembers it. "A New York visitor in Chicago looks at his watch, which is set an hour ahead of Chicago time, and tells a Chicago friend that it is twelve o'clock. The Chicago friend, not considering the difference in time between Chicago and New York, tells the New Yorker that he is hungry and that he must go to lunch."

Autosuggestion may be used to banish various fears and other negative conditions. A young singer was invited to give an audition. She had been looking forward to the interview, but on three previous occasions she had failed miserably due to fear of failure. This young lady had a very good voice, but she had been saying to herself,

"When the time comes for me to sing, maybe they won't like me. I will try, but I'm full of fear and anxiety."

Her subconscious mind accepted these negative autosuggestions as a request and proceeded to manifest them and bring them into her experience. The cause was an involuntary autosuggestion, i.e., silent fear thoughts, emotionalized and subjectified.

She overcame it by the following technique: Three times a day she isolated herself in a room. She sat down comfortably in an armchair, relaxed her body, and closed her eyes. She stilled her mind and body as best she could. Physical inertia favors mental passivity and renders the mind more receptive to suggestion. She counteracted the fear suggestion by saying to herself, "I sing beautifully, I am poised, serene, confident, and calm."

She repeated this statement slowly, quietly, and with feeling from five to ten times at each sitting. She had three such "sittings" every day and one immediately prior to sleep. At the end of a week she was completely poised and confident. When the invitation to audition came, she gave a remarkable, wonderful audition.

How She Restored Her Memory

A woman, aged seventy-five, was in the habit of saying to herself, "I am losing my memory." She reversed the procedure and practiced induced autosuggestion several times a day as follows: "My memory from today on is improving in every department. I shall always remember whatever I need to know at every moment of time and point of space. The impressions received will be clearer and more definite. I shall retain them automatically and with ease. Whatever I wish to recall will immediately present itself in the correct form in my mind. I am improving rapidly every day, and very soon my memory will be better than it has ever been before." At the end of three weeks, her memory was back to normal and she was delighted.

How He Overcame a Nasty Temper

Many men who complained of irritability and bad temper proved to be very susceptible to autosuggestion and obtained marvelous results by using the following statements three or four times a day—morning, noon, and night prior to sleep for about a month. "Henceforth, I shall grow more good-humored. Joy, happiness, and cheerfulness are now becoming my normal states of mind. Every day I am becoming more and more lovable and understanding. I am now becoming the center of cheer and good will to all those about me, infecting them with good humor. This happy, joyous, and cheerful mood is now becoming my normal, natural state of mind. I am grateful."

The Constructive and Destructive Power of Suggestion

Some illustrations and comments on heterosuggestion: Heterosuggestion means suggestions from another person. In all ages the power of suggestion has played a part in the life and thoughts of man in every period of time and in each country of the earth. In many parts of the world it is the controlling power in religion.

Suggestion may be used to discipline and control ourselves, but it can also be used to take control and command over others who do not know the laws of mind. In its constructive form it is wonderful and magnificent. In its negative aspects it is one of the most destructive of all the response patterns of the mind, resulting in patterns of misery, failure, suffering, sickness, and disaster.

Have You Accepted Any of These?

From infancy on, the majority of us have been given many negative suggestions. Not knowing how to thwart them, we unconsciously accepted them. Here are some of the negative suggestions: "You can't." "You'll never amount to anything." "You mustn't." "You'll fail." "You haven't got a chance." "You're all wrong." "It's no use." "It's not what you know, but who you know." "The world is going to the dogs." "What's the use? Nobody cares." "It's no use trying so hard." "You're too old now." "Things are getting worse and worse." "Life is an endless grind." "Love is for the birds." "You just can't win." "Pretty soon you'll be bankrupt." "Watch out, you'll get the virus." "You can't trust a soul," etc.

Unless, as an adult, you use constructive autosuggestion, which is reconditioning therapy, the impressions made on you in the past can cause behavior patterns that cause failure in your personal and social life. Autosuggestion is a means releasing you from the mass of negative verbal conditioning that might otherwise distort your life pattern, making the development of good habits difficult.

You Can Counteract Negative Suggestions

Pick up the paper any day and you can read dozens of items that could sow the seeds of futility, fear, worry, and impending doom. If accepted by you, these thoughts of fear could cause you to lose the will for life. Knowing that you can reject all these negative suggestions by giving your subconscious mind constructive autosuggestions, you counteract all these destructive ideas.

Check regularly on the negative autosuggestions that people make to you. You do not have to be influenced by destructive hetero-suggestion. All of us have suffered from it in our childhood and in our teens. If you look back, you can easily recall how parents, friends, relatives, teachers, and associates contributed in a campaign of negative suggestions. Study the things said to you and you will discover much of it was in the form of propaganda. The purpose of much of what was said was to control you or instill fear into you.

This heterosuggestion process goes on in every home, office, factory, and club. You will find that many of these suggestions are for the purpose of making you think, feel, and act as others want you to and in ways that are to their advantage.

How Suggestion Killed a Man

Here is an illustration of heterosuggestion: A relative of mine went to a crystal ball–gazer in India who told him that he had a bad heart and predicted that he would die at the next new moon. He began to tell all members of his family about this prediction, and he arranged his will.

This powerful suggestion entered into his subconscious mind because he accepted it completely. My relative also told me that this crystal gazer was believed to have some strange occult powers and she could do harm or good to a person. He died as predicted, not knowing that he was the cause of his own death. I suppose many of us have heard similar stupid, ridiculous, superstitious stories.

Let us look at what happened in the light of our knowledge of the way the subconscious mind works. Whatever the conscious, reasoning mind of man believes the subconscious mind will accept and act upon. My relative was happy, healthy, vigorous, and robust when he went to see the fortuneteller. She gave him a very negative suggestion, which he accepted.

He became terrified and constantly dwelt upon the fact that he was going to die at the next new moon. He proceeded to tell everyone about it, and he prepared for the end. The activity took place in his own mind and his own thought was the cause. He brought about his own so-called death, or rather destruction of the physical body, by his fear and expectation of the end.

The woman who predicted his death had no more power than the stones and sticks in the field. Her suggestion had no power to create or bring about the end she suggested. If he had known the laws of his mind, he would have completely rejected the negative suggestion and refused to give her words any attention, knowing in his heart that he was governed and controlled by his own thought and feeling. Like tin arrows aimed at a battleship, her prophecy could have been completely neutralized and dissipated without hurting him.

The suggestions of others in themselves have absolutely no power whatever over you except the power that you give them through your own thoughts. You have to give your mental consent; you have to entertain the thought. Then, it becomes your thought, and you do the thinking. Remember, you have the capacity to choose. Choose life! Choose love! Choose health! Choose abundance!

The Power of an Assumed Major Premise

Your mind works like a syllogism. This means that whatever major premise your conscious mind assumes to be true determines the conclusion your subconscious mind comes to in regard to any particular question or problem in your mind. If your premise is true, the conclusion must be true as in the following example:

- Every virtue is laudable.
- Kindness is a virtue.
- Therefore, kindness is laudable.

Another example:

- All formed things change and pass away.
- The pyramids of Egypt are formed things.
- Therefore, some day the pyramids will pass away.

The first statement is referred to as the major premise, and the right conclusion must necessarily follow the right premise.

A college professor, who attended some of my science of mind lectures in May 1962, at Town Hall, New York, said to me, "Everything in my life is topsy-turvy, and I have lost health, wealth, and friends. Everything I touch turns out wrong."

I explained to him that he should establish a major premise in his thinking, that the Infinite Intelligence of his subconscious mind was guiding, directing, and prospering him spiritually, mentally, and materially. Then his subconscious mind would automatically direct him wisely in his investments, decisions, and also heal his body and restore his mind to peace and tranquility.

This professor formulated an overall picture of the way he wanted his life to be, and this was his major premise: "Infinite Intelligence leads and guides me in all my ways. Perfect health is mine, and the Law of Harmony operates in my mind and body. Beauty, love, peace, and abundance are mine. The principle of right action and divine order govern my entire life. I know my major premise is based on the eternal truths of life, and I know, feel, and believe that my subconscious mind responds according to the nature of my conscious mind thinking."

He wrote me as follows: "I repeated the above statements slowly, quietly, and lovingly several times a day knowing that they were sinking deep down into my subconscious mind, and that results must follow. I am deeply grateful for the interview you gave me and

I would like to add that all departments of my life are changing for the better. It works!"

The Subconscious Does Not Argue Controversially

Your subconscious mind is all-wise and knows the answers to all questions. It does not argue with you or talk back to you. It does not say, "You must not impress me with that." For example, when you say, "I can't do this," "I am too old now," "I can't meet this obligation," "I was born on the wrong side of the tracks," "I don't know the right politician," you are impregnating your subconscious with these negative thoughts and it responds accordingly. You are actually blocking your own good, thereby bringing lack, limitation, and frustration into your life.

When you set up obstacles, impediments, and delays in your conscious mind, you are denying the wisdom and intelligence resident in your subconscious mind. You are actually saying in effect that your subconscious mind cannot solve your problem. This leads to mental and emotional congestion, followed by sickness and neurotic tendencies. To realize your desire and overcome your frustration, affirm boldly several times a day: "The Infinite Intelligence, which gave me this desire, leads, guides, and reveals to me the perfect plan for the unfolding of my desire. I know the deeper wisdom of my subconscious is now responding and what I feel and claim within is expressed in the without. There is a balance, equilibrium, and equanimity."

If you say, "There is no way out; I am lost; there is no way out of this dilemma; I am stymied and blocked," you will get no answer or response from your subconscious mind. If you want the subconscious to work for you, give it the right request, and attain its cooperation. It is always working for you. It is controlling your heartbeat this minute and also your breathing. It heals a cut on your finger and its tendency is lifeward, forever seeking to take care of you and preserve you. Your subconscious has a mind of its own, but it accepts your patterns of thought and imagery.

When you are seeking an answer to a problem, your subconscious will respond, but it expects you to come to a decision and to a true judgment in your conscious mind. You must acknowledge the answer is in your subconscious mind. However, if you say, "I don't think there is any way out; I am all mixed up and confused; why don't I get an answer?" you are neutralizing your prayer. Like the soldier marking time, you do not get anywhere.

Still the wheels of your mind, relax, let go, and quietly affirm, "My subconscious knows the answer. It is responding to me now. I give thanks because I know the Infinite Intelligence of my subconscious knows all things and is revealing the perfect answer to me now. My real conviction is now setting free the majesty and glory of my subconscious mind. I rejoice that it is so."

Review of Highlights

1. Think good, and good follows. Think evil, and evil follows. You are what you think all day long.

2. Your subconscious mind does not argue with you. It accepts what your conscious mind decrees. If you say, "I can't afford it," it may be true, but do not say it. Select a better thought, decree. "I'll buy it, I accept it in my mind."

3. You have the power to choose. Choose health and happiness. You can choose to be friendly or you can choose to be unfriendly.

Choose to be cooperative, joyous, friendly, lovable, and the whole world will respond. This is the best way to develop a wonderful personality.

4. Your conscious mind is the "watchman at the gate." Its chief function is to protect your subconscious mind from false impressions. Choose to believe that something good can happen and is happening now. Your greatest power is your capacity to choose. Choose happiness and abundance.

5. The suggestions and statements of others have no power to hurt you. The only power is the movement of your own thought. You can choose to reject the thoughts or statements of others and affirm the good. You have the power to choose how you will react.

6. Watch what you say. You have to account for every idle word. Never say, "I will fail; I will lose my job; I can't pay the rent." Your subconscious cannot take a joke. It brings all these things to pass.

7. Your mind is not evil. No force of nature is evil. It depends how you use the powers of nature. Use your mind to bless, heal, and inspire all people everywhere.

8. Never say, "I can't." Overcome that fear by substituting the following: "I can do all things through the power of my subconscious mind."

9. Begin to think from the standpoint of the eternal truths and principles of life and not from the standpoint of fear, ignorance, and superstition. Do not let others do your thinking for you. Choose your own thoughts and make your own decisions.

10. You are the captain of your soul (subconscious mind) and the master of your fate. Remember, you have the capacity to choose. Choose life! Choose love! Choose health! Choose happiness!

11. Whatever your conscious mind assumes and believes to be true, your subconscious mind will accept and bring to pass. Believe in good fortune, divine guidance, right action, and all the blessings of life.

3

The Miracle-Working Power
of Your Subconscious

The power of your subconscious is enormous. It inspires you, it guides you, and it reveals to you names, facts, and scenes from the storehouse of memory. Your subconscious started your heartbeat, controls the circulation of your blood, regulates your digestion, assimilation, and elimination. When you eat a piece of bread, your subconscious mind transmutes it into tissue, muscle, bone, and blood. This process is beyond the ken of the wisest man who walks the earth. Your subconscious mind controls all vital processes and functions of your body and knows the answer to all problems.

Your subconscious mind never sleeps, and never rests. It is always on the job. You can discover the miracle-working power of your subconscious by plainly stating to your subconscious prior to sleep that you wish a certain specific thing accomplished. You will be delighted to discover that forces within you will be "released," leading to the desired result. Here, then, is a source of power and wisdom which places you in touch with omnipotence, or the power that moves the world, guides the planets in their course, and causes the sun to shine.

Your subconscious mind is the source of your ideals, aspirations, and altruistic urges. It was through the subconscious mind that

Shakespeare perceived great truths hidden from the average man of his day. Undoubtedly, it was the response of his subconscious mind that caused the Greek sculptor, Phidias, to portray beauty, order, symmetry, and proportion in marble and bronze. It enabled the Italian artist, Raphael, to paint Madonnas, and Ludwig van Beethoven to compose symphonies.

In 1955, I lectured at the Yoga-Vendanta Forest Academy, Rishikesh, India, and there I chatted with a visiting surgeon from Bombay. He told me about Dr. James Esdaille, a Scotch surgeon, who worked in Bengal before ether or other modern methods of anesthesia were discovered. Between 1843 and 1846, Dr. Esdaille performed about four hundred major operations on the eye, ear, and throat. All operations were conducted under mental anesthesia only. This Indian doctor at Rishikesh informed me that the postoperative mortality rate of patients operated on by Dr. Esdaille was extremely low, probably 2 or 3 percent. Patients felt no pain and there were no deaths during the operations.

Dr. Esdaille suggested to the subconscious minds of all his patients, who were in a hypnotic state, that no infection or septic condition would develop. You must remember that this was before Louis Pasteur, Joseph Lister, and others who pointed out the bacterial origin of disease and causes of infection due to unsterilized instruments and virulent organisms.

This Indian surgeon said that the reason for the low mortality rate and the general absence of infection, which was reduced to a minimum, was undoubtedly due to the suggestions of Dr. Esdaille to the subconscious minds of his patients. They responded according to the nature of his suggestion.

It is simply wonderful, when you conceive how a surgeon, over 120 years ago, discovered the miraculous wonder-working powers of the subconscious mind. Doesn't it cause you to be seized with a sort of mystic awe when you stop and think of the transcendental powers of your subconscious mind? Consider its extrasensory perceptions, such as its capacity for clairvoyance and clairaudience, its independence of time and space, its capacity to render you free from all pain and suffering, and its capacity to get the answer to all problems, be they what they may.

All these and many more reveal to you that there is a power and an intelligence within you that far transcends your intellect, causing you to marvel at the wonders of it all. All these experiences cause you to rejoice and believe in the miracle-working powers of your own subconscious mind.

Your Subconscious Is Your Book of Life

Whatever thoughts, beliefs, opinions, theories, or dogmas you write, engrave, or impress on your subconscious mind, you shall experience them as the objective manifestation of circumstances, conditions, and events. What you write on the inside, you will experience on the outside. You have two sides to your life, objective and subjective, visible and invisible, thought and its manifestation.

Your thought is received by your brain, which is the organ of your conscious reasoning mind. When your conscious or objective mind accepts the thought completely, it is sent to the solar plexus, called the brain of your mind, where it becomes flesh and is made manifest in your experience.

As previously outlined, your subconscious cannot argue. It acts only from what you write on it. It accepts your verdict of the conclusions of your conscious mind as final. This is why you are always writing on the book of life, because your thoughts become your experiences. The American essayist Ralph Waldo Emerson said, "Man is what he thinks about all day long."

What Is Impressed in the Subconscious
Is Expressed

William James, the father of American psychology, said that the power to move the world is in your subconscious mind. Your subconscious mind is one with Infinite Intelligence and boundless wisdom. It is fed by hidden springs, and is called the law of life. Whatever you impress upon your subconscious mind, the latter will move heaven and earth to bring it to pass. You must, therefore, impress it with right ideas and constructive thoughts.

The reason there is so much chaos and misery in the world is because people do not understand the interaction of their conscious and subconscious minds. When these two principles work in accord, in concord, in peace, and synchronously together, you will have health, happiness, peace, and joy. There is no sickness or discord when the conscious and subconscious work together harmoniously and peacefully.

The tomb of Hermes was opened with great expectancy and a sense of wonder because people believed that the greatest secret of the ages was contained therein. The secret was "as within, so without; as above, so below."

In other words, whatever is impressed in your subconscious mind is expressed on the screen of space. This same truth was proclaimed by Moses, Isaiah, Jesus, Buddha, Zoroaster, Laotze, and all the illumined seers of the ages. Whatever you feel as true subjectively is expressed as conditions, experiences, and events. Motion and emotion must balance. As in heaven (your own mind), so on earth (in your body and environment). This is the great law of life.

You will find throughout all nature the law of action and reaction, of rest and motion. These two must balance, then there will be harmony and equilibrium. You are here to let the Life-Principle flow through you rhythmically and harmoniously. The intake and the outgo must be equal. The impression and the expression must be equal. All your frustration is due to unfulfilled desire.

If you think negatively, destructively, and viciously, these thoughts generate destructive emotions, which must be expressed and find an outlet. These emotions, being of a negative nature, are frequently expressed as ulcers, heart trouble, tension, and anxieties.

What is your idea or feeling about yourself now? Every part of your being expresses that idea. Your vitality, body, financial status, friends, and social status represent a perfect reflection of the idea you have of yourself. This is the real meaning of what is impressed in your subconscious mind, and which is expressed in all phases of your life.

We injure ourselves by the negative ideas which we entertain. How often have you wounded yourself by getting angry, fearful, jealous, or vengeful? These are the poisons that enter your subconscious mind. You were not born with these negative attitudes. Feed your subconscious mind life-giving thoughts and you will wipe out all the negative patterns lodged therein. As you continue to do this, all the past will be wiped out and remembered no more.

The Subconscious Heals a Malignancy of the Skin

A personal healing will ever be the most convincing evidence of the healing power of the subconscious mind. Over forty years ago I resolved a malignancy of the skin through prayer. Medical therapy had failed to check the growth, and it was getting progressively worse.

A clergyman, with a deep psychological knowledge, explained to me the inner meaning of the 139th Psalm wherein it says, *In thy book all my members were written which in continuance were fashioned, when as yet there was none of them.* He explained that the term "book" meant my subconscious mind, which fashioned and molded all my organs from an invisible cell. He also pointed out that inasmuch as my subconscious mind made my body, it could also recreate it and heal it according to the perfect pattern within it.

This clergyman showed me his watch and said, "This had a maker, and the watchmaker had to have the idea first in mind before the watch became an objective reality, and if the watch was out of order, the watchmaker could fix it." My friend reminded me that the subconscious intelligence, which created my body, was like a watchmaker, and it also knew exactly how to heal, restore, and direct all the vital functions and processes of my body, but that I had to give it the perfect idea of health. This would act as cause, and the effect would be a healing.

I prayed in a very simple way as follows: "My body and all its organs were created by the Infinite Intelligence in my subconscious mind. It knows how to heal me, its wisdom fashioned all my organs, tissues, muscles, and bones. This Infinite Healing Presence within me is now transforming every atom of my being making me whole and perfect now. I give thanks for the healing I know is taking place now. Wonderful are the works of the creative intelligence within me."

I prayed aloud for about five minutes two or three times a day, repeating the above simple prayer. In about three months my skin was whole and perfect.

As you can see, all I did was give life-giving patterns of wholeness, beauty, and perfection to my subconscious mind, thereby obliterating the negative images and patterns of thought lodged in my subconscious mind, which were the cause of all my trouble. Nothing appears on your body except when the mental equivalent is first in your mind, and as you change your mind by drenching it with incessant affirmatives, you change your body. This is the basis of all healing. *Marvelous are thy works; and that my soul* [subconscious mind] *knoweth right well* (Psalms 139:14).

How the Subconscious Controls All Functions of the Body

While you are awake or sound asleep upon your bed, the ceaseless, tireless action of your subconscious mind controls all the vital organs of your body without the help of your conscious mind. For example, while you are asleep your heart continues to beat rhythmically, your lungs do not rest, and the process of inhalation and exhalation, whereby your blood absorbs fresh air, goes on just the same as when you are awake. Your subconscious controls your digestive processes and glandular secretions, as well as all the other mysterious operations of your body. The hair on your face continues to grow whether you are asleep or awake. Scientists tell us that the skin secretes much more perspiration during sleep than during the waking hours. Your eyes, ears, and other senses are active during sleep.

For instance, many of our great scientists have received answers to perplexing problems while they were asleep. They saw the answers in a dream.

Oftentimes your conscious mind interferes with the normal rhythm of the heart, lungs, and functioning of the stomach and intestines by worry, anxiety, fear, and depression.

These patterns of thought interfere with the harmonious functioning of your subconscious mind. When mentally disturbed, the best procedure is to let go, relax, and still the wheels of your thought processes. Speak to your subconscious mind, telling it to take over in peace, harmony, and divine order. You will find that all the functions of your body will become normal again. Be sure to speak to your subconscious mind with authority and conviction and it will conform to your command.

Your subconscious seeks to preserve your life and restore you to health at all costs. It causes you to love your children, which also illustrates an instinctive desire to preserve all life. Let us suppose you accidentally ate some bad food. Your subconscious mind would cause you to regurgitate it.

If you inadvertently took some poison, your subconscious powers would proceed to neutralize it. If you completely entrusted yourself to its wonder-working power, you would be entirely restored to health.

How to Get the Subconscious to Work for You

The first thing to realize is that your subconscious mind is always working. It is active night and day, whether you act upon it or not. Your subconscious is the builder of your body, but you cannot consciously perceive or hear that inner silent process. Your business is with your conscious mind and not your subconscious mind. Just keep your conscious mind busy with the expectation of the best and make sure the thoughts you habitually think are based on whatsoever things are lovely, true, just, and of good report. Begin now to take care of your conscious mind, knowing in your heart and soul that your subconscious mind is always expressing, reproducing, and manifesting according to your habitual thinking.

Remember, just as water takes the shape of the pipe it flows through, the Life-Principle in you flows through you according to the nature of your thoughts. Claim that the healing presence in your subconscious is flowing through you as harmony, health, peace, joy, and abundance. Think of it as a living intelligence, a lovely companion on the way. Firmly believe it is continually flowing through you vivifying, inspiring, and prospering you. It will respond exactly this way. It is done unto you, as you believe.

Healing Principle of the Subconscious Restores Atrophied Optic Nerves

There is the well-known, duly authenticated case of Madame Bire of France, recorded in the archives of the medical department of Lourdes, France. She was blind; the optic nerves were atrophied and useless. She visited Lourdes and had what she termed a miraculous healing. Ruth Cranston, a Protestant young lady who investigated and wrote about healings at Lourdes in *McCall's* magazine, November 1955, writes about Madame Bire as follows: "At Lourdes she regained her sight incredibly, with the optic nerves still lifeless and useless, as several doctors could testify after repeated examinations. A month later, upon re-examination, it was found that the seeing mechanism had been restored to normal. But at first, so far as medical examination could tell, she was seeing with 'dead eyes.'"

I have visited Lourdes several times where I, too, witnessed some healings and, of course, as we shall explain in the next chapter, there is no doubt that healings take place at many shrines throughout the world, Christian and non-Christian.

Madame Bire, to whom we just referred, was not healed by the waters of the shrine, but by her own subconscious mind, which responded to her belief. The healing principle within her subconscious mind responded to the nature of her thought. Belief is a thought in the subconscious mind. It means to accept something as true. The thought accepted executes itself automatically. Undoubtedly, Madame Bire went to the shrine with expectancy and great faith, knowing in her heart she would receive a healing. Her subconscious mind, which created the eye, can certainly bring a dead nerve back to life. What the creative principle created, it can recreate. *According to your belief is it done unto you* (Matthew 9:29).

How to Convey the Idea of Perfect Health to Your Subconscious Mind

A Protestant minister I knew in Johannesburg, South Africa, told me the method he used to convey the idea of perfect health to his subconscious mind. He had cancer of the lung. His technique, as given to me in his own handwriting, is exactly as follows: "Several times a day I would make certain that I was completely relaxed, mentally and physically. I relaxed my body by speaking to it as follows: 'My heart and lungs are relaxed, my head is relaxed, my whole being is completely relaxed.' After about five minutes I would be in a sleepy, drowsy state, and then I affirmed the following truth, 'The perfection of God is now being expressed through me. The idea of perfect health is now filling my subconscious mind. The image God has of me is a perfect image, and my subconscious mind recreates my body in perfect accordance with the perfect image held in the mind of God.'" This minister had a remarkable healing. This is a simple, easy way of conveying the idea of perfect health to your subconscious mind.

Another wonderful way to convey the idea of health to your subconscious mind is through disciplined or scientific imagination. I told a man who was suffering from functional paralysis to make a vivid picture of himself walking around in his office, touching the desk, answering the telephone, and doing all the things he ordinarily would do if he were healed. I explained to him that this idea and mental picture of perfect health would be accepted by his subconscious mind.

He lived the role and actually felt himself back in the office. He knew that he was giving his subconscious mind something definite to work upon. His subconscious mind was the film upon which the picture was impressed. One day, after several weeks of frequent conditioning of the mind with this mental picture, the telephone rang by prearrangement and kept ringing while his wife and nurse were out. The telephone was about twelve feet away, but nevertheless he managed to answer it. He was healed at that hour. The healing power of his subconscious mind responded to his mental imagery and a healing followed.

This man had a mental block, which prevented impulses from the brain reaching his legs; therefore, he said he could not walk. When he shifted his attention to the healing power within him, the power flowed through his focused attention, enabling him to walk. *Whatsoever ye shall ask in prayer, believing, ye shall receive* (Matthew 21:22).

Ideas Worth Remembering

1. Your subconscious mind controls all the vital processes of your body and knows the answer to all problems.

2. Prior to sleep, turn over a specific request to your subconscious mind and prove its miracle-working power to yourself.

3. Whatever you impress on your subconscious mind is expressed on the screen of space as conditions, experiences, and events. Therefore, you should carefully watch all ideas and thoughts entertained in your conscious mind.

4. The law of action and reaction is universal. Your thought is action and the reaction is the automatic response of your subconscious mind to your thought. Watch your thoughts!

5. All frustration is due to unfulfilled desires. If you dwell on obstacles, delays, and difficulties, your subconscious mind responds accordingly and you are blocking your own good.

6. The Life-Principle will flow through you rhythmically and harmoniously if you consciously affirm: "I believe that the subconscious power, which gave me this desire, is now fulfilling it through me." This dissolves all conflicts.

7. You can interfere with the normal rhythm of your heart, lungs, and other organs by worry, anxiety, and fear. Feed your subconscious with thoughts of harmony, health, and peace and all the functions of your body will become normal again.

8. Keep your conscious mind busy with the expectation of the best and your subconscious will faithfully reproduce your habitual thinking.

9. Imagine the happy ending or solution to your problem, feel the thrill of accomplishment; and what you imagine and feel will be accepted by your subconscious mind and bring it to pass.

4

Mental Healings in Ancient Times

Down through the ages men of all nations have somehow instinctively believed that somewhere there resided a healing power, which would restore to normal the functions and sensations of man's body. They believed that this strange power could be invoked under certain conditions and that the alleviation of human suffering would follow. The history of all nations presents testimony in support of this belief.

In the early history of the world the power of secretly influencing men for good or evil, including the healing of the sick, was said to be possessed by the priests and holy men of all nations. Healing of the sick was supposed to be a power derived directly by them from God and the procedures and processes of healing varied throughout the world. The healing processes took the form of supplications to God attended by various ceremonies such as the laying on of hands, incantations, the application of amulets, talismans, rings, relics, and images.

For example, in the religions of antiquity, priests in the ancient temples gave drugs to the patient and practiced hypnotic suggestions prior to the patient's sleep, telling him that the gods would visit him in his sleep and heal him. Many healings followed. Obviously, all this was the work of potent suggestions to the subconscious mind.

After the performance of certain mysterious rites, the devotees of Hecate would see the goddess during sleep, provided that before going to sleep they had prayed to her according to weird and fantastic instructions. They were told to mix lizards with resin, frankincense, and myrrh and pound all this together in the open air under the crescent moon. Healings were reported in many cases following this grotesque procedure.

It is obvious that these strange procedures, as mentioned in the illustrations given, favored suggestion and acceptance by the subconscious mind of these people by making a powerful appeal to their imagination. Actually, in all these healings, the subconscious mind of the subject was the healer.

In all ages, unofficial healers have obtained remarkable results in cases where authorized medical skill has failed. This gives cause for thought. How do these healers in all parts of the world effect their cures? The answer to all these healings is due to the blind belief of the sick person, which released the healing power resident in his subconscious mind. Many of the remedies and methods employed were rather strange and fantastic, which fired the imagination of the patients, causing an aroused emotional state. This state of mind facilitated the suggestion of health, and was accepted both by the conscious and subconscious mind of the sick. This will be elaborated on further in the next chapter.

Biblical Accounts of the Use of the Subconscious Powers

What things soever ye desire, when ye pray believe that ye receive them, and ye shall have them (Mark 11:24). Note the difference in tenses. The inspired writer tells us to believe and accept as true the fact that our desire has already been accomplished and fulfilled, that it is already completed, and that its realization will follow as a thing in the future.

The success of this technique depends on the confident conviction that the thought, the idea, the picture is already a fact in mind. In order for anything to have substance in the realm of mind, it must be thought of as actually existing there.

Here, in a few cryptic words, is a concise and specific direction for making use of the creative power of thought by impressing upon the subconscious the particular thing which you desire. Your thought, idea, plan, or purpose is as real on its own plane as your hand or your heart. In following the biblical technique, you completely eliminate from your mind all consideration of conditions, circumstances, or anything which might imply adverse contingencies. You are planting a seed (concept) in the mind, which, if you leave it undisturbed, will infallibly germinate into external fruition.

The prime condition, which Jesus insisted upon, was faith. Over and over again you read in the Bible, "According to your faith is it done unto you." If you plant certain types of seeds in the ground, you have faith they will grow after their kind. This is the way of seeds, and trusting the laws of growth and agriculture, you know that the seeds will come forth after their kind. Faith as mentioned in the Bible is a way of thinking, an attitude of mind, an inner certitude, knowing that the idea you fully accept in your conscious mind will be embodied in your subconscious mind and made manifest. Faith is, in a sense, accepting as true what your reason and senses deny, i.e., a shutting out of the little, rational, analytical, conscious mind and embracing an attitude of complete reliance on the inner power of your subconscious mind.

A classical instance of Bible technique is recorded in Matthew 9:28–30:

*And when he was come into the house, the blind man came to
him; and Jesus saith unto them, Believe ye that I am able to do
this? They said unto him, Yea, Lord. Then touched he their eyes,
saying, according to your faith be it unto you. And their eyes
opened; and Jesus straightly charged them, saying, see that no
man know it.*

In the words, "according to your faith be it unto you," you
can see that Jesus was actually appealing to the cooperation of the
subconscious mind of the blind men. Their faith was their great
expectancy, their inner feeling, their inner conviction that something miraculous would happen, and that their prayer would be
answered, and it was. This is the time-honored technique of healing,
utilized alike by all healing groups throughout the world regardless
of religious affiliation.

In the words, "see that no man know it," Jesus enjoins the newly
healed patients not to discuss their healing because they might be subjected to the skeptical and derogatory criticisms of the unbelieving.
This might tend to undo the benefits they had received at the hand
of Jesus by depositing thoughts of fear, doubt, and anxiety in the subconscious mind.

*For with authority and power he commandeth the unclean spir-
its, and they came out* (Luke 4:36). When the sick came to Jesus to
be healed, they were healed by their faith together with his faith
and understanding of the healing power of the subconscious mind.
Whatever he decreed, he felt inwardly to be true. He and the people needing help were in the one universal, subjective mind, and his
silent inner knowing and conviction of the healing power changed
the negative, destructive patterns in the patients' subconscious. The
resultant healings were the automatic response to the internal mental change. His command was his appeal to the subconscious mind

of the patients plus his awareness, feeling, and absolute trust in the response of the subconscious mind to the words, which he spoke with authority.

Miracles at Various Shrines throughout the World

It is an established fact that cures have taken place at various shrines throughout the world, such as in Japan, India, Europe, and America. I have visited several of the famous shrines in Japan. At the world famous shrine called Daibutsu is a gigantic divinity of bronze where Buddha is seated with folded hands, and the head is inclined in an attitude of profound contemplative ecstasy. It is forty-two feet in height and is called the Great Buddha. Here I saw young and old making offerings at its feet. Money, fruit, rice, and oranges were offered. Candles were lit, incense was burned, and prayers of petition recited.

The guide explained the chant of a young girl as she murmured a prayer, bowed low, and placed two oranges as an offering. She also lit a candle. He said she had lost her voice, and it was restored at the shrine. She was thanking Buddha for restoring her voice. She had the simple faith that Buddha would give her back her singing voice if she followed a certain ritual, fasted, and made certain offerings. All this helped to kindle faith and expectancy, resulting in a conditioning of her mind to the point of belief. Her subconscious mind responded to her belief.

To illustrate further the power of imagination and blind belief, I will relate the case of a relative of mine who had tuberculosis. His lungs were badly diseased. His son decided to heal his father. He came home to Perth, Western Australia, where his father lived, and said to him that he had met a monk who had returned from one of the healing shrines in Europe. This monk sold him a piece of the true cross. He said he gave the monk the equivalent of five hundred dollars for it.

This young man had actually picked up a splinter of wood from the sidewalk, went to the jeweler's, and had it set in a ring so that it looked real. He told his father that many were healed just by touching the ring or the cross. He inflamed and fired his father's imagination to the point that the old gentleman snatched the ring from him, placed it over his chest, prayed silently, and went to sleep. In the morning he was healed. All the clinic's tests proved negative.

You know, of course, it was not the splinter of wood from the sidewalk that healed him. It was his imagination aroused to an intense degree, plus the confident expectancy of a perfect healing. Imagination was joined to faith or subjective feeling, and the union of the two brought about a healing. The father never learned of the trick that had been played upon him. If he had, he probably would have had a relapse. He remained completely cured and passed away fifteen years later at the age of eighty-nine.

One Universal Healing Principle

It is a well-known fact that all of the various schools of healing effect cures of the most wonderful character. The most obvious conclusion which strikes your mind is that there must be some underlying principle which is common to them all: namely, the subconscious mind, and the one process of healing is faith.

It will now be in order to recall to your mind once more the following fundamental truths:

First, that you possess mental functions, which have been distinguished by designating one the conscious mind and the other the subconscious mind.

Second, your subconscious mind is constantly amenable to the power of suggestion. Furthermore, your subconscious mind has complete control of the functions, conditions, and sensations of your body.

I venture to believe that all the readers of this book are familiar with the fact that symptoms of almost any disease can be induced in hypnotic subjects by suggestion. For example, a subject in the hypnotic state can develop a high temperature, flushed face, or chills according to the nature of the suggestion given. By experiment, you can also suggest to the person that he is paralyzed and cannot walk: it will be so. By illustration, you can hold a cup of cold water under the nose of the hypnotic subject and tell him, "This is full of pepper, smell it!" He will proceed to sneeze. What do you think caused him to sneeze, the water or the suggestion?

If a man says he is allergic to Timothy grass, you can place a synthetic flower or an empty glass in front of nose, when he is in a hypnotic state, and tell him it is Timothy grass. He will portray the usual allergic symptoms. This indicates that the cause of the disease is in the mind. The healing of the disease can also take place mentally.

You realize that remarkable healings take place through osteopathy, chiropractic medicine, and naturopathy, as well as through all the various religious bodies throughout the world, but it is obvious that all of these healings are brought about through the subconscious mind: the only healer there is.

Notice how it heals a cut on your face caused by shaving. It knows exactly how to do it. The doctor dresses the wound and says, "Nature heals it!"

Nature refers to natural law, the law of the subconscious mind, or self-preservation, which is the function of the subconscious mind. The instinct of self-preservation is the first law of nature. Your strongest instinct is the most potent of all autosuggestions.

Widely Different Theories

It would be tedious and unprofitable to discuss to any great extent the numerous theories advanced by different religious sects and prayer therapy groups. There are a great number who claim that because their theory produces results it is, therefore, the correct one. This, as explained in this chapter, cannot be true.

You are aware that there are all types of healing. Franz Anton Mesmer, an Austrian physician (1734–1815) who practiced in Paris, discovered that by applying magnets to the diseased body he could cure that disease miraculously. He also performed cures with various other pieces of glass and metals. He discontinued this form of healing and claimed that his cures were due to "animal magnetism," theorizing that this substance was projected from the healer to the patient.

His method of healing disease from then on was by hypnotism, which was called mesmerism in his day. Other physicians said that all his healings were due to suggestion and nothing else.

All of these groups, such as psychiatrists, psychologists, osteopaths, chiropractors, physicians, and all the churches, are using the one universal power resident in the subconscious mind. Each may proclaim the healings are due to their theory. The process of all healing is a definite, positive, mental attitude, an inner attitude, or a way of thinking, called faith. Healing is due to a confident expectancy, which acts as a powerful suggestion to the subconscious mind releasing its healing potency.

One man does not heal by a different power than another. It is true that he may have his own theory or method. There is only one process of healing and that is faith. There is only one healing power, namely, your subconscious mind. Select the theory and method you prefer. You can rest assured, if you have faith, you shall get results.

Views of Paracelsus

Philippus Paracelsus, a famous Swiss alchemist and physician, who lived from 1493 to 1541, was a great healer in his day. He stated what is now an obvious scientific fact when he uttered these words, "Whether the object of your faith be real or false, you will nevertheless obtain the same effects. Thus, if I believed in Saint Peter's statue as I should have believed in Saint Peter himself, I shall obtain the same effects that I should have obtained from Saint Peter. But that is superstition. Faith, however, produces miracles; and whether it is true or false faith, it will always produce the same wonders."

The views of Paracelsus were also entertained in the sixteenth century by Pietro Pomponazzi, an Italian philosopher and contemporary of Paracelsus, who said, "We can easily conceive the marvelous effects, which confidence and imagination can produce, particularly when both qualities are reciprocated between the subjects and the person who influences them. The cures attributed to the influence of certain relics are the effect of their imagination and confidence. Quacks and philosophers know that if the bones of any skeleton were put in place of the saint's bones, the sick would nonetheless experience beneficial effects, if they believed that they were veritable relics."

Then, if you believe in the bones of saints to heal, or if you believe in the healing power of certain waters, you will get results because of the powerful suggestion given to your subconscious mind. It is the latter that does the healing.

Bernheim's Experiments

Hippolyte Bernheim, professor of medicine at Nancy, France, 1910 to 1919, was the expounder of the fact that the suggestion of the physician to the patient was exerted through the subconscious mind.

Bernheim, in his *Suggestive Therapeutics*, tells a story of a man with paralysis of the tongue, which had yielded to no form of treatment. His doctor told the patient that he had a new instrument with which he promised to heal him. He introduced a pocket thermometer into the patient's mouth. The patient imagined it to be the instrument which was to save him. In a few moments he cried out joyfully that he could once more move his tongue freely.

"Among our cases," continues Bernheim, "facts of the same sort will be found. A young girl came into my office, having suffered from complete loss of speech for nearly four weeks. After making sure of the diagnosis, I told my students that loss of speech sometimes yielded instantly to electricity, which might act simply by its suggestive influence. I sent for the induction apparatus. I applied my hand over the larynx and moved a little, and said, 'Now you can speak aloud.' In an instant I made her say 'A,' then 'B,' then 'Maria.' She continued to speak distinctly; the loss of voice had disappeared." Here Bernheim is showing the power of faith and expectancy on the part of the patient, which acts as a powerful suggestion to the subconscious mind.

Producing a Blister by Suggestion

Bernheim states that he produced a blister on the back of a patient's neck by applying a postage stamp and suggesting to the patient that it was a fly-plaster [blister-plaster]. This had been confirmed by the experiments and experiences of many doctors in many parts of the world, which leave no doubt that structural changes are a possible result of oral suggestion to patients.

The Cause of Bloody Stigmata

In [Thomas Jay] Hudson's *Law of Psychic Phenomena*, he states,

> Hemorrhages and bloody stigmata may be induced in certain subjects by means of suggestion.
>
> Dr. M. Bourru put a subject into the somnambulistic condition, and gave him the following suggestion: "At four o'clock this afternoon, after the hypnosis, you will come into my office, sit down in the armchair, cross your arms upon your breast, and your nose will begin to bleed." At the hour appointed the young man did as directed. Several drops of blood came from the left nostril.
>
> On another occasion the same investigator traced the patient's name on both his forearms with the dull point of an instrument. Then when the patient was in the somnambulistic condition, he said, "At four o'clock this afternoon you will go to sleep, and your arms will bleed along the lines which I have traced, and your name will appear written on your arms in the letters of blood." He was watched at four o'clock and seen to fall asleep. On the left arm the letters stood out in bright relief and in several places there were drops of blood. The letters were still visible three months afterward, although they had gradually grown faint.

These facts demonstrate at once the correctness of the two fundamental propositions previously stated, namely, the constant amenability of the subconscious mind to the power of suggestion and the perfect control, which the subconscious mind exercises over the functions, sensations, and conditions of the body. All the foregoing phenomena dramatize vividly abnormal conditions induced by suggestion, and are conclusive proof of this line from Proverbs 23:7, *As a man thinketh in his heart* [subconscious mind] *so is he.*

Healing Points in Review

1. Remind yourself frequently that the healing power is in your own subconscious mind.

2. Know that faith is like a seed planted in the ground; it grows after its kind. Plant the idea (seed) in your mind, water, and fertilize it with expectancy and it will manifest.

3. The idea you have for a book, new invention, or play is real in your mind. This is why you can believe you have it now. Believe in the reality of your idea, plan, or invention, and as you do, it will become manifest.

4. In praying for another, know that your silent inner knowing of wholeness, beauty, and perfection can change the negative patterns of the other's subconscious mind and bring about wonderful results.

5. The miraculous healings you hear about at various shrines are due to imagination and blind faith, which act on the subconscious mind, releasing the healing power.

6. All disease originates in the mind. Nothing appears on the body unless there is a mental pattern corresponding to it.

7. The symptoms of almost any disease can be induced in you by hypnotic suggestion. This shows you the power of your thought.

8. There is only one process of healing and that is faith. There is only one healing power, namely, your subconscious mind.

9. Whether the object of your faith is real or false, you will get results. Your subconscious mind responds to the thought in your mind. Look upon faith as thought in your mind and that will suffice.

5

Mental Healings in Modern Times

Everyone is definitely concerned with the healing of bodily conditions and human affairs. What is it that heals? Where is this healing power? These are questions asked by everyone. The answer is that this healing power is in the subconscious mind of each person, and a changed mental attitude on the part of the sick person releases this healing power.

No mental or religious science practitioner, psychologist, psychiatrist, or medical doctor ever healed a patient. There is an old saying, "The doctor dressed the wound, but God heals it." The psychologist or psychiatrist proceeds to remove the mental blocks in the patient so that the healing principle may be released, restoring the patient to health. Likewise, the surgeon removes the physical block enabling the healing currents to function normally. No physician, surgeon or mental science practitioner claims that "he healed the patient." The one healing power is called by many names: Nature, Life, God, Creative Intelligence, Subconscious Power.

As previously outlined, there are many different methods used to remove the mental, emotional, and physical blocks, which inhibit the flow of the healing Life-Principle animating all of us. The healing principle in your subconscious mind can and will, if properly directed by you or some other person, heal your mind and body of all disease. This healing principle is operative in all men regardless of creed, color, or race. You do not have to belong to some particular church in order to use and participate in this healing process. Your subconscious will heal the burn or cut on your hand even though you profess to be an atheist or agnostic.

The modern mental therapeutic procedure is based on the truth that the Infinite Intelligence and power of your subconscious mind responds according to your faith. The mental science practitioner or minister follows the injunction of the Bible, i.e., he goes into his closet and shuts the door, which means he stills his mind, relaxes, lets go, and thinks of the Infinite Healing Presence within him. He closes the door of his mind to all outside distractions as well as appearances, and then he quietly and knowingly turns over his request or desire to his subconscious mind, realizing that the intelligence of his mind will answer him according to his specific needs.

The most wonderful thing to know is this: Imagine the end desired and feel its reality; then the infinite Life-Principle will respond to your conscious choice and your conscious request. This is the meaning of "Believe you have received, and you shall receive." This is what the modern mental scientist does when he practices prayer therapy.

One Process of Healing

There is only one universal healing principle operating through everything—the cat, the dog, the tree, the grass, the wind, the earth— for everything is alive. This Life-Principle operates through the animal, vegetable, and mineral kingdoms as instinct and the law of growth. Man is consciously aware of this Life-Principle, and he can consciously direct it to bless himself in countless ways.

There are many different approaches, techniques, and methods in using the universal power, but there is only process of healing, which is faith, *For according to your faith is it done unto you* (Matthew 9:29).

The Law of Belief

All religions of the world represent forms of belief, and these beliefs are explained in many ways. The law of life is belief. What do you believe about yourself, life, and the universe? It is done unto you as you believe.

Belief is a thought in your mind, which causes the power of your subconscious to be distributed into all phases of your life according to your thinking habits. You must realize the Bible is not talking about your belief in some ritual, ceremony, form, institution, man, or formula. It is talking about belief itself. The belief of your mind is simply the thought of your mind. *If thou canst believe, all things are possible to him that believeth* (Mark 9:23).

It is foolish to believe in something to hurt or harm you. Remember, it is not the thing believed in that hurts or harms you, but the belief or thought in your mind, which creates the result. All your experiences, all your actions, and all the events and circumstances of your life are but the reflections and reactions to your own thought.

Prayer Therapy Is the Combined Function of the Conscious and Subconscious Mind Scientifically Directed

Prayer therapy is the synchronized, harmonious, and intelligent function of the conscious and subconscious levels of mind specifically directed for a definite purpose. In scientific prayer or prayer therapy, you must know what you are doing and why you are doing it. You trust the law of healing.

Prayer therapy is sometimes referred to as mental treatment, and another term is scientific prayer.

In prayer therapy you consciously choose a certain idea, mental picture, or plan, which you desire to experience. You realize your capacity to convey this idea or mental image to your subconscious by feeling the reality of the state assumed. As you remain faithful in your mental attitude, your prayer will be answered. Prayer therapy is a definite mental action for a definite specific purpose.

Let us suppose that you decide to heal a certain difficulty by prayer therapy. You are aware that your problem or sickness, whatever it may be, must be caused by negative thoughts charged with fear and lodged in your subconscious mind, and that if you can succeed in cleansing your mind of these thoughts, you will get a healing.

You, therefore, turn to the healing power within your own subconscious mind and remind yourself of its infinite power and intelligence and its capacity to heal all conditions. As you dwell on these truths, your fear will begin to dissolve, and the recollection of these truths also corrects the erroneous beliefs. You give thanks for the healing that you know will come and then you keep your mind off the difficulty until you feel guided, after an interval, to pray again. While you are praying, you absolutely refuse to give any power to the negative conditions or to admit for a second that the healing will not come. This attitude of mind brings about the harmonious union of the conscious and subconscious mind, which releases the healing power.

Faith Healing, What It Means, and How Blind Faith Works

What is popularly termed faith healing is not the faith mentioned in the Bible, which means a knowledge of the interaction of the conscious and subconscious mind. A faith healer is one who heals without any real scientific understanding of the powers and forces involved. He may claim that he has a special gift of healing, and the sick person's blind belief in him or his powers may bring results.

The "voodoo" doctor in South Africa and other parts of the world may heal by incantations, or a person may be healed by touching the so-called bones of saints, or anything else which causes the patients to honestly believe in the method or process.

Any method which causes you to move from fear and worry to faith and expectancy will heal. There are many persons, each of whom claims that because his personal theory produces results, it is, therefore, the correct one. This, as already explained in this chapter, cannot be true.

To illustrate how blind faith works: You will recall our discussion of the Swiss physician, Franz Anton Mesmer. In 1776, he claimed many cures when he stroked diseased bodies with artificial magnets. Later on, he threw away his magnets and evolved the theory of animal magnetism. This he held to be a fluid, which pervades the universe, but is most active in the human organism.

He claimed that his magnetic fluid, which was going forth from him to his patients, healed them. People flocked to him and many wonderful cures were effected.

Mesmer moved to Paris, and while there the government appointed a commission composed of physicians and members of the Academy of Science, of which Benjamin Franklin was a member, to investigate his cures. The report admitted the leading facts claimed by Mesmer, but held that there was no evidence to prove the correctness of his magnetic fluid theory and said the effects were due to the imagination of the patients.

Soon after this, Mesmer was driven into exile and died in 1815. Shortly afterwards, Dr. Braid of Manchester undertook to show that magnetic fluid had nothing to do with the production of the healings of Dr. Mesmer. Dr. Braid discovered that patients could be thrown into hypnotic sleep by suggestion, during which many of the well-known phenomena ascribed to magnetism by Mesmer could be produced.

You can readily see that all these cures were undoubtedly brought about by the active imagination of the patients together with a powerful suggestion of health to their subconscious minds. All this could be termed "blind faith" as there was no understanding in those days as to how the cures were brought about.

Subjective Faith and What It Means

You will recall the proposition, which need not be repeated at length, that the subjective or subconscious mind of an individual is as amenable to the control of his own conscious or objective mind as it is by the suggestions of another. It follows that whatever may be your objective belief, if you will assume to have faith actively or passively, your subconscious mind will be controlled by the suggestions, and your desire will be fulfilled.

The faith required in mental healings is a purely subjective faith, and is attainable upon the cessation of active opposition on the part of the objective or conscious mind.

In the healing of the body it is, of course, desirable to secure the concurrent faith of both the conscious and subconscious mind. However, it is not always essential if you will enter into a state of passivity and receptivity by relaxing the mind and the body and getting into a sleepy state. In this drowsy state your passivity becomes receptive to subjective impression.

Recently, I was asked by a man, "How is it that I got a healing through a minister? I did not believe what he said when he told me that there is no such thing as disease and that matter does not exist."

This man at first thought his intelligence was being insulted, and he protested against such a palpable absurdity. The explanation is simple. He was quieted by soothing words and told to get into a perfectly passive condition, to say nothing, and think of nothing for the time being. His minister also became passive and affirmed quietly, peacefully, and constantly for about one half hour that this man would have perfect health, peace, harmony, and wholeness. He felt immense relief and was restored to health.

It is easy to see that his subjective faith had been made manifest by his passivity under treatment and the suggestions of perfect healthfulness by the minister were conveyed to his subconscious mind. The two subjective minds were then en rapport.

The minister was not handicapped by antagonistic auto-suggestions of the patient arising from objective doubt of the power of the healer or the correctness of the theory. In this sleepy, drowsy state the conscious mind resistance is reduced to a minimum and results followed. The subconscious mind of the patient being necessarily controlled by such suggestion exercised its functions in accordance therewith, and a healing followed.

The Meaning of Absent Treatment

Suppose you learned that your mother was sick in New York City and you lived in Los Angeles. Your mother would not be physically present where you are, but you could pray for her. *It is the Father within which doeth the work* (John 14:10).

The creative law of mind (subconscious mind) serves you and will do the work. Its response to you is automatic. Your treatment is for the purpose of inducing an inner realization of health and harmony in your mentality. This inner realization, acting through the subconscious mind, operates through your mother's subconscious mind, as there is but one creative mind. Your thoughts of health, vitality, and perfection operate through the one universal subjective mind, and set a law of motion on the subjective side of life, which manifests through her body as a healing.

In the mind principle there is no time or space. It is the same mind that operates through your mother, no matter where she may be. In reality there is no "absent treatment," as opposed to "present treatment," for the universal mind is omnipresent. You do not try to send out thoughts or hold a thought. Your treatment is a conscious movement of thought and, as you become conscious of the qualities of health, well-being, and relaxation, these qualities will be resurrected in the experience of your mother, and results will follow.

The following is a perfect example of what is called absent treatment. Recently, a listener of our radio program in Los Angeles prayed as follows for her mother in New York, who had a coronary thrombosis: "The healing presence is right where my mother is. Her bodily condition is but a reflection of her thought-life, like shadows cast on the screen. I know that in order to change the images on the screen I must change the projection reel. My mind is the projection reel, and I now project in my own mind the image of wholeness, harmony, and perfect health for my mother. The Infinite Healing Presence, which created my mother's body and all her organs, is now saturating every atom of her being, and a river of peace flows through every cell of her body. The doctors are divinely guided and directed, and whoever touches my mother is guided to do the right thing. I know that disease has no ultimate reality; if it had, no one could be healed. I now align myself with the infinite principle of love and life, and I know and decree that harmony, health, and peace are now being expressed in my mother's body."

She prayed in the above manner several times daily, and her mother had a most remarkable recovery after a few days, much to the amazement of her specialist. He complimented her on her great faith in the power of God.

The conclusion, arrived at in the daughter's mind, set the creative law of mind in motion on the subjective side of life, which manifested itself through her mother's body as perfect health and harmony. What the daughter felt as true about her mother was simultaneously resurrected in the experience of her mother.

Releasing the Kinetic Action of the Subconscious Mind

A psychologist friend of mind told me that one of his lungs was infected. X-rays and analysis showed the presence of tuberculosis. At night going to sleep he would quietly affirm, "Every cell, nerve, tissue, and muscle of my lungs is now being made whole, pure, and perfect. My whole body is being restored to health and harmony."

These are not his exact words, but they represent the essence of what he affirmed. A complete healing followed in about a month's time. Subsequent X-rays showed a perfect healing.

I wanted to know his method, so I asked him why he repeated the words prior to sleep. Here is his reply, "The kinetic action of the subconscious mind continues through your sleep time period. Hence, give the subconscious mind something good to work on as you drop off into slumber." This was very wise answer. In thinking of harmony and perfect health, he never mentioned his trouble by name.

I strongly suggest that you cease talking about your ailments or giving them a name. The only sap from which they draw life is your attention and fear of them. Like the above mentioned psychologist, become a mental surgeon. Then your troubles will be cut off like dead branches are pruned from a tree.

If you are constantly naming your aches and symptoms you inhibit the kinetic action, which means the release of the healing power and energy of your subconscious mind. Furthermore, by the law of your own mind, these imaginings tend to take shape *as the thing I greatly feared* (Job 3:25). Fill your mind with the great truths of life and walk forward in the light of love.

Summary of Your Aids to Health

1. Find out what it is that heals you. Realize that correct directions given to the subconscious mind will heal your mind and body.

2. Develop a definite plan for turning over your requests or desires to your subconscious mind.

3. Imagine the end desired and feel its reality. Follow it through and you will get definite results.

4. Decide what belief is. Know that belief is a thought in your mind, and what you think, you create.

5. It is foolish to believe in sickness and something to hurt or harm you. Believe in perfect health, prosperity, peace, wealth, and divine guidance.

6. Great and noble thoughts upon which you habitually dwell become great acts.

7. Apply the power of prayer therapy in your life. Choose a certain plan, idea, or mental picture. Mentally and emotionally unite with that idea and as you remain faithful to your mental attitude, your prayer will be answered.

8. Always remember, if you really want the power to heal, you can have it through faith, which means a knowledge of the working of your conscious and subconscious mind. Faith comes with understanding.

9. Blind faith means that a person may get results in healing without any scientific understanding of the powers and forces involved.

10. Learn to pray for your loved ones who my be ill. Quiet your mind and your thoughts of health, vitality, and perfection, operating through the one universal subjective mind, will be felt and resurrected in the mind of your loved one.

6

Practical Techniques in Mental Healing

An engineer has a technique and a process for building a bridge or an engine. Like the engineer, your mind also has a technique for governing, controlling, and directing your life. You must realize that methods and techniques are primary.

In building the Golden Gate Bridge, the chief engineer understood mathematical principles, stresses, and strains. Secondly, he had a picture of the ideal bridge across the bay. The third step was his application of tried-and-proven methods by which the principles were implemented, until the bridge took form and we drive on it. There also are techniques and methods by which your prayers are answered. If your prayer is answered, there is a way in which it is answered and this is a scientific way. Nothing happens by chance. This is a world of law and order. In this chapter you will find practical techniques for the unfolding and nurture of your spiritual life. Your prayers must not remain up in the air like a balloon. They must go somewhere and accomplish something in your life.

When we come to analyze prayer we discover there are many different approaches and methods. We will not consider in this book the formal, ritual prayers used in religious services. These have an important place in group worship. We are immediately concerned with the methods of personal prayer as it is applied in your daily life and as it is used to help others.

Prayer is the formulation of an idea concerning something we wish to accomplish. Prayer is the soul's sincere desire. Your desire is your prayer. It comes out of your deepest needs and it reveals the things you want in life. *Blessed are they that hunger and thirst after righteousness; for they shall be filled* (Matthew 5:6). That is really prayer, life's hunger and thirst for peace, harmony, health, joy, and all the other blessings of life.

The Passing-Over Technique for Impregnating the Subconscious

This consists essentially in inducing the subconscious mind to take over your request as handed it by the conscious mind. This passing-over is best accomplished in the reverie-like state. Know that in your deeper mind is Infinite Intelligence and Infinite Power. Just calmly think over what you want; see it coming into fuller fruition from this moment forward. Be like the little girl who had a very bad cough and a sore throat. She declared firmly and repeatedly: "It is passing away now. It is passing away now." It passed away in about an hour. Use this technique with complete simplicity and naivete.

Your Subconscious Will Accept Your Blueprint

If you were building a new home for yourself and your family, you know that you would be intensely interested in regard to the blueprint for your home; you would see to it that the builders conformed to the blueprint. You would watch the material and select only the best wood, steel, in fact, the best of everything. What about your mental home and your mental blueprint for happiness and abundance? All your experiences and everything that enters into your life depend upon the nature of the mental building blocks which you use in the construction of your mental home.

If your blueprint is full of mental patterns of fear, worry, anxiety, or lack and if you are despondent, doubtful, and cynical, then the texture of the mental material you are weaving into your mind will come forth as more toil, care, tension, anxiety, and limitation of all kinds.

The most fundamental and the most far-reaching activity in life is that which you build into your mentality every waking hour. Your word is silent and invisible; nevertheless, it is real.

You are building your mental home all the time, and your thought and mental imagery represent your blueprint. Hour by hour, moment by moment, you can build radiant health, success, and happiness by the thoughts you think, the ideas which you harbor, the beliefs you accept, and the scenes that you rehearse in the hidden studio of your mind. This stately mansion, upon the construction of which you are perpetually engaged, is your personality, your identity in this plane, your whole life story on this earth.

Get a new blueprint; build silently by realizing peace, harmony, joy, and good will in the present moment. By dwelling upon these things, and claiming them, your subconscious mind will accept your blueprint and bring all these things to pass. *By their fruits ye shall know them* (Matthew 7:16).

The Science and Art of True Prayer

The term "science" means knowledge, which is coordinated, arranged, and systematized. Let us think of the science and art of true prayer as it deals with the fundamental principles of life and the techniques and processes by which they can be demonstrated in your life, as well as in the life of every human being when he applies them faithfully. The art is your technique or process, and the science behind it is the definite response of creative mind to your mental picture or thought. *Ask, and it shall be given you; seek, and ye shall find; knock, and it shall be opened unto you* (Matthew 7:7).

Here you are told you shall receive that for which you ask. It shall be opened to you when you knock, and you shall find that for which you are searching. This teaching implies the definiteness of mental and spiritual laws. There is always a direct response from the Infinite Intelligence of your subconscious mind to your conscious thinking. If you ask for bread, you will not receive a stone. You must ask *believing*, if you are to receive.

Your mind moves from the thought to the thing. Unless there is first an image in the mind, it cannot move, for there would be nothing for it to move toward. Your prayer, which is your mental act, must be accepted as an image in your mind before the power from your subconscious will play upon it and make it productive. You must reach a point of acceptance in your mind, an unqualified and undisputed state of agreement.

This contemplation should be accompanied by a feeling of joy and restfulness in foreseeing the certain accomplishment of your desire. The sound basis for the art and science of true prayer is your knowledge and complete confidence that the movement of your conscious mind will gain a definite response from your subconscious mind, which is one with boundless wisdom and infinite power. By following this procedure, your prayers will be answered.

The Visualization Technique

The easiest and most obvious way to formulate an idea is to visualize it, to see it in your mind's eye as vividly as if it were alive. You can see with the naked eye only what already exists in the external world; in a similar way, that which you can visualize in your mind's eye already exists in the invisible realms of your mind. Any picture, which you have in your mind, is the substance of things hoped for and the evidence of things not seen. What you form in your imagination is as real as any part of your body. The idea and the thought are real and will one day appear in your objective world if you are faithful to your mental image.

This process of thinking forms impressions in your mind; these impressions in turn become manifested as facts and experiences in your life. The builder visualizes the type of building he wants; he sees it as he desires it to be completed. His imagery and thought processes become a plastic mold from which the building will emerge—a beautiful or an ugly one, a skyscraper or a very low one. His mental imagery is projected and is drawn on paper. Eventually, the contractor and his workers gather the essential materials and the building progresses until it stands finished, conforming perfectly to the mental patterns of the architect.

I use the visualization technique prior to speaking from the platform. I quiet the wheels of my mind in order that I may present to the subconscious mind my images of thought. Then, I picture the entire auditorium and the seats filled with men and women; each one of them illumined and inspired by the Infinite Healing Presence. I see them as radiant, happy, and free.

Having first built up the idea in my imagination, I quietly sustain it there as a mental picture while I imagine I hear men and women saying, "I am healed," "I feel wonderful," "I've had an instantaneous healing," "I'm transformed." I keep this up for about ten minutes or more, knowing and feeling that each person's mind and body are saturated with love, wholeness, beauty, and perfection. My awareness grows to the point where in my mind I can actually hear the voices of the multitude proclaiming their health and happiness; then I release the whole picture and go onto the platform. Almost every Sunday some people stop and say that their prayers were answered.

Mental Movie Method

The English say, "A picture is worth a thousand words." William James, the father of American psychology, stressed the fact that the subconscious mind will bring to pass any picture held in the mind and backed by faith. *Act as though I am, and I will be.*

A number of years ago I was in the Middle West lecturing in several states, and I desired to have a permanent location in the general area from which I could serve those who desired help. I traveled far, but the desire did not leave my mind. One evening, while in a hotel in Spokane, Washington, I relaxed completely on a couch, immobilized my attention, and in a quiet, passive manner imagined that I was talking to a large audience, saying, in effect, "I am glad to be here; I have prayed for the ideal opportunity." I saw in my mind's eye the imaginary audience and I felt the reality of it all. I played the role of the actor, dramatized this mental movie, and felt satisfied that this picture was being conveyed to my subconscious mind, which would bring it to pass in its own way. The next morning, on awakening, I felt a great sense of peace and satisfaction and in a few days' time I received a telegram asking me to take over an organization in the Midwest, which I did, and I enjoyed it immensely for several years.

The method outlined here appeals to many who have described it as "the mental movie method." I have received numerous letters from people who listen to my radio talks and weekly public lectures, telling me of the wonderful results they get using this technique in the sale of their property. I suggest to those who have homes or property for sale that they satisfy themselves in their own mind that their price is right. Then I claim that the Infinite Intelligence is attracting to them the buyer who really wants to have the property and who will love it and prosper in it. After having done this I suggest that they quiet their mind, relax, let go, and get into a drowsy, sleepy state, which reduces all mental effort to a minimum. Then they are to picture the check *in their hands*, rejoice in the check, give thanks for the check, and go off to sleep feeling the naturalness of the whole mental movie created in their own mind. They must act as though it were an objective reality, and the subconscious mind will take it as an impression, and through the deeper currents of the mind, the buyer and the seller are brought together. A mental picture held in the mind, backed by faith, will come to pass.

The Baudouin Technique

Charles Baudouin was a professor at the Rousseau Institute in France. He was a brilliant psychotherapist and a research director of the New Nancy School of Healing who, in 1910, taught that the best way to impress the subconscious mind was to enter into a drowsy, sleepy state, or a state akin to sleep, in which all effort was reduced to a minimum. Then, in a quiet, passive, receptive way, by reflection, he would convey the idea to the subconscious. The following is his formula: "A very simple way of securing this [impregnation of the subconscious mind] is to condense the idea, which is to be the object of suggestion, to sum it up in a brief phrase, which can be readily graven on the memory and to repeat it over and over again as a lullaby."

Some years ago, a young lady in Los Angeles was engaged in a prolonged bitter family lawsuit over a will. Her husband had bequeathed his entire estate to her, and his sons and daughters by a previous marriage were bitterly fighting to break the will. The Baudouin technique was outlined to her, and this is what she did: She relaxed her body in an armchair, entered into the sleepy state and, as suggested, condensed the idea of her need into a phrase consisting of six words easily graven on the memory. "It is finished in divine order." The significance to her of these words meant that Infinite Intelligence operating through the laws of her subconscious mind would bring about a harmonious adjustment through the principle of harmony. She continued this procedure every night for about ten nights. After she got into a sleepy state, she would affirm slowly, quietly, and feelingly the statement: "It is finished in divine order," over and over again, feeling a sense of inner peace and an all-pervading tranquility; then she went off into her deep, normal sleep. On the morning of the eleventh day, following the use of the above technique, she awakened with a sense of well-being, a conviction that it was finished. Her attorney called her the same day saying that the opposing attorney and his clients were willing to settle. A harmonious agreement was reached and litigation was discontinued.

The Sleeping Technique

By entering into a sleepy, drowsy state, effort is reduced to a minimum. The conscious mind is submerged to a great extent when in a sleepy state. The reason for this is that the highest degree of outcropping of the subconscious occurs prior to sleep and just after we awaken. In this state, the negative thoughts, which tend to neutralize your desire and so prevent acceptance by your subconscious mind, are no longer present.

Suppose you want to get rid of a destructive habit. Assume a comfortable posture, relax your body, and be still. Get into a sleepy state, and in that sleepy state, say quietly, over and over again as a lullaby, "I am completely free from this habit; harmony and peace of mind reign supreme." Repeat the above slowly, quietly, and lovingly for five or ten minutes, night and morning. Each time you repeat the words the emotional value becomes greater. When the urge comes to repeat the negative habit, repeat the above formula out loud to yourself. By this means you induce the subconscious to accept the idea, and a healing follows.

The Thank-You Technique

In the Bible, Paul recommends that we make known our requests with praise and thanksgiving. Some extraordinary results follow this simple method of prayer. The thankful heart is always close to the creative forces of the universe, causing countless blessings to flow toward it by the law of reciprocal relationship, based on a cosmic law of action and reaction.

For instance, a father promises his son a car for graduation; the boy has not yet received the car but he is very thankful and happy, and is as joyous as though he had actually received the car. He knows his father will fulfill his promise and he is full of gratitude and joy, even though he has not yet received the car, objectively speaking. He has, however, received it with joy and thankfulness in his mind.

I shall illustrate how Mr. Broke applied this technique with excellent results. He said, "Bills are piling up, I am out of work, I have three children and no money. What shall I do?" Regularly, every night and morning for a period of about three weeks, he repeated the words, "Thank you, Father, for my wealth," in a relaxed, peaceful manner until the feeling or mood of thankfulness dominated his mind. He imagined he was addressing the infinite power and intelligence within him knowing, of course, that he could not see the creative intelligence or infinite mind. He was seeing with the inner eye of spiritual perception, realizing that his thought-image of wealth was the *first* cause relative to the money, position, and food he needed. His thought-feeling was the substance of wealth untrammeled by antecedent conditions of any kind. By repeating, "Thank you, Father," over and over again, his mind and heart were lifted up to the point of acceptance, and when fear, thoughts of lack, poverty, and distress came into his mind, he would say, "Thank you, Father," as often as necessary. He knew that as he kept up the thankful attitude he would recondition his mind to the idea of wealth, which is what happened.

The sequel to his prayer is very interesting. After praying in the above-mentioned manner, he met a former employer of his on the street whom he had not seen for twenty years. The man offered him a very lucrative position and advanced him five hundred dollars on a temporary loan. Today, Mr. Broke is vice president of the company for which he works. His recent remark to me was, "I shall never forget the wonders of 'Thank you, Father.' It has worked wonders for me."

The Affirmative Method

The effectiveness of an affirmation is determined largely by your understanding of the truth and the meaning of the words, "In praying use not vain repetition." Therefore, the power of your affirmation lies in the intelligent application of definite and specific positives. For example, a boy adds three and three and puts down seven on the blackboard. The teacher affirms with mathematical certainty that three and three are six; therefore, the boy changes his figures accordingly. The teacher's statement did not make three and three equal six because the latter was already a mathematical truth. The mathematical truth caused the boy to rearrange the figures on the blackboard.

It is abnormal to be sick; it is normal to be healthy. Health is the truth of your being. When you affirm health, harmony, and peace for yourself or another, and when you realize these are universal principles of your own being, you will rearrange the negative patterns of your subconscious mind based on your faith and understanding of that which you affirm.

The result of the affirmative process of prayer depends on your conforming to the principles of life, regardless of appearances. Consider for a moment that there is a principle of mathematics and none of error; there is a principle of truth but none of dishonesty; there is a principle of intelligence but none of ignorance; there is a principle of harmony and none of discord; there is a principle of health but none of disease; and there is a principle of abundance but none of poverty.

The affirmative method was chosen by the author for use on his sister, who was to be operated on for the removal of gallstones in a hospital in England. The condition described was based on the diagnosis of hospital tests and the usual X-ray procedures. She asked me to pray for her. We were separated geographically about 6500 miles, but there is no time or space in the mind principle. Infinite mind or intelligence is present in its entirety at every point simultaneously.

I withdrew all thought from the contemplation of symptoms and from the corporeal personality altogether. I affirmed as follows: "This prayer is for my sister Catherine. She is relaxed and at peace, poised, balanced, serene, and calm. The healing intelligence of her subconscious mind, which created her body, is now transforming every cell, nerve, tissue, muscle, and bone of her being according to the perfect pattern of all organs lodged in her subconscious mind. Silently, quietly, all distorted thought patters in her subconscious mind are removed and dissolved, and the vitality, wholeness, and beauty of the Life-Principle are made manifest in every atom of her being. She is now open and receptive to the healing currents which are flowing through her like a river, restoring her to perfect health, harmony, and peace. All distortions and ugly images are now washed away by the infinite ocean of love and peace flowing through her, and it is so."

I affirmed the above several times a day and at the end of two weeks my sister had an examination which showed a remarkable healing and the X-ray proved negative.

To affirm is to state that it is so, and as you maintain this attitude of mind as true, regardless of all evidence to the contrary, you will receive an answer to your prayer. Your thought can only affirm, for even if you deny something, you are actually affirming the presence of what you deny. Repeating an affirmation, knowing what you are saying and why you are saying it, leads the mind to that state of consciousness where it accepts that which you state as true. Keep on affirming the truths of life until you get the subconscious reaction, which satisfies.

The Argumentative Method

This method is just what the word implies. It stems from the procedure of Dr. Phineas Parkhurst Quimby of Maine. Dr. Quimby, a pioneer in mental and spiritual healing, lived and practiced in Belfast, Maine, about one hundred years ago. A book called *The Quimby Manuscripts*, published in 1921 by Thomas Y. Crowell Company, New York City, and edited by Horatio Dresser, is available in your library. This book gives newspaper accounts of this man's remarkable results in prayer treatment of the sick. Quimby duplicated many of the healing miracles recorded in the Bible. In brief, the argumentative method employed according to Quimby consists of spiritual reasoning where you convince the patient and yourself that sickness is due to his false belief, groundless fears, and negative patterns lodged in his subconscious mind. You reason it out clearly in your mind and convince your patient that the disease or ailment is due only to a distorted, twisted pattern of thought, which has taken form in the body. This wrong belief in some external power and external causes has now externalized itself as sickness, and can be changed by changing the thought patterns.

You explain to the sick person that the basis of all healing is a change of belief. You also point out that the subconscious mind created the body and all its organs; therefore, it knows how to heal it, can heal it, and is doing so now as you speak. You argue in the courtroom of your mind that the disease is a shadow of the mind based on disease-soaked, morbid thought imagery. You continue to build up all the evidence you can muster on behalf of the healing power within, which created all the organs in the first place, and which has a perfect pattern of every cell, nerve, and tissue within it. Then, you render a verdict in the courthouse of your mind in favor of yourself and your patient. You liberate the sick one by faith and spiritual understanding. Your mental and spiritual evidence is overwhelming; there being but one mind, what you feel as true will be resurrected in the experience of the patient. This procedure is essentially the argumentative method used by Dr. Quimby of Maine from 1849 to 1869.

The Absolute Method Is Like Modern Sound Wave Therapy

Many people throughout the world practice this form of prayer treatment with wonderful results. The person using the absolute method mentions the name of the patient, such as John Jones, then quietly and silently thinks of God and His qualities and attributes, such as, "God is all bliss, boundless love, Infinite Intelligence, all-powerful, boundless wisdom, absolute harmony, indescribable beauty and perfection." As he quietly thinks along these lines he is lifted up in consciousness into a new spiritual wave length, at which times he feels the infinite ocean of God's love is now dissolving everything unlike itself in the mind and body of John Jones, for whom he is praying. He feels all the power and love of God are now focused on John Jones, and whatever is bothering or vexing him is now completely neutralized in the presence of the infinite ocean of life and love.

The absolute method of prayer might be likened to the sound wave or sonic therapy recently shown by a distinguished physician in Los Angeles. He has an ultrasound wave machine, which oscillates at a tremendous speed and sends sound waves to any area of the body to which it is directed. These sound waves can be controlled, and he told me of achieving remarkable results in dissolving arthritic, calcareous deposits, as well as the healing and removal of other disturbing conditions.

To the degree that we rise in consciousness by contemplating qualities and attributes of God, do we generate spiritual electronic waves of harmony, health, and peace. Many remarkable healings follow this technique of prayer.

A Cripple Walks

Dr. Phineas Parkhurst Quimby, of whom we spoke previously in this chapter, used the absolute method in the latter years of his healing career. He was really the father of psychosomatic medicine, and the first psychoanalyst. He had the capacity to diagnose clairvoyantly the cause of the patient's troubles, pains, and aches.

The following is a condensed account of the healing of a cripple as recorded in Quimby's *Manuscripts:* Quimby was called on to visit a woman who was lame, aged, and bedridden. He states that her ailment was due to the fact that she was imprisoned by a creed so small and contracted that she could not stand upright and move about. She was living in the tomb of fear and ignorance; furthermore, she was taking the Bible literally and it frightened her. "In this tomb," Quimby said, "was the presence and power of God trying to burst the bands, break through the bonds, and rise from the dead." When she would ask others for an explanation of some passage of the Bible, the answer would be a stone; then she would hunger for the bread of life. Dr. Quimby diagnosed her case as a mind cloudy and stagnated, due to excitation and fear caused by the inability to see clearly the meaning of the passage of the Bible, which she had been reading. This showed itself in the body by her heavy and sluggish feeling, which would terminate as paralysis.

At this point, Quimby asked her what was meant in the Bible verses: *Yet a little while am I with you, and then I go unto Him that sent me. Ye shall seek me, and shall not find me: and where I am, thither ye cannot come* (John 7:33–34). She replied that it meant Jesus went to heaven. Quimby explained what it really meant by telling her that *being with her a little while* meant his explanation of her symptoms, feelings, and their causes; i.e., he had compassion and sympathy for her momentarily, but he could not remain in that mental state. The next step was *to go to Him that sent us* which, as Quimby pointed out, was the creative power of God in all of us.

Quimby immediately traveled in his mind and contemplated the divine ideal; i.e. the vitality, intelligence, harmony, and power of God functioning in the sick person. This is why, he said to the woman, "Therefore, where I go you cannot come, for you are in your narrow, restricted belief, and I am in health." This prayer and explanation produced an instantaneous sensation, and a change came over her mind. She walked without her crutches! Quimby said it was one of the most singular of all his healings. She was, as it were, dead to error, and to bring her to life or truth was to raise her from the dead. Quimby quoted the resurrection of Christ and applied it to her own Christ or health; this produced a powerful effect on her. He also explained to her that the truth, which she accepted was the angel or idea, which rolled away the stone of fear, ignorance, and superstition, thereby releasing the healing power of God, which made her whole.

The Decree Method

Power goes into our word according to the feeling and faith behind it. When we realize the power that moves the world is moving on our behalf and is backing up our word, our confidence and assurance grow. You do not try and add power to power; therefore, there must be no mental striving, coercion, force, or mental wrestling.

A young girl used the decree method on a young man who was constantly phoning her, pressing her for dates, and meeting her at her place of business; she found it very difficult to get rid of him. She decreed as follows: "I release (man's name) unto God. He is in the true place at all times. I am free and he is free. I now decree that my words go forth into infinite mind and it brings it to pass. It is so." She said he vanished and she has never seen him since, adding, "It was as though the ground swallowed him up."

Thou shall decree a thing, and it shall be established unto thee: and the light shall shine upon thy ways (Job 22:28).

Serve Yourself With Scientific Truth

1. Be a mental engineer and use tried and proven techniques in building a grander and greater life.

2. Your desire is your prayer. Picture the fulfillment of your desire now and feel its reality and you will experience the joy of the answered prayer.

3. Desire to accomplish things the easy way with the sure aid of mental science.

4. You can build radiant health, success, and happiness by the thoughts you think in the hidden studio of your mind.

5. Experiment scientifically until you personally prove that there is always a direct response from the Infinite Intelligence of your subconscious mind to your conscious thinking.

6. Feel the joy and restfulness in foreseeing the certain accomplishment of your desire. Any mental picture which you have in your mind is the substance of things hoped for and the evidence of things not seen.

7. A mental picture is worth a thousand words. Your subconscious will bring to pass any picture held in the mind backed by faith.

8. Avoid all effort or mental coercion in prayer. Get into a sleepy, drowsy state, and lull yourself to sleep feeling and knowing that your prayer is answered.

9. Remember that the thankful heart is always close to the riches of the universe.

10. To affirm is to state that it is so, and as you maintain this attitude of mind as true, regardless of all evidence to the contrary, you will receive an answer to your prayer.

11. Generate electronic waves of harmony, health, and peace by thinking of the love and the glory of God.

12. What you decree and feel as true will come to pass. Decree harmony, health, peace, and abundance.

7

The Tendency of the Subconscious Is Lifeward

Over 90 percent of your mental life is subconscious, so men and women who fail to make use of this marvelous power live within very narrow limits. Your subconscious processes are always lifeward and constructive. Your subconscious is the builder of your body and maintains all its vital functions. It is on the job twenty-four hours a day and never sleeps. It is always trying to help and preserve you from harm.

Your subconscious mind is in touch with infinite life and boundless wisdom, and its impulses and ideas are always lifeward. The great aspirations, inspirations, and visions for a greater and nobler life spring from the subconscious. Your profoundest convictions are those you cannot argue about rationally because they do not come from your conscious mind; they come from your subconscious mind.

Your subconscious speaks to you in intuitions, impulses, hunches, intimations, urges, and ideas, and it is always telling you to rise, transcend grow, advance, adventure, and move forward to greater heights. The urge to love, to save the lives of others, comes from the depths of your subconscious. For example, during the great San Francisco earthquake and fire of April 18, 1906, invalids and cripples who had been confined to bed for long periods of time rose up and performed some of the most amazing feats of bravery and endurance. The intense desire welled up within them to save others at all costs, and their subconscious responded accordingly.

Great artists, musicians, poets, speakers, and writers tune in with their subconscious powers and become animated and inspired. For example, Robert Louis Stevenson, before he went to sleep, used to charge his subconscious with the task of evolving stories for him while he slept. He was accustomed to ask his subconscious to give him a good, marketable thriller when his bank account was low. Stevenson said the intelligence of his deeper mind gave him the story piece by piece, like a serial. This shows how your subconscious will speak lofty and wise sayings through you, which your conscious mind knows nothing about.

Mark Twain confided to the world on many occasions that he never worked in his life. All his humor and all his great writings were due to the fact that he tapped the inexhaustible reservoir of his subconscious mind.

How the Body Portrays the Workings of the Mind

The interaction of your conscious and subconscious mind requires a similar interaction between the corresponding system of nerves. The cerebrospinal system is the organ of the conscious mind, and the sympathetic system is the organ of the subconscious mind. The cerebrospinal system is the channel through which you receive conscious perception by means of your five physical senses and exercise control over the movement of your body. This system has its nerves in the brain, and it is the channel of your volitional and conscious mental function.

The sympathetic system, sometimes referred to as the involuntary nervous system, has its center in a ganglionic mass at the back of the stomach known as the solar plexus, and is sometimes spoken of as the abdominal brain. It is the channel of that mental action, which unconsciously supports the vital functions of the body.

The two systems may work separately or synchronously. Judge Thomas Troward, *The Edinburgh Lectures on Mental Science* (New York: Robert McBride and Co., 1909) says, "[The vagus nerve] passes out of the cerebral region as a portion of the voluntary system, and through it we control the vocal organs; then it passes onwards to the thorax sending out branches to the heart and lungs; and finally, passing through the diaphragm, it loses the outer coating which distinguishes the nerves of the voluntary system and becomes identified with those of the sympathetic system, so forming a connecting link between the two and making the man physically a single entity.

"Similarly different areas of the brain indicate their connection with the objective and subjective activities of the mind respectively, and speaking in a general way we may assign the frontal portion of the brain to the former and the posterior portion to the latter, while the intermediate portion partakes of the character of both."

A rather simple way of looking at the mental and physical interaction is to realize that your conscious mind grasps an idea, which induces a corresponding vibration in your voluntary system of nerves. This in turn causes a similar current to be generated in your involuntary system of nerves, thus handing the idea over to your subconscious mind, which is the creative medium.

This is how your thoughts become things.

Every thought entertained by your conscious mind and accepted as true is sent by your brain to your solar plexus, the brain of the subconscious mind, to be made into your flesh, and to be brought forth into your world as a reality.

There Is an Intelligence Which Takes Care of the Body

When you study the cellular system and the structure of the organs, such as eyes, ears, heart, liver, bladder, etc., you learn they consist of groups of cells, which form a group intelligence whereby they function together and are able to take orders and carry them out in deductive function at the suggestion of the master mind (conscious mind).

A careful study of the single-celled organism shows you what goes on in your complex body. Though the monocellular organism has no organs, it still gives evidence of mind action and reaction performing the basic functions of movement, alimentation, assimilation, and elimination.

Many say there is an intelligence which will take care of your body if you let it alone. That is true, but the difficulty is that the conscious mind always interferes with its five-sense evidence based on outer appearances, leading to the sway of false belief, fears, and mere opinion. When fear, false beliefs, and negative patterns are made to register in your subconscious mind through psychological, emotional conditioning, there is no other course open to the subconscious mind except to act on the blueprint specifications offered it.

The Subconscious Mind Works Continually for the Common Good

The subjective self within you works continuously for the general good, reflecting an innate principle of harmony behind all things. Your subconscious mind has its own will and it is a very real something in itself. It acts night and day, whether you act upon it or not. It is the builder of your body, but you cannot see, hear, or feel it building, as all this is a silent process. Your subconscious has a life of its own, which is always moving toward harmony, health, and peace. This is the divine norm within it seeking expression through you at all times.

How Man Interferes with the Innate Principle of Harmony

To think correctly, scientifically, we must know the "truth." To know the truth is to be in harmony with the Infinite Intelligence and power of your subconscious mind, which is always moving lifeward.

Every thought or action, which is not harmonious, whether through ignorance or design, will result in discord and limitation of all kinds.

Scientists inform us that you build a new body every eleven months; so you are really only eleven months old from a physical standpoint. If you build defects back into your body by thoughts of fear, anger, jealousy, and ill will, you have no one to blame but yourself.

You are the sum total of your own thoughts. You can keep from entertaining negative thoughts and imagery. The way to get rid of darkness is with light; the way to overcome cold is with heat; the way to overcome the negative thought is to substitute the good thought. Affirm the good and the bad will vanish.

Why It's Normal to Be Healthy, Vital, and Strong—It's Abnormal to Be Sick

The average child born into the world is perfectly healthy with all its organs functioning perfectly. This is the normal state, and we should remain healthy, vital, and strong. The instinct of self-preservation is the strongest instinct of your nature and it constitutes a most potent, ever-present and constantly operative truth, inherent in your nature. It is, therefore, obvious that all your thoughts, ideas, and beliefs must operate with greater potentiality when they are in harmony with the innate Life-Principle in you, which is forever seeking to preserve and protect you along all lines. It follows from this that normal conditions can be restored with greater ease and certainty than abnormal conditions can be induced.

It is abnormal to be sick; it simply means you are going against the stream of life and thinking negatively. The law of life is the law of growth; all nature testifies to the operation of this law by silently, constantly expressing itself in the law of growth. When there is growth and expression, there must be life; where there is life, there must be harmony; and where there is harmony, there is perfect health.

If your thought is in harmony with the creative principle of your subconscious mind, you are in tune with the innate principle of harmony. If you entertain thoughts which are not in accordance with the principle of harmony, these thoughts cling to you, harass you, worry you, and finally bring about disease; and if persisted in, possibly death.

In the healing of disease, you must increase the inflow and distribution of the vital forces of your subconscious mind throughout your system. This can be done by eliminating thoughts of fear, worry, anxiety, jealousy, hatred, and every other destructive thought which tends to tear down and destroy your nerves and glands—body tissue which controls the elimination of all waste material.

Pott's Disease Cured

In the *Nautilus* magazine of March 1917, there appears an article about a boy suffering from Pott's disease, or tuberculosis of the spine, who had a remarkable healing. His name was Frederick Elias Andrews of Indianapolis, now minister of Unity School of Christianity, Kansas City, Missouri. His physician pronounced him incurable. He began to pray, and from a crooked, twisted cripple going about on hands and knees, he became a strong, straight, well-formed man. He created his own affirmation, mentally absorbing the qualities he needed.

He affirmed over and over again many times a day, "I am whole, perfect, strong, powerful, loving, harmonious, and happy." He persevered and said that this prayer was the last utterance on his lips at night and the first in the morning. He prayed for others also by sending out thoughts of love and health. This attitude of mind and way of prayer returned to him multiplied many times. His faith and perseverance paid off with big dividends. When thoughts of fear, anger, jealousy, or envy drew his attention, he would immediately start his counteracting force of affirmation going in his mind. His subconscious mind responded according to the nature of his habitual thinking. This is the meaning of the statement in the Bible, *Go thy way, thy faith hath made thee whole* (Mark 10:52).

How Faith in Your Subconscious Powers Makes You Whole

A young man, who came to my lectures on the healing power of the subconscious mind, had severe eye trouble which his doctor said necessitated an operation. He said to himself, "My subconscious made my eyes, and it can heal me."

Each night, as he went to sleep, he entered into a drowsy, meditative state, the condition akin to sleep. His attention was immobilized and focused on the eye doctor. He imagined the doctor was in front of him, and he plainly heard, or imagined he heard, the doctor saying to him, "A miracle has happened!" He heard this over and over again every night for perhaps five minutes or so before going to sleep. At the end of three weeks he again went to the ophthalmologist who had previously examined his eyes, and the physician said to this man, "This is a miracle!" What happened? This man impressed his subconscious mind using the doctor as an instrument or a means of convincing it or conveying the idea. Through repetition, faith, and expectancy he impregnated his subconscious mind. His subconscious mind made his eye; within it was the perfect pattern and immediately it proceeded to heal the eye. This is another example of how faith in the healing power of your subconscious can make you whole.

Pointers to Review

1. Your subconscious is the builder of your body and is on the job twenty-four hours a day. You interfere with its life-giving patterns by negative thinking.

2. Charge your subconscious with the task of evolving an answer to any problem prior to sleep and it will answer you.

3. Watch your thoughts. Every thought accepted as true is sent by your brain to your solar plexus—your abdominal brain—and is brought into your world as a reality.

4. Know that you can remake yourself by giving a new blueprint to your subconscious mind.

5. The tendency of your subconscious is always lifeward. Your job is with your conscious mind. Feed your subconscious mind with

premises which are true. Your subconscious is always reproducing according to your habitual mental patterns

6. You build a new body every eleven months. Change your body by changing your thoughts and keeping them changed.

7. It is normal to be healthy. It is abnormal to be ill. There is within the innate principle of harmony.

8. Thoughts of jealousy, fear, worry, and anxiety tear down and destroy your nerves and glands bringing about mental and physical diseases of all kinds.

9. What you affirm consciously and feel as true will be made manifest in your mind, body, and affairs. Affirm the good and enter into the joy of living.

8

How to Get the Results You Want

The principle reasons for failure are: lack of confidence and too much effort. Many people block answers to their prayers by failing to fully comprehend the workings of the subconscious mind. When you know how your mind functions, you gain a measure of confidence. You must remember whenever your subconscious mind accepts an idea, it immediately begins to execute it. It uses all its mighty resources to that end and mobilizes all the mental and spiritual laws of your deeper mind. This law is true for good or bad ideas. Consequently, if you use it negatively, it brings trouble, failure, and confusion. When you use it constructively, it brings guidance, freedom, and peace of mind.

The right answer is inevitable when your thoughts are positive, constructive, and loving. From this it is obvious that the only thing you have to do in order to overcome failure is to get your subconscious to accept your idea or request by feeling its reality now, and the law of your mind will do the rest. Turn over your request with faith and confidence and your subconscious will take over and answer for you.

You will always fail to get results by trying to use mental coercion— your subconscious mind does not respond to coercion, it responds to your faith or conscious mind acceptance.

Your failure to get results may also arise from such statements as, "Things are getting worse," "I will never get an answer," "I see no way out," "It's hopeless," "I don't know what to do," "I'm all mixed up." When you use such statements, you get no response or cooperation from your subconscious mind. Like a soldier marking time, you neither go forward nor backward; in other words, you don't get anywhere.

If you get into a taxi and give a half dozen different directions to the driver in five minutes, he would become hopelessly confused and probably refuse to take you anywhere. It is the same when working with your subconscious mind. There must be a clear-cut idea in your mind. You must arrive at the definite decision that there is a way out, a solution to the vexing problem in sickness. Only the Infinite Intelligence within your subconscious knows the answer. When you come to that clear-cut conclusion in your conscious mind, your mind is then made up, and according to your belief is it done unto you.

Easy Does It

A house owner once remonstrated with a furnace repairman for charging two hundred dollars for fixing the boiler. The mechanic said, "I charged five cents for the missing bolt and one hundred and ninety-nine dollars and ninety-five cents for knowing what was wrong."

Similarly, your subconscious mind is the master mechanic, the all-wise one, who knows ways and means of healing any organ of your body, as well as your affairs. Decree health, and your subconscious will establish it, but relaxation is the key. ("Easy does it.") Do not be concerned with details and means, but know the end result. Get the feel of the happy solution to your problem whether it is health, finances, or employment. Remember how you felt after you had recovered from a severe state of illness. Bear in mind that your feeling is the touchstone of all subconscious demonstration. Your new idea must be felt subjectively in a finished state, not the future, but as coming about now.

Infer No Opponent, Use Imagination and Not Will Power

In using your subconscious mind you infer no opponent, you use no will power. You imagine the end and the freedom state. You will find your intellect trying to get in the way, but persist in maintaining a simple, childlike, miracle-making faith. Picture yourself without the ailment or problem. Imagine the emotional accompaniment of the freedom state you crave. Cut out all red tape from the process. The simple way is the best.

How Disciplined Imagination Works Wonders

A wonderful way to get a response from your subconscious mind is through disciplined or scientific imagination. As previously pointed out, your subconscious mind is the builder of the body and controls all its vital functions.

The Bible says, *Whatsoever ye shall ask in prayer, believing, ye shall receive* (Matthew 21:22). To believe is to accept something as true, or to live in the state of being it. As you sustain this mood, you shall experience the joy of the answered prayer!

The Three Steps to Success in Prayer

The usual procedure is as follows:

1. Take a look at the problem.

2. Turn to the solution or way out known only to the subconscious mind.

3. Rest in a sense of deep conviction that it is done.

Do not weaken your prayer by saying, "I wish I might be healed," or "I hope so." Your feeling about the work to be done is "the boss." Harmony is yours. Know that health is yours. Become intelligent by becoming a vehicle for the infinite healing power of the subconscious mind. Pass on the idea of health to your subconscious mind to the point of conviction, then relax. Get yourself off your hands. Say to the condition, and circumstance, "This, too, shall pass." Through relaxation you impress your subconscious mind enabling the kinetic energy behind the idea to take over and bring it into concrete realization.

The Law of Reversed Effort and Why You Get the Opposite of What You Pray For

Coué, the famous psychologist from France who visited America about forty years ago, defined the law of reversed effort as follows: "When your desires and imagination are in conflict, your imagination invariably gains the day."

If, for example, you were asked to walk a plank on the floor, you would do so without question. Now suppose the same plank were placed twenty feet up in the air between two walls. Would you walk it? Your desire to walk it would be counteracted by your imagination or fear of falling. Your dominant idea which would be the picture of falling would conquer. Your desire, will, or effort to walk on the plank would be reversed, and the dominant idea of failure would be reinforced.

Mental effort is invariably self-defeated, eventuating always in the opposite of what is desired. The suggestions of powerlessness to overcome the condition dominate the mind; your subconscious is always controlled by the dominant idea. Your subconscious will accept the strongest of two contradictory propositions. The effortless way is better.

If you say, "I want a healing, but I can't get it," "I try so hard," "I force myself to pray," "I use all of the will power I have," you must realize that your error lies in your effort. Never try to compel the subconscious mind to accept your idea by exercising will power. Such attempts are doomed to failure and you get the opposite of what you prayed for.

The following is a rather common experience. Students, when taking examinations and reading through their papers, find that all their knowledge has suddenly deserted them. Their minds become appalling blanks and they are unable to recall one relevant thought. The more they grit their teeth and summon the powers of the will, the further the answers seem to flee. But, when they have left the examination room and the mental pressure relaxes, the answers they were seeking flow tantalizingly back into their minds. Trying to force themselves to remember was the cause of their failure. This is an example of the law of reversed effort whereby you get the opposite of what you asked or prayed for.

The Conflict of Desire and Imagination Must Be Reconciled

To use mental force is to presuppose that there is opposition. When your mind is concentrated on the means to overcome a problem, it is no longer concerned with the obstacle. Matthew 18:19 says, *If two*

of you shall agree on earth as touching anything that they shall ask, it
shall be done for them of my Father which is in heaven.

Who are these two? It means the harmonious union between
your conscious and subconscious on any idea, desire, or mental
image. When there is no longer any quarrel in either part of your
mind, your prayer will be answered. The two agreeing may also be
represented as you and your desire, your thought and feeling, your
idea and emotion, your desire and imagination.

You avoid all conflict between your desires and imagination by
entering into a drowsy, sleepy state which brings all effort to a minimum. The conscious mind is submerged to a great extent when in a
sleepy state. The best time to impregnate your subconscious occurs
prior to sleep and just after we awaken. In this state the negative
thoughts and imagery which tend to neutralize your desire and so
prevent acceptance by your subconscious mind no longer present
themselves. When you imagine the reality of the fulfilled desire and
feel the thrill of accomplishment, your subconscious brings about
the realization of your desire.

A great many people solve all their dilemmas and problems by
the play of their controlled, directed, and disciplined imagination,
knowing that whatever they imagine and feel as true *will* and *must*
come to pass.

The following will clearly illustrate how a young girl overcame
the conflict between her desire and her imagination. She desired a
harmonious solution to her legal problem, yet her mental imagery
was constantly on failure, loss, bankruptcy, and poverty. It was a
complicated lawsuit and there was one postponement after another
with no solution in sight.

At my suggestion, she got into a sleepy, drowsy state each night
prior to sleep and she began to imagine the happy ending, feeling it to the best of her ability. She knew that the image in her

mind had to agree with her heart's desire. Prior to sleep she began to dramatize as vividly as possible her lawyer having an animated discussion with her regarding the outcome. She would ask him questions, and he would answer her appropriately. He would say to her over and over again, "There has been a perfect, harmonious solution. The case has been settled out of court." During the day, when fear thoughts came into her mind, she would run her mental movie with gestures, voice, and sound equipment. She could easily imagine the sound of his voice, smile, and mannerism. She ran this mental picture so often it became a subjective pattern, a regular train track. At the end of a few weeks her attorney called and confirmed objectively what she had been imagining and feeling as true subjectively.

This is really what the Psalmist meant when he wrote, *Let the words of my mouth* [your thoughts, mental images, good] *and the meditations of my heart* [your feeling, nature, emotion] *be acceptable in thy sight, O Lord* [the law of your subconscious mind], *my strength, and my redeemer* [the power and wisdom of your subconscious mind can redeem you from sickness, bondage, and misery] (Psalms 19:14).

Ideas Worth Remembering

1. Mental coercion or too much effort shows anxiety and fear which block your answer. Easy does it.

2. When your mind is relaxed and you accept an idea, your subconscious goes to work to execute the idea.

3. Think and plan independently of traditional methods. Know that there is always an answer and a solution to every problem.

4. Do not be overly concerned with the beating of your heart, with the breathing of your lungs or the functions of any part of your anatomy. Lean heavily upon your subconscious and proclaim frequently that divine right action is taking place.

5. The feeling of health produces health, the feeling of wealth produces wealth. How do you feel?

6. Imagination is your most powerful faculty. Imagine what is lovely and of good report. You are what you imagine yourself to be.

7. You avoid conflict between your conscious and subconscious in the sleepy state. Imagine the fulfillment of your desire over and over again prior to sleep. Sleep in peace and wake in joy.

9

How to Use the Power of Your Subconscious for Wealth

If you are having difficulties, if you are trying to make ends meet, it means you have not convinced your subconscious mind that you will always have plenty and some to spare. You know men and women who work a few hours a week and make fabulous sums of money. They do not strive or slave hard. Do not believe the story that the only way you can become wealthy is by the sweat of your brow and hard labor. It is not so; the effortless way of life is the best. Do the thing you love to do and do it for the joy and thrill of it.

I know an executive in Los Angeles who receives a salary of seventy-five thousand dollars yearly. Last year he went on a nine-month cruise, seeing the world and its beauty spots. He said to me that he had succeeded in convincing his subconscious mind that he is worth that much money. He told me that many men in his organization getting about one hundred dollars a week knew more about the business than he did, and could manage it better, but they had no ambition, no creative ideas, and were not interested in the wonders of their subconscious mind.

Wealth Is of the Mind

Wealth is simply a subconscious conviction on the part of the individual. You will not become a millionaire by saying, "I am a millionaire, I am a millionaire." You will grow into a wealth consciousness by building into your mentality the idea of wealth and abundance.

Your Invisible Means of Support

The trouble with most people is that they have no invisible means of support. When business falls away, the stock market drops, or they lose their investments, they seem helpless. The reason for such insecurity is that they do not know how to tap the subconscious mind. They are unacquainted with the inexhaustible storehouse within.

A man with a poverty-type mind finds himself in poverty-stricken conditions. Another man with a mind filled with ideas of wealth is surrounded with everything he needs. It was never intended that man should lead a life of indigence. You can have wealth, everything you need, and plenty to spare. Your words have power to cleanse your mind of wrong ideas and to instill right ideas in their place.

The Ideal Method for Building a Wealth Consciousness

Perhaps you are saying as you read this chapter, "I need wealth and success." This is what you do: Repeat for about five minutes to yourself three or four times a day, "Wealth. Success." These words have tremendous power. They represent the inner power of the subconscious mind. Anchor your mind on this substantial power within you; then conditions and circumstances corresponding to their nature and quality will be manifested in your life. You are not saying, "I am wealthy," you are dwelling on real powers within you. There is no conflict in the mind when you say, "Wealth." Furthermore, the feeling of wealth will well up within you as you dwell on the idea of wealth.

The feeling of wealth produces wealth; keep this in mind at all times. Your subconscious mind is like a bank, a sort of universal financial institution. It magnifies whatever you deposit or impress upon it whether it is the idea of wealth or of poverty. Choose wealth.

Why Your Affirmations for Wealth Fail

I have talked to many people during the past thirty-five years whose usual complaint is, "I have said for weeks and months, 'I am wealthy, I am prosperous,' and nothing has happened." I discovered that when they said, "I am wealthy, I am prosperous," they felt that they were lying to themselves.

One man told me, "I have affirmed that I am prosperous until I am tired. Things are now worse. I knew when I made the statement that it was obviously not true." His statements were rejected by the conscious mind, and the very opposite of what he outwardly affirmed and claimed was made manifest.

Your affirmation succeeds best when it is specific and when it does not produce a mental conflict or argument; hence the statements made by this man made matters worse because they suggested his lack. Your subconscious accepts what you really feel to be true, not just idle words or statements. The dominant idea or belief is always accepted by the subconscious mind.

How to Avoid Mental Conflict

The following is the ideal way to overcome this conflict for those who have this difficulty. Make this practical statement frequently, particularly prior to sleep: "By day and by night I am being prospered in all of my interests." This affirmation will not arouse any argument because it does not contradict your subconscious mind's impression of financial lack.

I suggested to one businessman, whose sales and finances were very low and who was greatly worried, that he sit down in his office, become quiet, and repeat this statement over and over again: "My sales are improving every day." This statement engaged the cooperation of the conscious and subconscious mind; results followed.

Don't Sign Blank Checks

You sign blank checks when you make such statements as, "There is not enough to go around." "There is a shortage." "I will lose the house because of the mortgage," etc. If you are full of fear about the future, you are also writing a blank check and attracting negative conditions to you. Your subconscious mind takes your fear and negative statement as your request and proceeds in its own way to bring obstacles, delays, lack, and limitation to your life.

Your Subconscious Gives You Compound Interest

To him that hath the feeling of wealth, more wealth shall be added; to him that hath the feeling of lack, more lack shall be added. Your subconscious multiplies and magnifies whatever you deposit in it. Every morning as you awaken deposit thoughts of prosperity, success, wealth, and peace. Dwell upon these concepts. Busy your mind with them as often as possible. These constructive thoughts will find their way as deposits in your subconscious mind, and bring forth abundance and prosperity.

Why Nothing Happened

I can hear you saying, "Oh, I did that and nothing happened." You did not get results because you indulged in fear thoughts perhaps ten minutes later and neutralized the good you had affirmed. When you place a seed in the ground, you do not dig it up. You let it take root and grow. Suppose, for example, you are going to say, "I shall not be able to make that payment." Before you get further than, "I shall . . ." stop the sentence and dwell on a constructive statement, such as, "By day and by night I am prospered in all my ways."

True Source of Wealth

Your subconscious mind is never short of ideas. There are within it an infinite number of ideas ready to flow into your conscious mind and appear as cash in your pocketbook in countless ways. This process will continue to go on in your mind regardless of whether the stock market goes up or down, or whether the pound sterling or dollar drops in value. Your wealth is never truly dependent on bonds, stocks, or money in the bank; these are really only symbols necessary and useful, of course, but only symbols.

The point I want to emphasize is that if you convince your subconscious mind that wealth is yours, and that it is always circulating in your life, you will always and inevitably have it, regardless of the form it takes.

Trying to Make Ends Meet and the Real Cause

There are people who claim that they are always trying to make ends meet. They seem to have a great struggle to meet their obligations. Have you listened to their conversation? In many instances their conversation runs along this vein. They are constantly condemning those who have succeeded in life and who have raised their heads above the crowd. Perhaps they are saying, "Oh, that fellow has a racket; he is ruthless; he is a crook." This is why they lack; they are condemning the thing they desire and want. The reason they speak critically of their more prosperous associates is because they are envious and covetous of the others' prosperity. The quickest way to cause wealth to take wings and fly away is to criticize and condemn others who have more wealth than you.

A Common Stumbling Block

There is one emotion which is the cause of the lack of wealth in the lives of many. Most people learn this the hard way. It is envy. For example, if you see a competitor depositing large sums of money in the bank and you have only a meager amount to deposit, does it make you envious? The way to overcome this emotion is to say to yourself, "Isn't it wonderful? I rejoice in that man's prosperity. I wish for him greater and greater wealth."

To entertain envious thoughts is devastating because it places you in a very negative position; therefore, wealth flows from you instead of to you. If you are ever annoyed or irritated by the prosperity or great wealth of another, claim immediately that you truly wish for him greater wealth in every possible way. This will neutralize the negative thoughts in your mind and cause an ever-greater measure of wealth to flow to you by the law of your own subconscious mind.

Rubbing Out a Great Mental Block to Wealth

If you are worried and critical about someone who you claim is making money dishonestly, cease worrying about him. You know such a person is using the law of mind negatively; the law of mind takes care of him. Be careful not to criticize him for the reasons previously indicated. Remember: the block or obstacle to wealth is in your own mind. You can now destroy that mental block. This you may do by getting on mental good terms with everyone.

Sleep and Grow Rich

As you go to sleep at night, practice the following technique. Repeat the word, "Wealth," quietly, easily, and feelingly. Do this over and over again, just like a lullaby. Lull yourself to sleep with the one word, "Wealth." You should be amazed at the result. Wealth should flow to you in avalanches of abundance. This is another example of the magic power of your subconscious mind.

Serve Yourself with the Powers of Your Mind

1. Decide to be wealthy the easy way, with the infallible aid of your subconscious mind.

2. Trying to accumulate wealth by the sweat of your brow and hard labor is one way to become the richest man in the graveyard. You do not have to strive or slave hard.

3. Wealth is a subconscious conviction. Build into your mentality the idea of wealth.

4. The trouble with most people is that they have no invisible means of support.

5. Repeat the word, "Wealth," to yourself slowly and quietly for about five minutes prior to sleep and your subconscious mind will bring wealth to pass in your experience.

6. The feeling of wealth produces wealth. Keep that in mind at all times.

7. Your conscious and subconscious mind must agree. Your subconscious accepts what you really feel to be true. The dominant idea is always accepted by your subconscious mind. The dominant idea should be wealth, not poverty.

8. You can overcome any mental conflict regarding wealth by affirming frequently, "By day and by night I am being prospered in all of my interests."

9. Increase your sales by repeating this statement over and over again, "My sales are improving every day; I am advancing, progressing, and getting wealthier every day."

10. Stop writing blank checks, such as, "There is not enough to go around," or "There is a shortage," etc. Such statements magnify and multiply your loss.

11. Deposit thoughts of prosperity, wealth, and success in your subconscious mind, and the latter will give you compound interest.

12. What you consciously affirm, you must not mentally deny a few moments later. This will neutralize the good you have affirmed.

13. Your true source of wealth consists of the ideas in your mind. You can have an idea worth millions of dollars. Your subconscious will give you the idea you seek.

14. Envy and jealousy are stumbling blocks to the flow of wealth. Rejoice in the prosperity of others.

15. The block to wealth is in your own mind. Destroy that block now by getting on good mental terms with everyone.

10

Your Right to Be Rich

It is your right to be rich. You are here to lead the abundant life and be happy, radiant, and free. You should, therefore, have all the money you need to lead a full, happy, and prosperous life.

You are here to grow, expand, and unfold spiritually, mentally, and materially. You have the inalienable right to fully develop and express yourself along all lines. You should surround yourself with beauty and luxury. Why be satisfied with just enough to go around when you can enjoy the riches of your subconscious mind?

In this chapter you can learn to make friends with money, and you should always have a surplus. Your desire to be rich is a desire for a fuller, happier, more wonderful life. It is a cosmic urge. It is not only good, but very good.

Money Is a Symbol

Money is a symbol of exchange. It means to you not only freedom from want, but beauty, luxury, abundance, and refinement. It is merely a symbol of the economic health of the nation. When your blood is circulating freely in your body, you are healthy. When money is circulating freely in your life, you are economically healthy. When people begin to hoard money, to put it away in tin boxes and become charged with fear, there is economic illness. Money has taken many forms as a medium of exchange down through the centuries, such as salt, beads, and trinkets of various kinds. In early times a man's wealth was determined by the number of sheep and oxen he had. Now we use currency, and other negotiable instruments, as it is much more convenient to write a check then carry some sheep around with you to pay bills.

How to Walk the Royal Road to Riches

Knowledge of the powers of your subconscious mind is the means to the royal road to riches of all kinds: spiritual, mental, or financial. The student of the laws of mind believes and knows definitely that, regardless of economic situations, stock market fluctuation, depression, strikes, war, or other conditions and circumstances, he will always be amply supplied, regardless of what form money takes. The reason for this is that he has conveyed the idea of wealth to his subconscious mind, and it keeps him supplied wherever he may be. He has convinced himself in his mind that money is forever flowing freely in his life and that there is always a wonderful surplus. Should there be a financial collapse of government tomorrow and all the man's present holdings become valueless, as the German marks did after the First World War, he would still attract wealth and be cared for, regardless of the form the new currency took.

Why You Do Not Have More Money

As you read this chapter, you are probably saying, "I am worthy of a higher salary than I am receiving." I believe most people are inadequately compensated. One of the causes many people do not have more money is that they are silently or openly condemning it.

They refer to money as "filthy lucre," or say, "the love of money is the root of all evil." Another reason they do not prosper is that they have a sneaky subconscious feeling there is some virtue in poverty. This subconscious pattern may be due to early childhood training, superstition, or it could be based on a false interpretation of scriptures.

Money and a Balanced Life

One time a man said to me, "I am broke. I do not like money. It is the root of all evil." These statements represent a confused, neurotic mind. Love of money to the exclusion of everything else will cause you to become lopsided and unbalanced. You are here to use your power or authority wisely. Some men crave power, others crave money. If you set your heart on money exclusively and say, "Money is all I want; I am going to give all my attention to amassing money; nothing else matters," you can get money and attain a fortune, but you have forgotten that you are here to lead a balanced life. You must also satisfy the hunger for peace of mind, harmony, love, joy, and perfect health.

By making money your sole aim, you simply made a wrong choice. You thought that was all you wanted, but you found after all your efforts that it was not only the money you needed. You also desired true expression of your hidden talents, true place in life, beauty, and the joy of contributing to the welfare and success of others. By learning the laws of your subconscious mind, you could have a million dollars or many millions, if you wanted them, and still have peace of mind, harmony, perfect health, and perfect expression.

Poverty Is a Mental Disease

There is no virtue in poverty; it is a disease like any other mental disease. If you were physically ill you would think there was something wrong with you. You would seek help and do something about the condition at once. Likewise, if you do not have money constantly circulating in your life, there is something radically wrong with you.

The urge of Life-Principle in you is toward growth, expansion, and the life more abundant. You are not here to live in a hovel, dress in rags, and go hungry. You should be happy, prosperous, and successful.

Why You Must Never Criticize Money

Cleanse your mind of all weird and superstitious beliefs about money. Do not ever regard money as evil or filthy. If you do, you cause it to take wing and fly away from you. Remember that you lose what you condemn. You cannot attract what you criticize.

Getting the Right Attitude toward Money

Here is a simple technique you may use to multiply money in your experience. Use the following statements several times a day, "I like money; I love it; I use it wisely, constructively, and judiciously. Money is constantly circulating in my life. I release it with joy and it returns to me multiplied in a wonderful way. It is good and very good. Money flows to me in avalanches of abundance. I only use it for good and I am grateful for my good and for the riches of my mind."

How the Scientific Thinker Looks at Money

Suppose, for example, you found gold, silver, lead, copper, or iron in the ground. Would you pronounce these things evil? All evil comes from man's darkened understanding, from his ignorance, from his false interpretation of life, and from his misuse of his subconscious mind. Uranium, lead, or some other metal could have been used as a medium of exchange. We use paper bills, checks, nickel, and silver; surely these things are not evil. Physicists and chemists know today that the only difference between one metal and another is the number and rate of motion of electrons revolving around a central nucleus. They can now change one metal into another through a bombardment of the atoms in the powerful cyclotron. Gold, under certain conditions, becomes mercury. I believe that our modern scientists in the near future will be able to make gold, silver, and other metals synthetically in the chemical laboratory. The cost may be prohibitive now, but it can be done. I cannot imagine any intelligent person seeing anything evil in electrons, neutrons, protons, and isotopes.

The piece of paper in your pocket is composed of atoms and molecules with their electrons and protons arranged differently. Their number and rate of motion are different. That is the only way the paper differs from the silver in your pocket.

How to Attract the Money You Need

Many years ago, I met a young boy in Australia who wanted to become a physician and surgeon, but he had no money. I explained to him how a seed deposited in the soil attracts to itself everything necessary for its unfolding, and that all he had to do was to take a lesson from the seed and deposit the required idea in his subconscious mind. For expenses, this young, brilliant boy used to clean out doctors' offices, wash windows, and do odd repair jobs. He told me that every night, as he went to sleep, he used to picture in his mind's eye a medical diploma on a wall with his name on it in big, bold letters. He used to clean and shine the framed diplomas in the medical building where he worked. It was not hard for him to engrave the image of a diploma in his mind and develop it there. Definite results followed as he persisted with his mental picture every night for about four months.

The sequel of this story was very interesting. One of the doctors took a great liking to this young boy and after training him in the art of sterilizing instruments, giving hypodermic injections, and other miscellaneous first aid work, he employed him as a technical assistant in his office. The doctor later sent him to medical school at his own expense. Today, this young man is a prominent medical doctor in Montreal, Canada. He discovered the law of attraction by using his subconscious mind the right way. He operated an age-old law, described by Thomas Troward, "Having seen and felt the end, you have willed the means to the realization of the end." The *end* in this case was to become a medical doctor.

This young man was able to imagine, see, and feel the reality of being a doctor. He lived with that idea, sustained it, nourished it and loved it until through his imagination it penetrated the layers of his subconscious mind and became a conviction, thereby attracting to him everything necessary for the fulfillment of his dream.

Why Some Men Do Not Get a Raise in Pay

If you are working in a large organization and you are silently thinking of and resenting the fact you are underpaid, that you are not appreciated, and that you deserve more money and great recognition, you are subconsciously severing your ties with that organization. You are setting a law in motion, and the superintendent or manager will say to you, "We have to let you go." Actually, you dismissed yourself. The manager was simply the instrument through which your own negative mental state was confirmed. It was an example of the law of action and reaction. The action was your thought and the reaction was the response of your subconscious mind.

Obstacles and Impediments on the Pathway to Riches

I am sure you have heard men say, "That fellow has a racket." "He is a racketeer." "He is getting money dishonestly." "He is a faker." "I knew him when he had nothing." "He is a crook, a thief, and a swindler."

If you analyze the man who talks like that, you discover he is usually in want or suffering from some financial or physical illness. Perhaps his former college friends went up the ladder of success and excelled him. Now he is bitter and envious. In many instances this is the cause of his downfall. Thinking negatively of these classmates and condemning their wealth causes the wealth and prosperity he is praying for to vanish and flee away. He is condemning the thing he is praying for.

He is praying two ways. On the one hand he is saying, "Wealth is flowing to me now," and in the next breath, silently or audibly, he is saying, "I resent that fellow's wealth." Always make it a special point to rejoice in the wealth of the other person.

Protect Your Investments

If you are seeking wisdom regarding investments, or if you are worried about your stocks or bonds, quietly claim, "Infinite Intelligence governs and watches over all my financial transactions, and whatsoever I do shall prosper." Do this frequently and you will find that your investments will be wise; moreover, you will be protected from loss, as you will be prompted to sell your securities or holdings before any loss accrues to you.

You Cannot Get Something for Nothing

In large stores the management employs store detectives to prevent people from stealing. They catch a number of people every day trying to get something for nothing. All such people are living in the mental atmosphere of lack and limitation and are stealing from themselves peace, harmony, faith, honesty, integrity, good will, and confidence. Furthermore, they are attracting to themselves all manner of loss, such as loss of character, prestige, social status, and peace of mind. These people lack faith in the source of supply and the understanding of how their minds work. If they would mentally call on the powers of their subconscious mind and claim that they are guided to their true expression, they would find work and constant supply. Then by honesty, integrity, and perseverance they would become a credit to themselves and to society at large.

Your Constant Supply of Money

Recognizing the powers of your subconscious mind and the creative power of your thought or mental image is the way to opulence, freedom, and constant supply. Accept the abundant life in your own mind. Your mental acceptance and expectancy of wealth has its own mathematics and mechanics of expression. As you enter in to the mood of opulence, all things necessary for the abundant life will come to pass.

Let this be your daily affirmation; write it in your heart: "I am one with the infinite riches of my subconscious mind. It is my right to be rich, happy, and successful. Money flows to me freely, copiously, and endlessly. I am forever conscious of my true worth. I give of my talents freely and I am wonderfully blessed financially. It is wonderful!"

Step Up This Way to Riches

1. Be bold enough to claim that it is your right to be rich and your deeper mind will honor your claim.

2. You don't want just enough to go around. You want all the money you need to do all the things you want to do and when you want to do them. Get acquainted with the riches of your subconscious mind.

3. When money is circulating freely in your life, you are economically healthy. Look at money like the tide; you will always have plenty of it. The ebb and flow of the tide is constant. When the tide is out, you are absolutely sure that it will return.

4. Knowing the laws of your subconscious mind, you will always be supplied regardless of what form money takes.

5. One reason many people simply make ends meet and never have enough money is that they condemn money. What you condemn takes wings and flies away.

6. Do not make a god of money. It is only a symbol. Remember that the real riches are in your mind. You are here to lead a balanced life—this includes acquiring all the money you need.

7. Don't make money your sole aim. Claim wealth, happiness, peace, true expression, and love, and personally radiate love and good will to all. Then your subconscious mind will give you compound interest in all these fields of expression.

8. There is no virtue in poverty. It is a disease of the mind and you should heal yourself of this mental conflict or malady at once.

9. You are not here to live in a hovel, to dress in rags, or to go hungry. You are here to lead the life more abundant.

10. Never use the terms "filthy lucre" or "I despise money." You lose what you criticize. There is nothing good or bad, but thinking of it in either light makes it so.

11. Repeat frequently, "I like money. I use it wisely, constructively, and judiciously. I release it with joy and it returns a thousand fold."

12. Money is not evil any more so than copper, lead, tin, or iron which you find in the ground. All evil is due to ignorance or misuse of the mind's powers.

13. To picture the end result in your mind causes your subconscious to respond and fulfill your mental picture.

14. Stop trying to get something for nothing. There is no such thing as a free lunch. You must give to receive. You must give mental attention to your goals, ideals, and enterprises and your deeper mind will back you up. The key to wealth is application of the laws of the subconscious mind by impregnating it with the idea of wealth.

11

Your Subconscious Mind as a Partner in Success

Success means successful living. A long period of peace, joy, and happiness on this plane may be termed success. The eternal experience of these qualities is the everlasting life spoken of by Jesus. The real things of life, such as peace, harmony, integrity, security, and happiness, are intangible. They come from the deep self of man. Meditating on these qualities builds these treasures of heaven in our subconscious . . . it is where *moth and rust do not consume, and where thieves do not break through and steal* (Matthew 6:20).

The Three Steps to Success

Let us discuss three steps to success.

First Step

The first step to success is to find out the thing you love to do, then do it. Success is in loving your work. Although, if a man is a psychiatrist, it is not adequate for him to get a diploma and place it on the wall; he must keep up with the times, attend conventions, and continue studying the mind and its workings. The successful psychiatrist visits clinics and reads the latest scientific articles. In other words, he is informed in the most advanced methods of alleviating human suffering. The successful psychiatrist or doctor must have the interest of his patients at heart.

Someone may say, "How can I put the first step into operation? I do not know what I should do." In such a case, pray for guidance as follows: "The Infinite Intelligence of my subconscious mind reveals to me my true place in life." Repeat this prayer quietly, positively, and lovingly to your deeper mind. As you persist with faith and confidence, the answer will come to you as a feeling, a hunch, or a tendency in a certain direction. It will come to you clearly and in peace, and as an inner silent awareness.

Second Step

The second step to success is to specialize in some particular branch of work and know more about it than anyone else. For example, if a young man chooses chemistry as his profession, he should concentrate on one of the many branches in this field. He should give all of his time and attention to his chosen specialty. He should become sufficiently enthusiastic to try to know all there is available about his field; if possible, he should know more than anyone else. The young man should become ardently interested in his work and should desire to serve the world.

He that is great among you, let him become your servant (Matthew 20:26). There is a great contrast in this attitude of mind in comparison to that of the man who only wants to make a living or just "get by." Getting by is not true success. Man's motive must be great, nobler, and more altruistic. He must serve others, thereby casting his bread upon the waters.

Third Step

The third step is the most important one. You must be sure that the thing you want to do does not redound to your success only. Your desire must not be selfish; it must benefit humanity. The path of a complete circuit must be formed. In other words, your idea must go forth with the purpose of blessing or serving the world. It will then come back to you pressed down, shaken together, and running over. If it is to benefit yourself exclusively, the circle or complete circuit is not formed, and you may experience a short circuit in your life which may consist of limitation or sickness.

The Measure of True Success

Some people may say, "But Mr. James made a fortune in selling fraudulent oil stock." A man may seem to succeed for a while, but the money he obtained by fraud usually takes wings and flies away.

When we rob from another, we rob from ourselves, because we are in a mood of lack and limitation which may manifest itself in our body, home life, and affairs. What we think and feel, we create. We create what we believe. Even though a man may have accumulated a fortune fraudulently, he is not successful. There is no success without peace of mind. What good is man's accumulated wealth if he cannot sleep nights, is sick, or has a guilt complex?

I knew a man in London who told me of his exploits. He had been a professional pickpocket and had amassed a large amount of money. He had a summer home in France and lived in a royal fashion in England. His story was that he was in constant dread of being arrested by Scotland Yard. He had many inner disorders which were undoubtedly caused by his constant fear and deep-seated guilt complex. He knew he had done wrong. This deep sense of guilt attracted all kinds of trouble to him. Subsequently, he voluntarily surrendered to the police and served a prison sentence. After his release from prison, he sought psychological and spiritual counsel and became transformed. He went to work and became an honest, law-abiding citizen. He found what he loved to do and was happy.

A successful person loves his work and expresses himself fully. Success is contingent upon a higher ideal than the mere accumulation of riches. The man of success is the man who possesses great psychological and spiritual understanding. Many of the great industrialists today depend upon the correct use of the subconscious minds for their success.

There was an article published some years ago about Henry Flagler, an oil magnate. He admitted that the secret of his success was his ability to see a project in its completion. For instance, in his case, he closed his eyes, imagined a big oil industry, saw trains running on tracks, heard whistles blowing, and saw smoke. Having seen and felt the fulfillment of his prayer, his subconscious mind brought about its realization. If you imagine an objective clearly, you will be provided with the necessities, in ways you know not of, through the wonder-working power of your subconscious mind.

In considering the three steps to success you must never forget the underlying power of the creative forces of your subconscious mind. This is the energy in back of all steps in any plan of success. Your thought is creative. Thought fused with feeling becomes a subjective faith or belief, and *according to your belief it is done unto you.* (Matthew 9:29).

A knowledge of a mighty force in you which is capable of bringing to pass all your desires gives you confidence and a sense of peace. Whatever your field of action may be, you should learn the laws of your subconscious mind. When you know how to apply the powers of your mind, and when you are expressing yourself fully and giving of your talents to others, you are on the sure path to true success. If you are about God's business, or any part of it, God, by His very nature, is for you, so who can be against you? With this understanding there is no power in heaven or on earth to withhold success from you.

How He Made His Dream Come True

A movie actor told me that he had very little education, but he had a dream as a boy of becoming a successful movie actor. Out in the field mowing hay, driving the cows home, or even when milking them, he said, "I would constantly imagine I saw my name in big lights at a large theater. I kept this up for years until finally I ran away from home. I got extra jobs in the motion picture field and the day finally came when I saw my name in great big lights as I did when I was a boy!" Then he added, "I know the power of sustained imagination to bring success."

His Dream Pharmacy Became a Reality

Thirty years ago I knew a young pharmacist who was receiving forty dollars a week plus commission on sales. "After twenty-five years," he said to me, "I will get a pension and retire."

I said to this young man, "Why don't you own your own store? Get out of this place. Raise your sights! Have a dream for your children. Maybe your son wants to be a doctor, perhaps your daughter desires to be a great musician."

His answer was that he had no money! He began to awaken to the fact that whatever he could conceive as true, he could give conception.

The first step toward his goal was his awakening to the powers of his subconscious mind which I briefly elaborated on for his benefit.

His second step was his realization that if he could succeed in conveying an idea to his subconscious mind, the latter would somehow bring it to pass.

He began to imagine that he was in his own store. He mentally arranged the bottles, dispensed prescriptions, and imagined several clerks in the store waiting on customers. He also visualized a big bank balance. Mentally he worked in that imaginary store. Like a good actor he lived the role. (*Act as though I am, and I will be.*) This pharmacist put himself wholeheartedly into the act, living, moving, and acting on the assumption that he owned the store.

The sequel was interesting. He was discharged from his position. He found new employment with a large chain store, became manager, and later on, district manager. He saved enough money in four years to provide a down payment on a drugstore of his own. He called it his "dream pharmacy."

"It was," he said, "exactly the store I saw in my imagination." He became a recognized success in his chosen field and was happy doing what he loved to do.

Using the Subconscious Mind in Business

Some years ago I gave a lecture to a group of businessmen on the powers of imagination and the subconscious mind.

In this lecture I pointed out how Johann von Goethe used his imagination wisely when confronted with difficulties and predicaments. His biographers point out that he was accustomed to fill many hours quietly holding imaginary conversations. It is well-known that his custom was to imagine one of his friends before him in a chair answering him in the right way. In other words, if he were concerned over any problems, he imagined his friends giving him the right or appropriate answer, accompanied with the usual gestures and tonal qualities of the voice, and he made the entire imaginary scene as real and as vivid as possible.

One of the men present at my lecture was a young stockbroker. He proceeded to adopt the technique of Goethe. He began to have mental, imaginary conversations with a multimillionaire banker friend of his who used to congratulate him on his wise and sound judgment and compliment him on his purchase of the right stocks. He used to dramatize this imaginary conversation until he had psychologically fixed it as a form of belief in his mind.

The broker's inner talking and controlled imagination certainly agreed with his aim which was to make sound investments for his clients. His main purpose was to make money for his clients and to see them prosper financially by his wise counsel. He is still using his subconscious mind in his business, and he is a brilliant success in his field of endeavor.

Boy of Sixteen Years Turns Failure into Success

A young boy who was attending high school said to me, "I am getting very poor grades. My memory is failing, I do not know what is the matter." I discovered that the only thing wrong with this boy was his attitude, which was one of indifference and resentment toward some of his teachers and fellow students. I taught him how to use his subconscious mind, and how to succeed in his studies.

He began to affirm certain truths several times a day particularly at night prior to sleep, and also in the morning after awakening. These are the best times to impregnate the subconscious mind.

He affirmed as follows: "I realize that my subconscious mind is a storehouse of memory. It retains everything I read and hear from my teachers. I have a perfect memory and the Infinite Intelligence in my subconscious mind constantly reveals to me everything I need to know at all my examinations, whether written or oral. I radiate love and good will to all my teachers and fellow students. I sincerely wish for them success and all good things."

This young man is now enjoying a greater freedom than he has ever known. He is now receiving all A's. He constantly imagines the teachers and his mother congratulating him on his success in his studies.

How to Become Successful in Buying and Selling

In buying and selling, remember that your conscious mind is the starter and your subconscious mind is the motor. You must start the motor to enable it to perform its work. Your conscious mind is the dynamo that awakens the power of your subconscious mind.

The first step in conveying your clarified desire, idea, or image to the deeper mind is to relax, immobilize the attention, get still, and be quiet. This quiet, relaxed, and peaceful attitude of mind prevents extraneous matter and false ideas from interfering with your mental absorption of your ideal. Furthermore in the quiet, passive, and receptive attitude of mind, effort is reduced to a minimum.

The second step is to begin to imagine the reality of that which you desire. For example, you may wish to buy a home, and in your relaxed state of mind affirm as follows: "The Infinite Intelligence of my subconscious mind is all-wise. It reveals to me now the ideal home which is central, ideal, is in a lovely environment, meets all my requirements, and is commensurate with my income. I am now turning this request over to my subconscious mind, and I know it responds according to the nature of my request. I release this request with absolute faith and confidence in the same way that a farmer deposits a seed in the ground, trusting implicitly in the laws of growth."

The answer to your prayer may come through an advertisement in the paper, through a friend, or you may be guided directly to a particular home which is exactly what you are seeking. There are many ways by which your prayer may be answered. The principle knowledge, in which you may place your confidence, is that the answer always comes, provided you trust the working of your deeper mind.

You may wish to sell a home, land, or any kind of property. In private consultation with real estate brokers I have told them of the way I sold my own home on Orlando Avenue in Los Angeles. Many of them have applied the technique I used with remarkable and speedy results. I placed a sign which read, "For sale by owner," in the garden in front of my home. The day after, I said to myself as I was going to sleep, "Supposing you sold your house, what would you do?"

I answered my own question and I said, "I would take that sign down and throw it into the garage." In my imagination I took hold of the sign, pulled it up from the ground, placed it on my shoulder, went to the garage, threw it on the floor and said jokingly to the sign, "I don't need you anymore!" I felt the inner satisfaction of it all, realizing it was finished.

The next day a man gave me a deposit of a thousand dollars and said to me, "Take your sign down. We will go into escrow now."

Immediately I pulled the sign up and took it to the garage. The outer action conformed to the inner. There is nothing new about this. As within, so without, meaning according to the image impressed on your subconscious mind, so it is on the objective screen of life. The outside mirrors the inside. External action follows internal action.

Here is another very popular method used in selling homes, land, or any kind of property. Affirm slowly, quietly, and feelingly as follows: "Infinite Intelligence attracts to me the buyer for this home who wants and who prospers in it. This buyer may look at many other homes, but mine is the only one he wants and will buy, because he is guided by the Infinite Intelligence within him. I know the buyer is right, the time is right, and the price is right. Everything about it is right. The deeper currents of my subconscious mind are now in operation bringing both of us together in divine order. I know that it is so."

Remember always that what you are seeking is also seeking you, and whenever you want to sell a home or property of any kind, there is always someone who wants what you have to offer. By using the powers of your subconscious mind correctly, you free your mind of all sense of competition and anxiety in buying and selling.

How She Succeeded in Getting What She Wanted

There is a young lady who regularly comes to my lectures and classes. She had to change buses three times; it took her one and a half hours each time to come to the lectures. In one lecture I explained how a young man needed a car in his work and received one.

She went home and experimented as outlined in my lecture. Here is her letter in part, narrating her application of my method, and published with her permission:

Dear Dr. Murphy,

This is how I received a Cadillac car: I wanted one to come to the lectures regularly. In my imagination, I went through the identical process I would go through if I were actually driving a car. I went to the showroom and the salesman took me for a ride in one. I also drove it several blocks.

I claimed the Cadillac car as my own over and over again. I kept the mental picture of getting into the car, driving it, feeling the upholstery etc., consistently for over two weeks. Last week I drove to your lectures in a Cadillac. My uncle in Inglewood passed away and left me his Cadillac and his entire estate.

A Success Technique Employed by Many Outstanding Executives and Businessmen

There are many prominent businessmen who quietly use the abstract term "success," over and over many times a day until they reach a conviction that success is theirs. They know that the idea of success contains all the essential elements of success. Likewise, you can begin now to repeat the word, "success," to yourself with faith and conviction. Your subconscious mind will accept it as true of you and you will be under a subconscious compulsion to succeed.

You are compelled to express your subjective beliefs, impressions, and convictions. What does success imply to you? You want, undoubtedly, to be successful in your home life and in your relationship with others. You wish to be outstanding in your chosen work or profession. You wish to possess a beautiful home and all the money you need to live comfortably and happily. You want to be successful in your prayer life and in your contact with the powers of your subconscious mind.

You are a businessman also because you are in the business of living. Become a successful businessman by imagining yourself doing what you long to do, and possessing the things you long to possess. Become imaginative, mentally participate in the reality of the successful state. Make a habit of it. Go to sleep feeling successful every night, and perfectly satisfied, and you will eventually succeed in implanting the idea of success in your subconscious mind. Believe you were born to succeed and wonders will happen as you pray!

Profitable Pointers

1. Success means successful living. When you are peaceful, happy, joyous, and doing what you love to do, you are successful.

2. Find out what you love to do, then do it. If you don't know your true expression, ask for guidance and the lead will come.

3. Specialize in your particular field and try to know more about it than anyone else.

4. A successful man is not selfish. His main desire in life is to serve humanity.

5. There is no true success without peace of mind.

6. A successful man possesses great psychological and spiritual understanding.

7. If you imagine an objective clearly, you will be provided with the necessities through the wonder-working power of your subconscious mind.

8. Your thought fused with feeling becomes a subjective belief, and "according to your belief is it done unto you."

9. The power of sustained imagination draws forth the miracle-working powers of your subconscious mind.

10. If you are seeking promotion in your work, imagine your employer, supervisor, or loved one congratulating you on your promotion.

Make the picture vivid and real. Hear the voice, see the gestures, and feel the reality of it all. Continue to do this frequently and through frequent occupancy of your mind, you will experience the joy of the answered prayer.

11. Your subconscious mind is a storehouse of memory. For a perfect memory, affirm frequently: "The Infinite Intelligence of my subconscious mind reveals to me everything I need to know at all times, everywhere."

12. If you wish to sell a home or property of any kind, affirm slowly, quietly, and feelingly as follows: "Infinite Intelligence attracts to me the buyer for this house or property, who wants it, and who prospers in it." Sustain the awareness and the deeper currents of your subconscious mind will bring it to pass.

13. The idea of success contains all the elements of success. Repeat the word "success" to yourself frequently with faith and conviction and you will be under a subconscious compulsion to succeed.

12

Scientists Use the
Subconscious Mind

Many scientists realize the true importance of the subconscious mind. Edison, Marconi, Kettering, Poincare, Einstein, and many others have used the subconscious mind. It has given them the insight and the "know-how" for all their great achievements in modern science and industry. Research has shown that the ability to bring into action the subconscious power has determined the success of all the great scientific and research workers.

An instance of how a famous chemist, Friedrich von Stradonitz, used his subconscious mind to solve his problem is as follows: He had been working laboriously for a long time trying to rearrange the six carbon and the six hydrogen atoms on the benzine formula, and he was constantly perplexed and unable to solve the matter. Tired and exhausted, he turned the request over completely to his subconscious mind. Shortly afterward, as he was about to board a London bus, his subconscious presented his conscious mind with a sudden flash of a snake biting its own tail and turning around like a pinwheel. This answer, from his subconscious mind, gave him the long-sought answer of the circular rearrangement of the atoms that is known as the benzine ring.

How a Distinguished Scientist Brought Forth His Inventions

Nikola Tesla was a brilliant electrical scientist who brought forth the most amazing innovations. When an idea for a new invention came into his mind, he would build it up in his imagination, knowing that his subconscious mind would reconstruct and reveal to his conscious mind all the parts needed for its manufacture in concrete form. Through quietly contemplating every possible improvement, he spent no time in correcting defects and was able to give the technicians the perfect product of his mind.

He said, "Invariably, my device works as I imagined it should. In twenty years there has not been a single exception."

How a Famous Naturalist Solved His Problem

Professor Louis Agassiz, a distinguished American naturalist, discovered the indefatigable activities of his subconscious mind while he slept. The following has been reported by his widow in her biography of her famous husband.

He had been for two weeks striving to decipher the somewhat obscure impression of a fossil fish on the stone slab in which it was preserved. Weary and perplexed, he put his work aside at last, and tried to dismiss it from his mind. Shortly after, he waked one night persuaded that while asleep he had seen his fish with all the missing features perfectly restored. But when he tried to hold and make fast the image it escaped him. Nevertheless, he went early to the Jardin des Plantes, thinking that on looking anew at the impression he should see something which would put him on the track of his vision. In vain the blurred record was as black as ever. The next night he saw the fish again, but with no more satisfactory result. When he awoke it disappeared from his memory as before. Hoping that the same experience might be repeated, on the third night he placed a pencil and paper beside the bed before going to sleep.

Accordingly, toward morning the fish reappeared in his dream, confusedly at first, but at last with such distinctness that he had no longer any doubt as to its zoological characters. Still half dreaming, in perfect darkness, he traced these characters on the sheet of paper at the bedside. In the morning he was surprised to see in his nocturnal sketch features which he thought it impossible the fossil itself should reveal. He hastened to the Jardin des Plantes, and, with his drawing as a guide, succeeded in chiseling away the surface of the stone under which portions of the fish proved to be hidden. When wholly exposed it corresponded with his dream and his drawing, and he succeeded in classifying it with ease.

An Outstanding Physician Solved the Problem of Diabetes

Some years ago I received a clipping from a magazine describing the origin of the discovery of insulin. This is the essence of the article as I recall it.

About forty years ago or more, Dr. Frederick Banting, a brilliant Canadian physician and surgeon, was concentrating his attention on the ravages of diabetes. At that time medical science offered no effective method of arresting the disease. Dr. Banting spent considerable time experimenting and studying the international literature on the subject. One night he was exhausted and fell asleep. While asleep, his subconscious mind instructed him to extract the residue from the degenerated pancreatic duct of dogs. This was the origin of insulin, which has helped millions of people.

You will note that Dr. Banting had been consciously dwelling on the problem for some time, seeking a solution, a way out, and his subconscious responded accordingly.

It does not follow that you will always get an answer overnight. The answer may not come for some time. Do not be discouraged. Keep on turning the problem over every night to the subconscious mind prior to sleep, as if you had never done it before.

One of the reasons for the delay may be that you look upon it as a major problem. You may believe it will take a long time to solve it.

Your subconscious mind is timeless and spaceless. Go to sleep believing you have the answer. No, do not postulate the answer in the future. Have an abiding faith in the outcome. Become convinced now as you read this book that there is an answer and a perfect solution for you.

How a Famous Scientist and Physicist Escaped from a Russian Concentration Camp

Dr. Lothar von Blenk-Schmidt, a member of the Rocket Society and an outstanding research electronic engineer, gives the following condensed summary of how he used his subconscious mind to free himself from certain death at the hands of brutal guards in a Russian prison camp coal mine. He states as follows:

> I was a prisoner of war in a coal mine in Russia, and I saw men dying all around me in that prison compound. We were watched over by brutal guards, arrogant officers, and sharp, fast-thinking commissars. After a short medical checkup, a

quota of coal was assigned to each person. My quota was three hundred pounds per day. In case any man did not fill his quota, his small food ration was cut down, and in a short time he was resting in the cemetery.

I started concentrating on my escape. I knew that my subconscious mind would somehow find a way. My home in Germany was destroyed, my family wiped out, all my friends and former associates were either killed in the war or were in concentration camps.

I said to my subconscious mind, I want to go to Los Angeles, and you will find the way. I had seen pictures of Los Angeles and I remembered some of the boulevards very well as well as some of the buildings.

Every day and night I would imagine I was walking down Wilshire Boulevard with an American girl whom I met in Berlin prior to the war (she is now my wife). In my imagination we would visit the stores, ride buses, and eat in restaurants. Every night I made it a special point to drive my imaginary American automobile up and down the boulevards of Los Angeles. I made all this vivid and real. These pictures in my mind were as real and as natural to me as one of the trees outside the prison camp.

Every morning the chief guard would count the prisoners as they were lined up. He would call out, "One, two, three," etc., and when seventeen was called out, which was my number in sequence, I stepped aside. In the meantime, the guard was called away for a minute or so, and on his return he started by mistake on the next man as number seventeen. When the crew returned in the evening, the number of men was the same, and I was not missed, and the discovery would take a long time.

I walked out of the camp undetected and kept walking for twenty-four hours, resting in a deserted town the next day.

I was able to live by fishing and killing some wildlife. I found coal trains going to Poland and traveled on them by night, until finally I reached Poland. With the help of friends, I made my way to Lucerne, Switzerland.

One evening at the Palace Hotel, Lucerne, I had a talk with a man and his wife from the United States of America. This man asked me if I would care to be a guest at his home in Santa Monica, California. I accepted, and when I arrived in Los Angeles, I found that their chauffeur drove me along Wilshire Boulevard and many other boulevards which I had imagined so vividly in the long months in the Russian coal mines. I recognized the buildings which I had seen in my mind so often. It actually seemed as if I had been in Los Angeles before. I had reached my goal.

I will never cease to marvel at the wonders of the subconscious mind. Truly, it has ways we know not of.

How Archaeologists and Paleontologists Reconstruct Ancient Scenes

These scientists know that their subconscious mind has a memory of everything that has ever transpired. As they study the ancient ruins and fossils, through their imaginative perception, their subconscious mind aids them in reconstructing the ancient scenes. The dead past becomes alive and audible once more. Looking at these ancient temples and studying the pottery, statuary, tools, and household utensils of these ancient times, the scientist tells us of an age when there was no language. Communication was done by grunts, groans, and signs.

The keen concentration and disciplined imagination of the scientist awakens the latent powers of his subconscious mind, enabling him to clothe the ancient temples with roofs, and surround them with gardens, pools, and fountains. The fossil remains are clothed with eyes, sinews, and muscles and they again walk and talk. The past becomes the living present and we find that in mind there is no time or space. Through disciplined, controlled, and directed imagination, you can be a companion of the most scientific and inspired thinkers of all time.

How to Receive Guidance from Your Subconscious

When you have what you term "a difficult decision" to make, or when you fail to see the solution to your problem, begin at once to think constructively about it. If you are fearful and worried, you are not really thinking. True thinking is free from fear.

Here is a simple technique you can use to receive guidance on any subject: Quiet the mind and still the body. Tell the body to relax; it has to obey you. It has no volition, initiative, or self-conscious intelligence. Your body is an emotional disk which records your beliefs and impressions. Mobilize your attention; focus your thought on the solution to your problem. Try to solve it with your conscious mind. Think how happy you would be about the perfect solution. Sense the feeling you would have if the perfect answer were yours now. Let your mind play with this mood in a relaxed way; then drop off to sleep. When you awaken, and you do not have the answer, get busy about something else. Probably, when you are preoccupied with something else, the answer will come into your mind like toast pops out of a toaster.

In receiving guidance from the subconscious mind, the simple way is the best. This is an illustration: I once lost a valuable ring which was an heirloom. I looked everywhere for it and could not locate it. At night I talked to the subconscious in the same manner that I would talk to anyone. I said to it prior to dropping off to sleep, "You know all things; you know where that ring is, and you now reveal to me where it is."

In the morning I awoke suddenly with the words ringing in my ear, "Ask Robert!"

I thought it very strange that I should ask Robert, a young boy about nine years of age; however, I followed the inner voice of intuition.

Robert said, "Oh yes, I picked it up in the yard while I was playing with the boys. I placed it on the desk in my room. I did not think it worth anything so I did not say anything about it."

The subconscious mind will always answer you if you trust it.

His Subconscious Revealed the Location of His Father's Will

A young man who attends my lectures had this experience. His father died and apparently left no will. However, this man's sister told him that their father had confided to her that a will had been executed which was fair to all. Every attempt to locate the will failed.

Prior to sleep he talked to his deeper mind as follows: "I now turn this request over to the subconscious mind. It knows just where that will is and reveals it to me." Then he condensed his request down to one word, "Answer," repeating it over and over again as a lullaby. He lulled himself to sleep with the word, "Answer."

The next morning this young man had an overpowering hunch to go to a certain bank in Los Angeles where he found a safe deposit vault registered in the name of his father, the contents of which solved all his problems.

Your thought, as you go to sleep, arouses the powerful latency which is within you. For example, let us suppose you are wondering whether to sell your home, buy a certain stock, sever partnership, move to New York or stay in Los Angeles, dissolve the present contract or take a new one. Do this: Sit quietly in your armchair or at the desk in your office. Remember that there is a universal law of action and reaction. The action is your thought. The reaction is the response from your subconscious mind. The subconscious mind is reactive and reflexive; this is its nature. It rebounds, rewards, and repays. It is the law of correspondence. It responds by corresponding. As you contemplate right action, you will automatically experience a reaction or response in yourself which represents the guidance or answer of your subconscious mind.

In seeking guidance, you simply think quietly about right action which means that you are using the Infinite Intelligence resident in the subconcious mind to the point where it begins to use you. From there on, your course of action is directed and controlled by the subjective wisdom within you which is all-wise and omnipotent. Your decision will be right. There will only be right action because you are under a subjective compulsion to do the right thing. I use the word *compulsion* because the law of the subconscious is compulsion.

The Secret of Guidance

The secret of guidance or right action is to mentally devote yourself to the right answer, until you find its response in you. The response is a feeling, an inner awareness, an overpowering hunch whereby you know that you know. You have used the power to the point where it begins to use you. You cannot possibly fail or make one false step while operating under the subjective wisdom within you. You will find that all your ways are pleasantness and all your paths are peace.

Highlights to Recall

1. Remember that the subconscious mind has determined the success and wonderful achievements of all great scientific workers.

2. By giving your conscious attention and devotion to the solution of a perplexing problem, your subconscious mind gathers all the necessary information and presents it full blow to the conscious mind.

3. If you are wondering about the answer to a problem, try to solve it objectively. Get all the information you can from research and also from others. If no answer comes, turn it over to your subconscious mind prior to sleep, and the answer always comes. It never fails.

4. You do not always get the answer overnight. Keep on turning your request over to your subconscious "until the day breaks and the shadows flee away."

5. You delay the answer by thinking it will take a long time or that it is a major problem. Your subconscious has no problem, it knows only the answer.

6. Believe that you have the answer now. Feel the joy of the answer and the way you would feel if you had the perfect answer. Your subconscious will respond to your feeling.

7. Any mental picture, backed by faith and perseverance, will come to pass through the miracle-working power of your sub-

conscious. Trust it, believe in its power, and wonders will happen as you pray.

8. Your subconscious is the storehouse of memory and within your subconscious are recorded your experiences since childhood.

9. Scientists meditating on ancient scrolls, temples, fossils, etc., are able to reconstruct scenes of the past and make them alive today. Their subconscious mind comes to their aid.

10. Turn over your request for a solution to your subconscious prior to sleep. Trust it and believe in it and the answer will come. It knows all and sees all, but you must not doubt or question its powers.

11. The action is your thought, and the reaction is the response of your subconscious mind. If your thoughts are wise, your actions and decisions will be wise.

12. Guidance comes as a feeling, an inner awareness, an overpowering hunch whereby you know that you know. It is an inner sense of touch. Follow it.

13

Your Subconscious and the Wonders of Sleep

You spend about eight out of every twenty-four hours, or one-third of your entire life, in sleep. This is an inexorable law of life. This also applies to the animal and vegetable kingdoms. Sleep is a divine law and many answers to our problems come to us when we are sound asleep upon the bed.

Many people have advocated the theory that you get tired during the day, that you go to sleep to rest the body, and that a reparative process takes place while you sleep. Nothing rests in sleep. Your heart, lungs, and all your vital organs function while you are asleep. If you eat prior to sleep, the food is digested and assimilated; also, your skin secretes perspiration, and your nails and hair continue to grow.

Your subconscious mind never rests or sleeps. It is always active, controlling all your vital forces. The healing process takes place more rapidly while you are asleep as there is no interference from your conscious mind. Remarkable answers are given to you while you are asleep.

Why We Sleep

Dr. John Bigelow, a famous research authority on sleep (*The Mystery of Sleep*, New York and London: Harper Brothers, 1903), demonstrated that at night while asleep you receive impressions showing that the nerves of the eyes, ears, nose, and taste buds are active during sleep and also that the nerves of your brain are quite active. He says that the main reason we sleep is because "the nobler part of the soul is united by abstraction to our higher nature and becomes a participant in the wisdom and foreknowledge of the gods."

Dr. Bigelow states also, "The results of my studies have not only strengthened my convictions that the supposed exemption from customary tolls and activities was not the final purpose of sleep, but have also made clearer to my mind the conviction that no part of a man's life deserves to be considered more indispensable to its symmetrical and perfect spiritual development than while he is separated from the phenomenal world in sleep."

Prayer, a Form of Sleep

Your conscious mind gets involved with vexations, strife, and contentions of the day and it is very necessary to withdraw periodically from sense evidence and the objective world, and commune silently with the inner wisdom of your subconscious mind. By claiming guidance, strength, and greater intelligence in all phases of your life, you will be enabled to overcome all difficulties and solve your daily problems.

This regular withdrawal from sense evidence and the noise and confusion of everyday living is also a form of sleep, i.e., you become asleep to the world of the senses and alive to the wisdom and power of your subconscious mind.

Startling Effects of Sleep Deprivation

Lack of sleep can cause you to become irritable, moody, and depressed. Dr. George Stevenson of the National Association for Mental Health says, "I believe it can safely be said that all human beings need a minimum of six hours' sleep to be healthy. Most people need more. Those who think they can get along on less are fooling themselves."

Medical research scholars, investigating sleep processes and deprivation of sleep, point out that severe insomnia has preceded psychotic breakdown in some instances. Remember, you are spiritually recharged during sleep, and adequate sleep is essential to produce joy and vitality in life.

You Need More Sleep

Robert O'Brien, in an article, "Maybe You Need More Sleep," in a February 1960 issue of *Reader's Digest*, reports the following experiments on sleep:

> For the last three years experiments have been in progress at Walter Reed Army Institute of Research in Washington, DC. Subjects—more than one hundred military and civilian volunteers—have been kept awake for as long as four days. Thousands of tests have measured the effects on their behavior and personality. Results of these tests have given scientists astonishingly new insights into the mysteries of sleep.
>
> They now know that the tired brain apparently craves sleep so hungrily that it will sacrifice anything to get it. After only a few hours of sleep loss, fleeting stolen naps called lapses, or micro sleep, occurred at the rate of three or four an hour. As in real sleep, eyelids dropped, and heartbeat slowed. Each lapse

lasted just a fraction of a second. Sometimes the lapses were periods of blankness; sometimes they were filled with images, wisps of dreams. As hours of sleep loss mounted, the lapses took place more often and lasted longer, perhaps two or three seconds. Even if the subjects had been piloting an airliner in a thunderstorm, they still couldn't have resisted micro sleeps for those few priceless seconds. And it can happen to you, as many who have fallen asleep at the wheel of a car can testify.

Another startling effect of sleep deprivation was its attack on human memory and perception. Many sleep deprived subjects were unable to retain information long enough to relate it to the task they were supposed to perform. They were totally befuddled in situations requiring them to hold several factors in mind and act on them, as a pilot must when he skilfully integrates wind direction, air speed, altitude, and glide path to make a safe landing.

Sleep Brings Counsel

A young lady in Los Angeles who listens to my morning radio talks told me that she had been offered a lucrative position in New York City at twice her present salary. She was wondering whether to accept or not and prayed prior to sleep as follows: "The creative intelligence of my subconscious mind knows what is best for me. Its tendency is always lifeward, and it reveals to me the right decision which blesses me and all concerned. I give thanks for the answer which I know will come to me."

She repeated this simple prayer over and over again as a lullaby prior to sleep and in the morning she had a persistent feeling that she should not accept the offer. She rejected the offer and subsequent events verified her inward sense of knowing, because the company went bankrupt a few months following their offer of employment to her.

The conscious mind may be correct on the facts objectively known, but the intuitive faculty of her subconscious mind saw the failure of the concern in question and prompted her accordingly.

Saved from Certain Disaster

I will illustrate how the wisdom of your subconscious mind can instruct you and protect you relative to your request for right action as you go to sleep.

Many years ago, before the Second World War, I was offered a very lucrative assignment in the Orient, and I prayed for guidance and right decision as follows: "Infinite Intelligence within me knows all things, and the right decision is revealed to me in divine order. I will recognize the answer when it comes."

I repeated this simple prayer over and over again as a lullaby prior to sleep and in a dream came the vivid realization of things to come three years hence. An old friend appeared in the dream and said, "Read these headlines—do not go!" The headlines of the newspaper which appeared in the dream related to war and the attack on Pearl Harbor.

Occasionally, the writer dreams literally. The aforementioned dream was undoubtedly a dramatization of the subconscious mind which projected a person whom I trusted and respected. To some, a warning may come in the form of a mother who appears in a dream. She tells the person not to go here or there, and the reason for the warning. Your subconscious mind is all-wise. It knows all things. Oftentimes it will speak to you only in a voice that your conscious mind will immediately accept as true. Sometimes your sub-conscious mind will warn you in a voice which sounds like that of your mother or some loved one which may cause you to stop on the street, and you find, if you had gone another foot, a falling object from a window might have struck you on the head.

My subconscious mind is one with the universal subconscious and it knew the Japanese were planning a war, and it also knew when the war would start.

Dr. Joseph Rhine, director of the Department of Psychology at Duke University, has gathered together a vast amount of evidence showing that a great number of people all over the world see events before they happen, and in many instances are, therefore, able to avoid the tragic event which was foreseen vividly in a dream.

The dream I had showed clearly the headlines in the *New York Times* about three years prior to the tragedy of Pearl Harbor. In consequence of this dream, I immediately canceled the trip as I felt a subconscious compulsion to do so. Three years later the Second World War proved the truth of the inner voice of intuition.

Your Future Is in Your Subconscious Mind

Remember that the future, the result of your habitual thinking, is already in your mind except when you change it through prayer. The future of a country, likewise, is in the collective subconscious of the people of that nation. There is nothing strange in the dream I had wherein I saw the headlines of the New York newspapers long before the war began. The war had already taken place in mind, and all the plans of attack were already engraved on that great recording instrument, the subconscious mind, or collective unconscious of the universal mind. Tomorrow's events are in your subconscious mind, so are next week's and next month's and they may be seen by a highly psychic or clairvoyant person.

No disaster or tragedy can happen to you if you decide to pray. Nothing is predetermined or foreordained. Your mental attitude, i.e., the way you think, feel, and believe, determines your destiny. You can, through scientific prayer, which is explained in a previous chapter, mold, fashion, and create your own future. *Whatsoever a man soweth, that shall he also reap* (Galatians 6:7).

A Catnap Nets Him Fifteen Thousand Dollars

One of my students mailed me a newspaper clipping three or four years ago about a man called Ray Hammerstrom, a roller at the steel works in Pittsburgh, operated by Jones and Laughlin Steel Corporation. He received fifteen thousand dollars for his dream.

According to the article, the engineers could not fix a faulty switch in a newly installed bar mill which controlled the delivery of straight bars to the cooling beds. The engineers worked on the switch about eleven or twelve times to no avail.

Hammerstrom thought a lot about the problem and tried to figure out a new design which might work. Nothing worked. One afternoon he lay down for a nap and prior to sleep he began to think about the answer to the switch problem. He had a dream in which the perfect design for the switch was portrayed. When he awoke, he sketched his new design according to the outline of his dream.

This visionary catnap won Hammerstrom a check for fifteen thousand dollars, the largest award the firm ever gave an employee for a new idea.

How a Famous Professor Solved His Problem in Sleep

Dr. H. V. Hilprecht, Professor of Assyrian at the University of Pennsylvania, wrote as follows:

One Saturday evening I had been wearying myself in the vain attempt to decipher two small fragments of agate which were supposed to belong to the finger rings of some Babylonians.

About midnight, weary and exhausted, I went to bed and dreamed the following remarkable dream: A tall thin priest of Nippur, about forty years of age, led me to the treasure chamber of the temple . . . a small, low-ceilinged room without windows, with scraps of agate and lapis-lazuli scattered on the floor. Here he addressed me as follows: "The two fragments, which you have published separately on pages 22 and 26, belong together, and are not finger rings. The first two rings served as earrings for the statue of God; the two fragments you have are the portions of them. If you will put them together you will have confirmation of my words."

I awoke at once. I examined the fragments and to my astonishment found the dream verified. The problem was then at last solved.

This demonstrates clearly the creative manifestation of his subconscious mind which knew the answer to all his problems.

How the Subconscious Worked for a Famous Writer While He Slept

Robert Louis Stevenson in one of his books, *Across the Plains*, devotes a whole chapter to dreams. He was a vivid dreamer and had the persistent habit of giving specific instructions to his subconscious every night prior to sleep. He would request his subconscious to evolve stories for him while he slept. For example, if Stevenson's funds were at a low ebb, his command to his subconscious would be something like this: "Give me a good thrilling novel which will be marketable and profitable." His subconscious responded magnificently.

Stevenson says, "These little brownies [the intelligences and powers of his subconscious] can tell me a story piece by piece, like a serial, and keep me, its supposed creator, all the while in total ignorance of where they aim." And he added: "That part of my work which is done when I am up and about [which he is consciously aware and awake] is by no means necessarily mine, since all goes to show that the *brownies* have a hand in it even then."

Sleep in Peace and Wake in Joy

To those who suffer from insomnia, you will find the following prayer very effective. Repeat it slowly, quietly, and lovingly prior to sleep:

> My toes are relaxed, my ankles are relaxed, my abdominal muscles are relaxed, my heart and lungs are relaxed, my hands and arms are relaxed, my neck is relaxed, my brain is relaxed, my face is relaxed, my eyes are relaxed, my whole mind and body are relaxed. I fully and freely forgive everyone, and I sincerely wish for them harmony, health, peace, and all the blessings of life. I am at peace; I am poised, serene, and calm. I rest in security and in peace. A great stillness steals over me, and a great calm quiets my whole being as I realize the divine presence within me. I know that the realization of life and love heals me. I wrap myself in the mantle of love and fall asleep filled with good will for all. Throughout the night peace remains with me and in the morning I shall be filled with life and love. A circle of love is drawn around me. *I will fear no evil, for Thou art with*

me, I sleep in peace, I wake in joy, and in Him I live, move, and have my being (Psalms 23).

Summary of Your Aids to the Wonders of Sleep

1. If you are worried that you will not wake up on time, suggest to your subconscious mind prior to sleep the exact time you wish to arise, and it will awaken you. It needs no clock. Do the same thing with all problems. There is nothing too hard for your subconscious.

2. Your subconscious never sleeps. It is always on the job. It controls all your vital functions. Forgive yourself and everyone else before you go to sleep and healing will take place much more rapidly.

3. Guidance is given to you while you are asleep, sometimes in a dream. The healing currents are also released and in the morning you feel refreshed and rejuvenated.

4. When troubled by the vexations and strife of the day, still the wheels of your mind and think about the wisdom and intelligence lodged in your subconscious mind which is ready to respond to you. This will give you peace, strength, and confidence.

5. Sleep is essential for peace of mind and health of body. Lack of sleep can cause irritation, depression, and mental disorders. You need eight hours' sleep.

6. Medical research scholars point out that insomnia precedes psychotic disorders.

7. You are spiritually recharged during sleep. Adequate sleep is essential for joy and vitality in life.

8. Your tired brain craves sleep so hungrily that it will sacrifice anything to get it. Many who have fallen asleep at the wheel of an automobile can testify to this.

9. Many sleep-deprived people have poor memories and lack proper coordination. They become befuddled, confused, and disorientated.

10. Sleep brings counsel. Prior to sleep, claim that the Infinite Intelligence of your subconscious mind is guiding and directing you. Then, watch for the lead which comes, perhaps on awakening.

11. Trust your subconscious completely. Know that its tendency is always lifeward. Occasionally, your subconscious answers you in a very vivid dream and a vision in the night. You can be forewarned in a dream in the same way as the author of this book was warned.

12. Your future is in your mind now, based on your habitual thinking and beliefs. Claim that Infinite Intelligence leads and guides you, and that all good is yours, and your future will be wonderful. Believe it and accept it. Expect the best and invariably the best will come to you.

13. If you are writing a novel, play, or book or are working on an invention, speak to your subconscious mind at night and claim boldly that its wisdom, intelligence, and power are guiding, directing, and revealing to you the ideal play, novel, book, or revealing the perfect solution whatever it may be. Wonders will happen as you pray this way.

14

Your Subconscious Mind and Marital Problems

Ignorance of the functions and powers of the mind is the cause of all marital trouble. Friction between husband and wife can be solved by each using the law of mind correctly. By praying together they stay together. The contemplation of divine ideals, the study of the laws of life, the mutual agreement on a common purpose and plan, and the enjoyment of personal freedom bring about that harmonious marriage, that wedded bliss, that sense of oneness where the two become one.

The best time to prevent divorce is before marriage. It is not wrong to try to get out of a very bad situation. But, why get into the bad situation in the first place? Would it not be better to give attention to the real cause of marital problems, in other words, to really get at the root of the matter involved?

As with all other problems of men and women, the problems of divorce, separation, annulment, and endless litigation are directly traceable to lack of knowledge of the working and interrelationship of the conscious and subconscious mind.

The Meaning of Marriage

Marriage to be real must first be on a spiritual basis. It must be of the heart and the heart is the chalice of love. Honesty, sincerity, kindness, and integrity are also forms of love. Each partner should be perfectly honest and sincere with the other. It is not a true marriage when a man marries a woman for her money, social position, or to lift his ego, because this indicates a lack of security, honesty, and true love. Such a marriage is a farce, a sham, and a masquerade.

When a woman says, "I am tired of working; I want to get married because I want security," her premise is false. She is not using the laws of mind correctly. Her security depends upon her knowledge of the interaction of the conscious and subconscious mind and its application.

For example, a woman will never lack for wealth or health if she applies the techniques outlined in the respective chapters of this book. Her wealth can come to her independent of her husband, father, or anyone else. A woman is not dependent on her husband for health, peace, joy, inspiration, guidance, love, wealth, security, happiness, or anything in the world. Her security and peace of mind come from her knowledge of the inner powers within her and from the constant use of the laws of her own mind in a constructive fashion.

How to Attract the Ideal Husband

You are now acquainted with the way your subconscious mind works. You know that whatever you impress upon it will be experienced in your world. Begin now to impress your subconscious mind with the qualities and characteristics you desire in a man.

The following is an excellent technique: Sit down at night in your armchair, close your eyes, let go, relax your body, become very quiet, passive, and receptive. Talk to your subconscious mind and say to it,

I am now attracting a man into my experience who is honest, sincere, loyal, faithful, peaceful, happy, and prosperous. These qualities which I admire are sinking down into my subconscious mind now. As I dwell upon these characteristics, they become a part of me and are embodied subconsciously.

I know there is an irresistible law of attraction and that I attract to me a man according to my subconscious belief. I attract that which I feel to be true in my subconscious mind.

I know I can contribute to his peace and happiness. He loves my ideals, and I love his ideals. He does not want to make me over, neither do I want to make him over. There is mutual love, freedom, and respect.

Practice this process of impregnating your subconscious. Then you will have the joy of attracting to you a man possessing the qualities and characteristics you mentally dwelt upon. Your subconscious intelligence will open up a pathway whereby both of you will meet, according to the irresistible and changeless flow of your own subconscious mind. Have a keen desire to give the best that is in you of love, devotion, and cooperation. Be receptive to this gift of love which you have given to your subconscious mind.

How to Attract the Ideal Wife

Affirm as follows:

I now attract the right woman who is in complete accord with me. This is a spiritual union because it is divine love functioning through the personality of someone with whom I blend perfectly. I know I can give to this woman love, light, peace, and joy. I feel and believe I can make this woman's life full, complete, and wonderful.

I now decree that she possesses the following qualities and attributes: She is spiritual, loyal, faithful, and true. She is harmonious, peaceful, and happy. We are irresistibly attracted to each other. Only that which belongs to love, truth, and beauty can enter my experience. I accept my ideal companion now.

As you think quietly and with interest on the qualities and attributes which you admire in the companion you seek, you will build the mental equivalent into your mentality. Then the deeper currents of your subconscious mind will bring both of you together in divine order.

No Need for Third Mistake

Recently a teacher said to me, "I have had three husbands and all three have been passive, submissive, and dependent on me to make all decisions and govern everything. Why do I attract such type men?"

I asked her whether she had known that her second husband was the effeminate type, and she replied, "Of course not. Had I known, I would not have married him." Apparently she had not learned anything from the first mistake. The trouble was with her own personality make up. She was very masculine, domineering, and unconsciously wanted someone who would be submissive and passive so that she could play the dominant role. All this was unconscious motivation, and her subconscious picture attracted to her what she subjectively wanted. She had to learn to break the pattern by adopting the right prayer process.

How She Broke the Negative Pattern

The above-mentioned woman learned a simple truth. When you believe you can have the type of man you idealize, it is done unto you as you believe. The following is the specific prayer she used to break the old subconscious pattern and attract to her the ideal mate: "I am building into my mentality the type of man I deeply desire. The man I attract for a husband is strong, powerful, loving, very masculine, successful, honest, loyal, and faithful. He finds love and happiness with me. I love to follow where he leads.

"I know he wants me, and I want him. I am honest, sincere, loving, and kind. I have wonderful gifts to offer him. They are good will, a joyous heart, and a healthy body. He offers me the same. It is mutual; I give and I receive. Divine Intelligence knows where this man is, and the deeper wisdom of my subconscious mind is now bringing both of us together in its own way and we recognize each other immediately. I release this request to my subconscious mind which knows how to bring my request to pass. I give thanks for the perfect answer."

She prayed in the above manner night and morning, affirming these truths and knowing that through frequent occupation of the mind she would reach the mental equivalent of that which she sought.

The Answer to Her Prayer

Several months went by. She had a great number of dates and social engagements, none of which was agreeable to her. When she was about to question, waiver, doubt, and vacillate, she reminded herself that the Infinite Intelligence was bringing it to pass in its own way and that there was nothing to be concerned about. Her final decree in her divorce proceedings was granted which brought her a great sense of release and mental freedom.

Shortly afterward she went to work as a receptionist in a doctor's office. She told me that the minute she saw the physician she knew he was the man she was praying about. Apparently he knew it too, because he proposed to her the first week she was in the office and their subsequent marriage was ideally happy. This physician was not the passive or submissive type, but was a real man, a former football player, an outstanding athlete, and was a deeply spiritual man though he was completely devoid of any sectarian or denominational affiliation.

She got what she prayed for because she claimed it mentally until she reached the point of saturation. In other words, she mentally and emotionally united with her idea, and it become a part of her in the same way that an apple becomes a part of her bloodstream.

Should I Get a Divorce?

Divorce is an individual problem. It cannot be generalized. In some cases, of course, there never should have been a marriage. In some cases, divorce is not the solution, no more so than marriage is the solution for a lonely man. Divorce may be right for one person and wrong for another. A divorced woman may be far more sincere and noble than any of her married sisters who perhaps are living a lie.

For example, I once talked with a woman whose husband was a dope fiend, an exconvict, a wife-beater, and a nonprovider. She had been told it was wrong to get a divorce. I explained to her that marriage is of the heart. If two hearts blend harmoniously, lovingly, and sincerely, that is the ideal marriage. The pure action of the heart is love.

Following this explanation she knew what to do. She knew in her heart that there is no divine law which compelled her to be browbeaten, intimidated, and beaten because someone said, "I pronounce you man and wife." If you are in doubt as to what to do, ask for guidance, knowing that there is always an answer, and you will receive it. Follow the *lead* that comes to you in the silence of your soul. It speaks to you in peace.

Drifting into Divorce

Recently, a young couple, married only for a few months, were seeking a divorce. I discovered that the young man had a constant fear that his wife would leave him. He expected rejection and he believed that she would be unfaithful. These thoughts haunted his mind and became an obsession with him. His mental attitude was one of separation and suspicion. She felt unresponsive to him; it was his own feeling or atmosphere of loss and separation operating through them. This brought about a condition or action in accordance with the mental pattern behind it. There is a law of action and reaction, or cause and effect. The thought is the action and the response of the subconscious mind is the reaction.

His wife left home and asked for a divorce which is what he feared and believed she would do.

Divorce Begins in the Mind

Divorce takes place first in the mind; the legal proceedings follow after. These two young people were full of resentment, fear, suspicion, and anger. These attitudes weaken, exhaust, and debilitate the whole being.

They learned that hate divides and that love unites. They began to realize what they had been doing with their minds. Neither one of them knew the law of mental action, and they were misusing their minds and bringing on chaos and misery. These two people went back together at my suggestion and experimented with prayer therapy.

They began to radiate love, peace, and good will to each other. Each one practiced radiating harmony, health, peace, and love to the other and they alternated in the reading of the Psalms every night. Their marriage is growing more beautiful every day.

The Nagging Wife

Many times the reason the wife nags is because she gets no attention. Oftentimes, it is a craving for love and affection. Give your wife attention and show your appreciation. Praise and exalt all her many good points. There is also the nagging type of woman who wants to make the man conform to her particular pattern. This is about the quickest way in the world to get rid of a man.

The wife and the husband must cease being scavengers always looking at the petty faults or errors in each other. Let each give attention and praise for the constructive and wonderful qualities in the other.

The Brooding Husband

If a man begins to brood, grows morbid against his wife because of the things she said or did, he is, psychologically speaking, committing adultery. One of the meanings of adultery is idolatry, i.e., giving attention to or uniting mentally with that which is negative and destructive. When a man is silently resenting his wife and is full of hostility toward her, he is unfaithful. He is not faithful to his marriage vows which are to love, cherish, and honor her all the days of his life.

The man who is brooding, bitter, and resentful can swallow his sharp remarks, abate his anger, and he can go to great lengths to be considerate, kind, and courteous. He can deftly skirt the differences. Through praise and mental effort, he can get out of the habit of antagonism. Then he will be able to get along better, not only with his wife, but with business associates also. Assume the harmonious state and eventually you will find peace and harmony.

The Great Mistake

A great mistake is to discuss your marital problems or difficulties with neighbors and relatives. Suppose, for example, a wife says to the neighbor, "John never gives me any money. He treats my mother abominably, drinks to excess, and is constantly abusive and insulting."

Now, this wife is degrading and belittling her husband in the eyes of all the neighbors and relatives. He no longer appears as the ideal husband to them. Never discuss your marital problems with anyone except a trained counselor. Why cause numerous people to think negatively of your marriage? Moreover, as you discuss and dwell upon these shortcomings of your husband, you are actually creating these states within yourself. Who is thinking and feeling it? You are! As you think and feel, so are you.

Relatives will usually give you the wrong advice. It is usually biased and prejudiced because it is not given in an impersonal way. Any advice you receive which violates the Golden Rule, which is a cosmic law, is not good or sound.

It is well to remember that no two human beings ever lived beneath the same roof without clashes of temperament, periods of hurts and stain. Never display the unhappy side of your marriage to your friends. Keep your quarrels to yourself. Refrain from criticism and condemnation of your partner.

Don't Try to Make Your Wife Over

A husband must not try to make his wife into a second edition of himself. The tactless attempt to change her in many ways is foreign to her nature. These attempts are always foolish and many times result in a dissolution of the marriage. These attempts to alter her destroy her pride and self-esteem, and arouse a spirit of contrariness and resentment that proves fatal to the marriage bond.

Adjustments are needed, of course, but if you have a good look inside your own mind, and study your character and behavior, you will find so many shortcomings they will keep you busy the rest of your life. If you say, "I will make her over into what I want," you are looking for trouble and the divorce court. You are asking for misery. You will have to learn the hard way that there is no one to change but yourself.

Pray Together and Stay Together through Steps in Prayer

The First Step

Never carry over from one day to another accumulated irritations arising from little disappointments. Be sure to forgive each other for any sharpness before you retire at night. The moment you awaken in the morning, claim Infinite Intelligence is guiding you in all your ways. Send out loving thoughts of peace, harmony, and love to your marriage partner, to all members of the family, and to the whole world.

The Second Step

Say grace at breakfast. Give thanks for the wonderful food, for your abundance, and for all your blessings. Makes sure that no problems, worries, or arguments shall enter into the table conversation; the same applies at dinner time. Say to your wife or husband, "I appreciate all you are doing and I radiate love and good will to you all day long."

The Third Step

The husband and wife should alternate in praying each night. Do not take your marriage partner for granted. Show your appreciation and love. Think appreciation and good will, rather than condemnation, criticism, and nagging. The way to build a peaceful home and a happy marriage is to use a foundation of love, beauty, harmony, mutual respect, faith in God, and all things good. Read the 23rd, 27th, and 91st Psalms, the 11th chapter of Hebrews, the 13th chapter of 1 Corinthians and other great texts of the Bible before going to sleep. As you practice these truths, your marriage will grow more and more blessed through the years.

Review Your Actions

1. Ignorance of mental and spiritual laws is the cause of all marital unhappiness. By praying scientifically together, you stay together.

2. The best time to prevent divorce is before marriage. If you learn how to pray in the right way, you will attract the right mate for you.

3. Marriage is the union of a man and woman who are bound together by love. Their hearts beat as one and they move onward, upward, and Godward.

4. Marriage does not bequeath happiness. People find happiness by dwelling on the eternal truths of God and the spiritual values of life. Then, the man and woman can contribute to each other's happiness and joy.

5. You attract the right mate by dwelling on the qualities and characteristics you admire in a woman or a man, and then your subconscious mind will bring you together in divine order.

6. You must build into your mentality the mental equivalent of what you want in a marriage partner. If you want to attract an honest, sincere, and loving partner in life, you must be honest, sincere, and loving yourself.

7. You do not have to repeat mistakes in marriage. When you really believe you can have the type of man or woman you idealize, it is done unto you as you believe. To believe is to accept something as true. Accept your ideal companion now mentally.

8. Do not wonder how, why, or where you will meet that mate you are praying for. Trust implicitly the wisdom of your subconscious mind. It has the know-how; you don't have to assist it.

9. You are mentally divorced when you indulge in peeves, grudges, ill will, and hostility toward your marriage partner. You are mentally dwelling with error in the bed of your mind. Adhere to your

marriage vows, "I promise to cherish, love and honor him/her all the days of my life."

10. Cease projecting fear patterns to your marriage partner. Project love, peace, harmony, and good will and your marriage will grow more beautiful and more wonderful through the years.

11. Radiate love, peace, and good will to each other. These vibrations are picked up by the subconscious mind resulting in mutual trust, affection, and respect.

12. A nagging wife is usually seeking attention and appreciation. She is craving for love and affection. Praise and exalt her many good points. Show her that you love her and appreciate her.

13. A man who loves his wife does not do anything unloving or unkind in word, manner, or action. Love is what love does.

14. In marital problems, always seek expert advice. You would not go to a carpenter to pull a tooth; neither should you discuss your marriage problems with relatives or friends. You should go to a trained person for counsel.

15. Never try to make your wife or husband over. These attempts are always foolish and tend to destroy the pride and self-esteem of the other. Moreover, it arouses a spirit of resentment that proves fatal to the marriage bond. Cease trying to make the other a second edition of yourself.

16. Pray together and you will stay together. Scientific prayer solves all problems. Mentally picture your wife as she ought to be,

joyous, happy, healthy, and beautiful. See your husband as he ought to be, strong, powerful, loving, harmonious, and kind. Maintain this mental picture and you will experience the marriage made in heaven, which is harmony and peace.

15

Your Subconscious Mind and Your Happiness

William James, father of American psychology, said that the greatest discovery of the nineteenth century was not in the realm of physical science. The greatest discovery was the power of the subconscious touched by faith. In every human being is that limitless reservoir of power which can overcome any problem in the world.

True and lasting happiness will come into your life the day you get the clear realization that you can overcome any weakness—the day you realize that your subconscious can solve your problems, heal your body, and prosper you beyond your fondest dream.

You might have felt very happy when your child was born, when you got married, when you graduated from college, or when you won a great victory or a prize. You might have been very happy when you became engaged to the loveliest girl or the most handsome man. You could go on and list innumerable experiences which have made you happy. However, no matter how marvelous these experiences are, they do not give real lasting happiness—they are transitory.

The Book of Proverbs gives the answer: *Whosoever trusteth in the Lord, happy is he.* When you trust in the Lord (the power and wisdom of your subconscious mind) to lead, guide, govern, and direct all your ways, you will become poised, serene, and relaxed. As you radiate love, peace, and good will to all, you are building a superstructure of happiness for all the days of your life.

You Must Choose Happiness

Happiness is a state of mind. There is a phrase in the Bible which says, *Choose ye this day whom ye will serve.* You have the freedom to choose happiness. This may seem extraordinarily simple, and it is. Perhaps this is why people stumble over the way to happiness; they do not see the simplicity of the key to happiness. The great things of life are simple, dynamic, and creative. They produce well-being and happiness.

St. Paul reveals to you how you can think your way into a life of dynamic power and happiness in these words: *Finally, brethren, whatsoever things are true, whatsoever things are honest, whatsoever things are just, whatsoever things are pure, whatsoever things are lovely, whatsoever things are of good report; if there be any virtue, and if there be any praise, think on these things* (Philippians 4:8).

How to Choose Happiness

Begin now to choose happiness. This is how you do it: When you open your eyes in the morning, say to yourself,

> Divine order takes charge of my life today and every day. All things work together for good for me today. This is a new and wonderful day for me. There will never be another day like this one. I am divinely guided all day long and whatever I do will prosper. Divine love surrounds me, enfolds me, and enwraps

me, and I go forth in peace. Whenever my attention wanders away from that which is good and constructive, I will immediately bring it back to the contemplation of that which is lovely and of good report. I am a spiritual and mental magnet attracting to myself all things which bless and prosper me. I am going to be a wonderful success in all my undertakings today. I am definitely going to be happy all day long.

Start each day in this manner; then you will be choosing to be a joyous person.

He Made It a Habit to Be Happy

A number of years ago, I stayed for about a week in a farmer's house in Connemara on the west coast of Ireland. He seemed to be always singing and whistling and was full of humor. I asked him the secret of happiness, and his reply was: "It is a habit of mine to be happy. Every morning when I awaken and every night before I go to sleep, I bless my family, the crops, the cattle, and I thank God for the wonderful harvest."

This farmer had made a practice of this for over forty years. As you know, thoughts repeated regularly and systematically sink into the subconscious mind and become habitual. He discovered that happiness is a habit.

You Must Desire to Be Happy

There is one very important point about being happy. You must sincerely desire to be happy. There are people who have been depressed, dejected, and unhappy so long that were they suddenly made happy by some wonderful, good, joyous news, they would actually be like the woman who said to me, "It is wrong to be so happy!" They have been so accustomed to the old mental patterns that they do not feel at home being happy! They long for the former, depressed, unhappy state.

I knew a woman in England who had rheumatism for many years. She would pat herself on the knee and say, "My rheumatism is bad today. I cannot go out. My rheumatism keeps me miserable."

This dear elderly lady got a lot of attention from her son, daughter, and the neighbors. She really wanted her rheumatism. She enjoyed her "misery" as she called it. This woman did not really want to be happy.

I suggested a curative procedure for her. I wrote down some biblical verses and told her that if she gave attention to these truths, her mental attitude would undoubtedly change and would result in her faith and confidence being restored to health. She was not interested. There seems to be a peculiar, mental, morbid streak in many people, whereby they seem to enjoy being miserable and sad.

Why Choose Unhappiness?

Many people choose unhappiness by entertaining these ideas: "Today is a black day; everything is going to be wrong." "I am not going to succeed." "Everyone is against me." "Business is bad, and it is going to get worse." "I'm always late." "I never get the breaks." "He can, but I can't." If you have this attitude of mind first thing in the morning, you will attract all these experiences to you and you will be very unhappy.

Begin to realize that the world you live in is determined by what goes on in your mind. Marcus Aurelius, the great Roman philosopher and sage said, "A man's life is what his thoughts make of it."

Emerson, America's foremost philosopher, said, "A man is what he thinks about all day long." The thoughts you habitually entertain in your mind have the tendency to actualize themselves in physical conditions.

Make certain you do not indulge in negative thoughts, defeatist thoughts, or unkind, depressing thoughts. Recall frequently to your mind that you can experience nothing outside your own mentality.

If I Had a Million Dollars, I Would Be Happy

I have visited many men in mental institutions who were millionaires, but they insisted they were penniless and destitute. They were incarcerated because of psychotic, paranoid, and manic depressive tendencies. Wealth in and of itself will not make you happy. On the other hand, it is not a deterrent to happiness. Today, there are many people trying to buy happiness through the purchase of radios, television sets, automobiles, a home in the country, a private yacht, and a swimming pool, but happiness cannot be purchased or procured in that way.

The kingdom of happiness is in your thought and feeling. Too many people have the idea that it takes something artificial to produce happiness. Some say, "If I were elected mayor, made president of the organization, promoted to general manager of the corporation, I would be happy."

The truth is that happiness is a mental state. None of these positions mentioned will necessarily bequeath happiness. Your strength, joy, and happiness consist in finding out the law of divine order and right action lodged in your subconscious mind and by applying these principles in all phases of your life.

He Found Happiness to Be the
Harvest of a Quiet Mind

Lecturing in San Francisco some years ago, I interviewed a man who was very unhappy and dejected over the way his business was going. He was the general manager. His heart was filled with resentment toward the vice president and the president of the organization. He claimed that they opposed him. Because of this internal strife, business was declining; he was receiving no dividends or stock bonuses.

This is how he solved his business problem: The first thing in the morning he affirmed quietly as follows,

> All those working in our corporation are honest, sincere, cooperative, faithful, and full of good will to all. They are mental and spiritual links in the chain of this corporation's growth, welfare, and prosperity. I radiate love, peace, and good will in my thoughts, words, and deeds to my two associates and to all those in the company. The president and the vice president of our company are divinely guided in all their undertakings. The Infinite Intelligence of my subconscious mind makes all decisions through me. There is only right action in all our business transactions and in our relationship with each other. I send the messengers of peace, love, and good will before me to the office. Peace and harmony reign supreme in the minds and hearts of all those in the company including myself. I now go forth into a new day, full of faith, confidence, and trust.

This business executive repeated the above meditation slowly three times in the morning, feeling the truth of what he affirmed. When fearful or angry thoughts came into his mind during the day, he would say to himself, "Peace, harmony, and poise govern my mind at all times."

As he continued disciplining his mind in this manner, all the harmful thoughts ceased to come and peace came into his mind. He reaped the harvest.

Subsequently, he wrote me to the effect that at the end of about two weeks of reordering his mind, the president and vice president called him into the office, praised his operations and his new constructive ideas, and remarked how fortunate they were in having him as a general manager.

He was very happy in discovering that man finds happiness within himself.

The Block or Stump Is Not Really There

I read a newspaper article some years ago which told about a horse who had shied when he came to a stump on the road. Subsequently, every time the horse came to that same stump, he shied. The farmer dug the stump out, burned it, and leveled the old road. Yet, for twenty-five years, every time the horse passed the place where the former stump was, he shied. The horse was shying at the memory of a stump.

There is no block to your happiness save in your own thought-life and mental imagery. Are fear or worry holding you back? Fear is a thought in your mind. You can dig it up this very moment by supplanting it with faith in success, achievement, and victory over all problems.

I knew a man who failed in business. He said to me, "I made mistakes. I've learned a lot. I am going back into business and I will be a tremendous success." He faced up to that stump in his mind. He did not whine or complain, but he tore up the stump of failure and through believing in his inner powers to back him up, he banished all fear thoughts and old depressions. Believe in yourself and you will succeed and be happy.

The Happiest People

The happiest man is he who constantly brings forth and practices what is best in him. Happiness and virtue complement each other. The best are not only the happiest, but the happiest are usually the best in the art of living life successfully. God is the highest and best in you. Express more of God's love, light, truth, and beauty and you will become one of the happiest persons in the world today.

Epictetus, the Greek stoic philosopher, said, "There is but one way to tranquility of mind and happiness: let this, therefore, be always ready at hand with thee, both when thou wakest early in the morning, and all day long, and when thou goest late to sleep, to account no external things thine own, but commit all these to God."

Summary of Steps to Happiness

1. William James said that the greatest discovery of the nineteenth century was the power of the subconscious mind touched by faith.

2. There is tremendous power within you. Happiness will come to you when you acquire a sublime confidence in this power. Then, you will make your dreams come true.

3. You can rise victorious over any defeat and realize the cherished desires of your heart through the marvelous power of your subconscious mind. This is the meaning of *Whosoever trusteth in the Lord* [spiritual laws of the subconscious mind], *happy is he.*

4. You must choose happiness. Happiness is a habit. It is a good habit to ponder often on *Whatsoever things are true, whatsoever things are honest, whatsoever things are just, whatsoever things are pure, whatsoever things are lovely, whatsoever things are of good report; if there be any virtue, and if there be any praise, think on these things* (Philippians 4:8).

5. When you open your eyes in the morning, say to yourself, "I choose happiness today. I choose success today. I choose right action today. I choose love and good will for all today. I choose peace today." Pour life, love, and interest into this affirmation, and you have chosen happiness.

6. Give thanks for all your blessings several times a day. Furthermore, pray for the peace, happiness, and prosperity of all members of your family, your associates, and all people everywhere.

7. You must sincerely desire to be happy. Nothing is accomplished without desire. Desire is a wish with wings of imagination and faith. Imagine the fulfillment of your desire, and feel its reality, and it will come to pass. Happiness comes in answered prayer.

8. By constantly dwelling on thoughts of fear, worry, anger, hate, and failure you will become very depressed and unhappy. Remember, your life is what your thoughts make of it.

9. You cannot buy happiness with all the money in the world. Some millionaires are very happy, some are very unhappy. Many people with very little worldly goods are very happy and some are very unhappy. Some married people are happy and some are very unhappy. Some single people are happy and some are very

unhappy. The kingdom of happiness is in your thought and
feeling.

10. Happiness is the harvest of a quiet mind. Anchor your thoughts
    on peace, poise, security, and divine guidance and your mind will
    be productive of happiness.

11. There is no block to your happiness. External things are not caus-
    ative, these are effects, not cause. Take your cue from the only
    creative principle within you. Your thought is cause, and new
    cause produces a new effect. Choose happiness.

12. The happiest man is he who brings forth the highest and the best
    in him. God is the highest and best in him, for the kingdom of
    God is within.

16

Your Subconscious Mind and
Harmonious Human Relations

In studying this book, you learn that your subconscious mind is a recording machine which faithfully reproduces whatever you impress upon it. This is one of the reasons for the application of the Golden Rule in human relations.

Matthew 7:12 says, *All things whatsoever ye would that men should do unto you, do ye even so to them.* This quotation has outer and inner meanings. You are interested in its inner meaning from the standpoint of your subconscious mind which is: As you would that men should think about you, think you about them in like manner. As you would that men should feel about you, feel you also about them in like manner. As you would want men to act toward you, act you toward them in like manner.

For example, you may be polite and courteous to someone in your office, but when his back is turned, you are very critical and resentful toward him in your mind. Such negative thoughts are highly destructive to you. It is like taking poison. You are actually taking mental poisons which rob you of vitality, enthusiasm, strength, guidance, and good will. These negative thoughts and emotions sink down into your subconscious, and cause all kinds of difficulties and maladies in your life.

The Master Key to Happy Relationships with Others

Judge not, that ye be not judged. For with that judgment ye judge, ye shall be judged: and with what measure ye mete, it shall be measured to you again (Matthew 7:1–2). A study of these verses and the application of the inner truths therein contained represent the real key to harmonious relations. To judge is to think, to arrive at a mental verdict or conclusion in your mind. The thought you have about the other person is your thought, because you are thinking it. Your thoughts are creative; therefore, you actually create in your own experience what you think and feel about the other person. It is also true that the suggestion you give to another, you give to yourself because your mind is the creative medium.

This is why it is said, "for with what judgment ye judge, ye shall be judged." When you know this law and the way your subconscious mind works, you are careful to think, feel, and act right toward the other. These verses teach you about the emancipation of man and reveal to you the solution to your individual problems. And with "What measure ye mete, it shall be measured to you again," the good you do for others comes back to you in like measure; and the evil you do returns to you by the law of your own mind. If a man cheats and deceives another, he is actually cheating and deceiving himself, his sense of guilt and mood of loss inevitably will attract loss to him in some way, at some time. His subconscious records his mental act and reacts according to the mental intention or motivation.

Your subconscious mind is impersonal and unchanging, neither considering persons nor respecting religious affiliations or institutions of any kind. It is neither compassionate not vindictive. The way you think, feel, and act toward others returns at least upon yourself.

The Daily Headlines Made Him Sick

Begin now to observe yourself. Observe your reactions to people, conditions, and circumstances. How do you respond to the events and news of the day? It makes no difference if all the other people were wrong and you alone were right. If the news disturbs you, it is your evil because your negative emotions robbed you of peace and harmony.

A woman wrote me about her husband, saying that he goes into a rage when he reads what certain newspaper columnists write in the newspaper. She added that his constant reaction of anger and suppressed rage on his part brought on bleeding ulcers and his physician recommended an emotional reconditioning.

I invited this man to see me and I explained to him the way his mind functions, indicating how emotionally immature it was to get angry when others write articles with which he disapproves or disagrees.

He began to realize that he should give the newspaperman freedom to express himself even though the latter disagreed with him politically, religiously, or in any other way. In the same manner, the newspaperman would give him freedom to write a letter to the newspaper disagreeing with his published statements. He learned that he could disagree without being disagreeable. He awakened to the simple truth that it is never what a person says or does that affects him, it is his reaction to what is said or done that matters.

This explanation was the cure for this man, and he realized that with a little practice he could master his morning tantrums. His wife told me, subsequently, that he laughed at himself and also at what the columnists say. They no longer have power to disturb, annoy, or irritate him. His ulcers have disappeared due to his emotional poise and serenity.

I Hate Women, But I Like Men

A private secretary was very bitter toward some of the girls in her office because they were gossiping about her, and as she said, spreading vicious lies about her. She admitted that she did not like women. She said, "I hate women, but I like men." I discovered also that she spoke to the girls who were under her in the office in a very haughty, imperious, and irritable tone of voice. She pointed out that they took delight in making things difficult for her. There was a certain pomposity in her way of speaking, and I could see where her tone of voice would affect some people unpleasantly.

If all the people in the office or factory annoy you, isn't it a possibility that the vibration, annoyance, and turmoil may be due to some subconscious pattern or mental projection from you? We know that a dog will react ferociously if you hate or fear dogs. Animals pick up your subconscious vibrations and react accordingly. Many undisciplined human beings are just as sensitive as dogs, cats, and other animals.

I suggested a process of prayer to this private secretary who hated women, explaining to her that when she began to identify herself with spiritual virtues and commenced to affirm the truths of life, her voice, mannerisms, and hatred of women would completely disappear. She was surprised to know that the emotion of hatred shows up in a person's speech, actions, in his writings, and in all phases of his life. She ceased reacting in the typical, resentful, and angry way. She established a pattern of prayer, which she practiced regularly, systematically, and conscientiously in the office.

The prayer was as follows: "I think, speak, and act lovingly, quietly, and peacefully. I now radiate love, peace, tolerance, and kindness to all the girls who criticized me and gossiped about me. I anchor my thoughts on peace, harmony, and good will to all. Whenever I am about to react negatively, I say firmly to myself, 'I am going to think, speak, and act from the standpoint of the principle of harmony, health, and peace within myself.' Creative intelligence leads, rules, and guides me in all my ways."

The practice of this prayer transformed her life and she found that all criticism and annoyance ceased. The girls became coworkers and friends along life's journey. She discovered that "there is no one to change but myself."

His Inner Speech Held Back His Promotion

One day a salesman came to see me and described his difficulties in working with the sales manager of his organization. He had been with the company ten years and had received no promotion or recognition of any kind. He showed me his sales figures, which were greater proportionately than the other men in the territory. He said that his sales manager did not like him, that he was unjustly treated, and that at conferences the manager was rude to him and at times ridiculed his suggestions.

I explained that undoubtedly the cause was to a great degree within himself, and that his concept and belief about his superior bore witness to the reaction of this man. *The measure we mete, shall be measured to us again*. His mental measure or concept of the sales manager was that he was mean and cantankerous. He was filled with bitterness and hostility toward the executive. On his way to work he conducted a vigorous conversation with himself filled with criticism, mental arguments, recriminations, and denunciations of his sales manager.

What he gave out mentally, he was inevitably bound to get back. This salesman realized that his inner speech was highly destructive because of the intensity and force of his silent thoughts and emotions, and personally conducted mental condemnation and vilification of the sales manager entered into his own subconscious mind. This brought about the negative response from his boss as well as creating many other personal, physical, and emotional disorders.

He began to pray frequently as follows: "I am the only thinker in my universe. I am responsible for what I think about my boss. My sales manager is not responsible for the way I think about him. I refuse to give power to any person, place, or thing to annoy me or disturb me. I wish health, success, peace of mind, and happiness for my boss. I sincerely wish him well, and I know he is divinely guided in all his ways."

He repeated this prayer out loud slowly, quietly, and feelingly, knowing that his mind is like a garden, and that whatever he plants in the garden will come forth like seeds after their kind.

I also taught him to practice mental imagery prior to sleep in this way: He imagined that his sales manager was congratulating him on his fine work, on his zeal and enthusiasm, and on his wonderful response from customers. He felt the reality of all this, felt his handshake, heard the tone of his voice, and saw him smile. He made a real mental movie, dramatizing it to the best of his ability. Night after night he conducted this mental movie, knowing that his subconscious mind was the receptive plate on which his conscious imagery would be impressed.

Gradually, by a process of what may be termed mental and spiritual osmosis, the impression was made on his subconscious mind, and the expression automatically came forth. The sales manager subsequently called him up to San Francisco, congratulated him, and gave him a new assignment as division sales manager over one hundred men with a big increase in salary. He changed his concept and estimate of his boss, and the latter responded accordingly.

Becoming Emotionally Mature

What the other person says or does cannot really annoy or irritate you except you permit him to disturb you. The only way he can annoy you is through your own thought. For example, if you get angry, you have to go through four stages in your mind. You begin to think about what he said. You decide to get angry and generate an emotion of rage. Then, you decide to act. Perhaps you talk back and react in kind. You see that the thought, emotion, reaction, and action all take place in your mind. When you become emotionally mature, you do not respond negatively to the criticism and resentment of others. To do so would mean that you had descended to that state of low mental vibration and become one with the negative atmosphere of the other. Identify yourself with your aim in life, and do not permit any person, place, or thing to deflect you from your inner sense of peace, tranquility, and radiant health.

The Meaning of Love in Harmonious Human Relations

Sigmund Freud, the Austrian founder of psychoanalysis, said that unless the personality has love, it sickens and dies. Love includes understanding, good will, and respect for the divinity in the other person. The more love and good will you emanate and exude, the more comes back to you.

If you puncture the other fellow's ego and wound his estimate of himself, you cannot gain his good will. Recognize that every man wants to be loved and appreciated, and made to feel important in the world. Realize that the other man is conscious of his true worth, and that, like yourself, he feels the dignity of being an expression of the One Life-Principle animating all men. As you do this consciously and knowingly, you build the other person up, and he returns your love and good will.

He Hated Audiences

An actor told me that the audience booed and hissed him on his first appearance on the stage. He added that the play was badly written and that undoubtedly he did not play a good role. He admitted openly to me that for months afterward he hated audiences. He called them dopes, dummies, stupid, ignorant, gullible, etc. He quit the stage in disgust and went to work in a drugstore for a year.

One day a friend invited him to hear a lecture in Town Hall, New York City, on "How to Get Along with Ourselves." This lecture changed his life. He went back to the stage and began to pray sincerely for the audience and himself. He poured out love and good will every night before appearing on the stage. He made it a habit to claim that the peace of God filled the hearts of all present, and that all present were lifted up and inspired. During each performance he sent out love vibrations to the audience. Today, he is a great actor, and he loves and respects people. His good will and esteem are transmitted to others and are felt by them.

Handling Difficult People

There are difficult people in the world who are twisted and distorted mentally. They are malconditioned. Many are mental delinquents, argumentative, uncooperative, cantankerous, cynical, and sour on life. They are sick psychologically. Many people have deformed and distorted minds, probably warped during childhood. Many have congenital deformities. You would not condemn a person who had tuberculosis, nor should you condemn a person who is mentally ill.

No one, for example, hates or resents a hunchback; there are many mental hunchbacks. You should have compassion and understanding. To understand all is to forgive all.

Misery Loves Company

The hateful, frustrated, distorted, and twisted personality is out of tune with the Infinite. He resents those who are peaceful, happy, and joyous. Usually he criticizes, condemns, and vilifies those who have been very good and kind to him. His attitude is this: Why should they be so happy when he is so miserable? He wants to drag them down to his own level. Misery loves company. When you understand this you remain unmoved, calm, and dispassionate.

The Practice of Empathy in Human Relations

A girl visited me recently stating that she hated another girl in her office. She gave her reason that the other girl was prettier, happier, and wealthier than she, and, in addition, was engaged to the boss of the company where they worked. One day after the marriage had taken place, the crippled daughter (by a former marriage) of the woman whom she hated came into the office. The child put her arms around her mother and said, "Mommy, mommy, I love my new daddy! Look what he gave me!" She showed her mother a wonderful new toy.

She said to me, "My heart went out to that little girl, and I knew how happy she must feel. I got a vision of how happy this woman was. All of a sudden I felt love for her, and I went into the office and wished her all the happiness in the world, and I meant it."

In psychological circles today, this is called empathy, which simply means the imaginative projection of your mental attitude into that of another. She projected her mental mood or the feeling of her heart into that of the other woman, and began to think and look out through the other woman's brain. She was actually thinking and feeling as the other woman, and also as the child, because she likewise had projected herself into the mind of the child. She was looking out from that vantage point on the child's mother.

If tempted to injure or think ill of another, project yourself mentally into the mind of Moses and think from the standpoint of the Ten Commandments. If you are prone to be envious, jealous, or angry, project yourself into the mind of Jesus and think from that standpoint, and you will feel the truth of the words *Love ye one another* (John 13:34).

Appeasement Never Wins

Do not permit people to take advantage of you and gain the point by temper tantrums, crying jags, or so-called heart attacks. These people are dictators who try to enslave you and make you do their bidding. Be firm but kind, and refuse to yield. Appeasement never wins. Refuse to contribute to their delinquency, selfishness, and possessiveness. Remember, do that which is right. You are here to fulfill your ideal and remain true to the eternal verities and spiritual values of life, which are eternal.

Give no one in all the world the power to deflect you from your goal, your aim in life, which is to express your hidden talents to the world, to serve humanity, and to reveal more and more of God's wisdom, truth, and beauty to all people in the world. Remain true to your ideal. Know definitely and absolutely that whatever contributes to your peace, happiness, and fulfillment must of necessity bless all men who walk the earth. The harmony of the part is the harmony of the whole, for the whole is in the part, and the part is in the whole.

All you owe the other, as Paul says, is love, and love is the fulfilling of the law of health, happiness, and peace of mind.

Profitable Pointers in Human Relations

1. Your subconscious mind is a recording machine which reproduces your habitual thinking. Think good of the other, and you are actually thinking good about yourself.

2. A hateful or resentful thought is a mental poison. Do not think ill of another for to do so is to think ill of yourself. You are the only thinker in your universe, and your thoughts are creative.

3. Your mind is a creative medium; therefore, what you think and feel about the other you are bringing to pass in your own experience. This is the psychological meaning of the Golden Rule. As you would that man should think about you, think you about them in the same manner.

4. To cheat, rob, or defraud another brings lack, loss, and limitation to yourself. Your subconscious mind records your inner motivations, thoughts, and feelings. These being of a negative nature, loss, limitation, and trouble come to you in countless ways. Actually, what you do to the other, you are doing to yourself.

5. The good you do, the kindness proffered, the love and good will you send forth, will all come back to you multiplied in many ways.

6. You are the only thinker in your world. You are responsible for the way you think about the other. Remember, the other person is

210 | *Dr. Joseph Murphy*

not responsible for the way you think about him. Your thoughts are reproduced. What are you thinking about the other fellow?

7. Become emotionally mature and permit other people to differ from you. They have a perfect right to disagree with you, and you have the same freedom to disagree with them. You can disagree without being disagreeable.

8. Animals pick up your fear vibrations and snap at you. If you love animals, they will never attack you. Many undisciplined human beings are just as sensitive as dogs, cats, and other animals.

9. Your inner speech, representing your silent thoughts and feelings, is experienced in the reactions of others toward you.

10. Wish for the other what you wish for yourself. This is the key to harmonious human relations.

11. Change your concept and estimate of your employer. Feel and know he is practicing the Golden Rule and the Law of Love, and he will respond accordingly.

12. The other person cannot annoy you or irritate you except you permit him. Your thought is creative; you can bless him. If someone calls you a skunk, you have the freedom to say to the other, "God's peace fills your soul."

13. Love is the answer to getting along with others. Love is understanding, good will, and respecting the divinity of the other.

14. You would not hate a hunchback or cripple. You would have compassion. Have compassion and understanding for mental hunchbacks who have been conditioned negatively. To understand all is to forgive all.

15. Rejoice in the success, promotion, and good fortune of the other. In doing so, you attract good fortune to yourself.

16. Never yield to emotional scenes and tantrums of others. Appeasement never wins. Do not be a doormat. Adhere to that which is right. Stick to your ideal, knowing that the mental outlook which gives you peace, happiness, and joy is right, good, and true. What blesses you, blesses all. All you owe any person in the world is love, and love is wishing for everyone what you wish for yourself—health, happiness, and all the blessings of life.

17

How to Use Your Subconscious for Forgiveness

Life plays no favorites. God is life, and this Life-Principle is flowing through you this moment. God loves to express Himself as harmony, peace, beauty, joy, and abundance through you. This is called the will of God or the tendency of life.

If you set up resistance in your mind to the flow of life through you, this emotional congestion will get snarled up in your subconscious mind and cause all kinds of negative conditions. God has nothing to do with unhappy or chaotic conditions in the world. All these conditions are brought about by man's negative and destructive thinking. Therefore, it is silly to blame God for your trouble or sickness.

Many persons habitually set up mental resistance to the flow of life by accusing and reproaching God for the sin, sickness, and suffering of mankind. Others cast blame on God for their pains, aches, loss of loved ones, personal tragedies, and accidents. They are angry at God and they believe He is responsible for their misery.

As long as people entertain such negative concepts about God, they will experience the automatic negative reactions from their subconscious minds. Actually, such people do not know that they are punishing themselves. They must see the truth, find release, and give up all condemnation, resentment, and anger against anyone or any power outside themselves. Otherwise, they cannot go forward into a healthy, happy, or creative activity. The minute these people entertain a God of love in their minds and hearts, and when they believe that God is the loving Father who watches over them, cares for them, guides them, sustains them, and strengthens them, this concept and belief about God or the Life-Principle will be accepted by their subconscious mind, and they will find themselves blessed in countless ways.

Life Always Forgives You

Life forgives you when you cut your finger. The subconscious intelligence within you sets about immediately to repair it. New cells build bridges over the cut. Should you take some tainted food by error, life forgives you and causes you to regurgitate it in order to preserve you. If you burn your hand, the Life-Principle reduces the edema and congestion, and gives you new skin, tissue, and cells. Life holds no grudges against you, and it is always forgiving you. Life brings you back to health, vitality, harmony, and peace, if you cooperate by thinking in harmony with nature. Negative, hurtful memories, bitterness, and ill will clutter up and impede the free flow of the Life-Principle in you.

How He Banished That Feeling of Guilt

I knew a man who worked every night until about one o'clock in the morning. He paid no attention to his two boys or his wife. He was always too busy working hard. He thought people should pat him on the back because he was working so arduously and persistently past midnight every night. He had a blood pressure over two hundred and was full of guilt. Unconsciously, he proceeded to punish himself by hard work and he completely ignored his children. A normal man does not do that. He is interested in his boys and in their development. He does not shut his wife out of his world.

I explained to him why he was working so arduously, "There is something eating you inside, otherwise, you would not act this way. You are punishing yourself, and you have to learn to forgive yourself." He did have a deep sense of guilt. It was toward a brother.

I explained to him that God was not punishing him, but that he was punishing himself. For example, if you misuse the laws of life, you will suffer accordingly. If you put your hand on a naked charged wire, you will get burned. The forces of nature are not evil; it is your use of them that determines whether they have a good or evil effect. Electricity is not evil, it depends on how you use it, whether to burn down a structure or light up a home. The only sin is ignorance of the law, and the only punishment is the automatic reaction of man's misuse of the law.

If you misuse the principle of chemistry, you may blow up the office or the factory. If you strike your hand on a board, you may cause your hand to bleed. The board is not for that purpose. Its purpose may be to lean upon or to support your feet.

This man realized that God does not condemn or punish anyone, and that all his suffering was due to the reaction of his subconscious mind to his own negative and destructive thinking. He had cheated his brother at one time and the brother had now passed on. Still, he was full of remorse and guilt.

I asked him, "Would you cheat your brother now?"

He said, "No."

"Did you feel you were justified at the time?"

His reply was, "Yes."

"But, you would not do it now?"

He added, "No, I am helping others to know how to live."

I added the following comment, "You have a greater reason and understanding now. Forgiveness is to forgive yourself. Forgiveness is getting your thoughts in line with the divine law of harmony. Self-condemnation is called hell (bondage and restriction); forgiveness is called heaven (harmony and peace)."

The burden of guilt and self-condemnation was lifted from his mind, and he had a complete healing. The doctor tested his blood pressure and it had become normal. The explanation was the cure.

A Murderer Learned to Forgive Himself

A man who murdered his brother in Europe visited me many years ago. He was suffering from great mental anguish and torture believing that God must punish him. He explained that his brother had been having an affair with his wife and that he had shot him on the spur of the moment. This had happened about fifteen years previous to his interview with me. In the meantime, this man had married an American girl and had been blessed with three lovely children. He was in a position where he helped many people and he was a transformed man.

My explanation to him was that physically and psychologically he was not the same man who shot his brother, since scientists inform us that every cell of our bodies changes every eleven months. Moreover, mentally and spiritually he was a new man. He was now full of love and good will for humanity. The "old" man who committed the crime fifteen years before was mentally and spiritually dead. Actually, he was condemning an innocent man!

This explanation had a profound effect upon him and he said it was as if a great weight had been lifted from his mind. He realized the significance of the following truth in the Bible: *Come now, let us reason together, saith the Lord: though your sins be as scarlet, they shall be as white as snow; though they be red like crimson, they shall be as wool* (Isaiah 1:18).

Criticism Cannot Hurt You without Your Consent

A school teacher told me that one of her associates criticized a speech she had given, saying to her that she spoke too fast, she swallowed some of her words, she couldn't be heard, her diction was poor, and her speech ineffective. This teacher was furious and full of resentment toward her critic.

She admitted to me that the criticisms were just. Her first reaction was really childish and she agreed that the letter was really a blessing and a marvelous corrective. She proceeded immediately to supplement her deficiencies in her speech by enrolling in a course in public speaking at City College. She wrote and thanked the writer of the note for her interest, expressing appreciation for her conclusions and findings which enabled the teacher to correct the matter at once.

How to Be Compassionate

Suppose none of the things mentioned in the letter had been true of the teacher? The latter would have realized that her class material had upset the prejudices, superstitions, or narrow sectarian beliefs of the writer of the note, and that a psychologically ill person was simply pouring forth her resentment because a psychological boil had been hurt.

To understand this fact is to be compassionate. The next logical step would be to pray for the other person's peace, harmony, and understanding. You cannot be hurt when you know that you are master of your thoughts, reactions, and emotions. Emotions follow thoughts, and you have the power to reject all thoughts which may disturb or upset you.

Left at the Altar

Some years ago, I visited a church to perform a marriage ceremony. The young man did not appear and at the end of two hours, the bride-to-be shed a few tears and then said to me, "I prayed for divine guidance. This might be the answer for He never faileth."

That was her reaction—faith in God and all things good. She had no bitterness in her heart because as she said, "It must not have been right action because my prayer was for right action for both of us." Someone else having a similar experience would have gone into a tantrum, have had an emotional fit, required sedation, and perhaps needed hospitalization. Tune in with the Infinite Intelligence within your subconscious depths, trusting the answer in the same way that you trusted your mother when she held you in her arms. This is how you can acquire poise and mental and emotional health.

It Is Wrong to Marry, Sex Is Evil, and I Am Evil

Some time ago I talked to a young lady, aged twenty-two. She was taught that it was a sin to dance, to play cards, to swim, and to go out with men. She was threatened by her mother who told her she would burn eternally in hellfire if she disobeyed her will and her religious teachings. This girl wore a black dress and black stockings. She wore no rouge, lipstick, or any form of makeup because her mother said that these things were sinful. Her mother told her that all men were evil, and that sex was of the devil and simply diabolic debauchery.

This girl had to learn how to forgive herself as she was full of guilt. To forgive means "to give for." She had to give up all these false beliefs for the truths of life and new estimate of herself. When she went out with young men in the office where she worked, she had a deep sense of guilt and thought that God would punish her. Several eligible young men proposed to her but she said to me, "It is wrong to marry. Sex is evil and I am evil." This was her conscience of early conditioning speaking.

She came to me once weekly for about ten weeks and I taught her the workings of the conscious and subconscious mind set forth in this book. This young girl gradually came to see that she had been completely brainwashed, mesmerized, and conditioned by an ignorant, superstitious, bigoted, and frustrated mother. She broke away completely from her family and started to live a wonderful life.

At my suggestion she dressed up and had her hair attended to. She took lessons in dancing from a man, and she also took driving lessons. She learned to swim, play cards, and had a number of dates. She began to love life. She prayed for a divine companion by claiming that Infinite Spirit would attract to her a man who harmonized with her thoroughly. Eventually this came to pass. As she left my office one evening, there was a man waiting to see me and I casually introduced them. They are now married and harmonize with each other perfectly.

Forgiveness Is Necessary for Healing

And when ye stand praying, forgive, if ye have ought against any (Mark 11:25). Forgiveness of others is essential to mental peace and radiant health. You must forgive everyone who has ever hurt you if you want perfect health and happiness. Forgive yourself by getting your thoughts in harmony with divine law and order. You cannot really forgive yourself completely until you have forgiven others first. To refuse to forgive yourself is nothing more or less than spiritual pride or ignorance.

In the psychosomatic field of medicine today, it is being constantly stressed that resentment, condemnation of others, remorse, and hostility are behind a host of maladies ranging from arthritis to cardiac disease. They point out that these sick people, who were hurt, mistreated, deceived, or injured, were full of resentment and hatred for those who hurt them. This caused inflamed and festering wounds in their subconscious minds. There is only one remedy. They have to cut out and discard their hurts, and the one and only sure way is by forgiveness.

Forgiveness Is Love in Action

The essential ingredient in the art of forgiveness is the willingness to forgive. If you sincerely desire to forgive the other, you are 51 percent over the hurdle. I feel sure you know that to forgive the other does not necessarily mean that you like him or want to associate with him. You cannot be compelled to like someone, neither can a government legislate good will, love, peace, or tolerance. It is quite impossible to like people because someone in Washington issues an edict to that effect. We can, however, love people without liking them.

The Bible says, *Love ye one another*. This, anyone can do who really wants to do it. Love means that you wish for the other health, happiness, peace, joy, and all the blessings of life. There is only one prerequisite and that is sincerity. You are not being magnanimous when you forgive, you are really being selfish, because what you wish for the other, you are actually wishing for yourself. The reason is that you are thinking it and you are feeling it. As you think and feel, so are you. Could anything be simpler than that?

Technique of Forgiveness

The following is a simple method which works wonders in your life as you practice it. Quiet your mind, relax, and let go. Think of God and His love for you, and then affirm, "I fully and freely forgive (mention the name of the offender); I release him mentally and spiritually. I completely forgive everything connected with the matter in question. I am free, and he/she is free. It is a marvelous feeling. It is my day of general amnesty. I release anybody and everybody who has ever hurt me, and I wish for each and everyone health, happiness, peace, and all the blessings of life. I do this freely, joyously, and lovingly and whenever I think of the person or persons who hurt me, I say, 'I have released you, and all the blessings of life are yours.' I am free and you are free. It is wonderful!"

The great secret of true forgiveness is that once you have forgiven the person, it is unnecessary to repeat the prayer. Whenever the person comes to your mind, or the particular hurt happens to enter your mind, wish the delinquent well, and say, "Peace be to you." Do this as often as the thought enters your mind. You will find that after a few days the thought of the person or experience will return less and less often, until it fades into nothingness.

The Acid Test for Forgiveness

There is an acid test for gold. There is also an acid test for forgiveness. If I should tell you something wonderful about someone who has wronged you, cheated you, or defrauded you, and you sizzled at hearing the good news about this person, the roots of hatred would still be in your subconscious mind, playing havoc with you.

Let us suppose you had a painful abscess on your jaw a year ago, and you told me about it, I would casually ask you if you had any pain now. You would automatically say, "Of course not, I have memory of it but no pain." That is the whole story. You may have a memory of the incident but no sting or hurt anymore. This is the acid test, and you must meet it psychologically and spiritually, otherwise, you are simply deceiving yourself and not practicing the true art of forgiveness.

To Understand All Is to Forgive All

When man understands the creative law of his own mind, he ceases to blame other people and conditions for making or marring his life. He knows that his own thoughts and feelings create his destiny. Furthermore, he is aware that externals are not the causes and conditioners of his life and his experiences. To think that others can mar your happiness, that you are the football of a cruel fate, that you must oppose and fight others for a living, all these and others like them, are untenable when you understand that thoughts are things. The Bible says the same thing. *For as a man thinketh in his heart, so is he* (Proverbs 23:7).

Summary of Your Aids to Forgiveness

1. God, or life, is no respecter of persons. Life plays no favorites. Life, or God, seems to favor you when you align yourself with the principle of harmony, health, joy, and peace.

2. God, or life, never sends disease, sickness, accident, or suffering. We bring these things on ourselves by our own negative thinking based upon the law *as we sow, so shall we reap.*

3. Your concept of God is the most important thing in your life. If you really believe in a God of love, your subconscious mind will respond in countless blessings to you. Believe in a God of love.

4. Life, or God, holds no grudge against you. Life never condemns you. Life heals a severe cut on your hand. Life forgives you if you burn your finger. It reduces the edema and restores the part to wholeness and perfection.

5. Your guilt complex is a false concept of God and life. God, or life, does not punish or judge you. You do this to yourself by your false beliefs, negative thinking, and self condemnation.

6. God, or life, does not condemn or punish you. The forces of nature are not evil. The effect of their use depends on how you use the power within you. You can use electricity to kill someone or to light the house. You can use water to drown a child or quench his thirst. Good and evil come right back to the thought and purpose in man's own mind.

7. God, or life, never punishes. Man punishes himself by his false concepts of God, life, and the universe. His thoughts are creative and he creates his own misery.

8. If another criticizes you, and these faults are within you, rejoice, give thanks, and appreciate the comments. This gives you the opportunity to correct the particular fault.

9. You cannot be hurt by criticism when you know that you are master of your thoughts, reactions, and emotions. This gives you the opportunity to pray and bless the other, thereby blessing yourself.

10. When you pray for guidance and right action, take what comes. Realize it is good and very good. Then there is no cause for self pity, criticism, or hatred.

11. There is nothing good or bad, but thinking makes it so. There is no evil in sex, the desire for food, wealth, or true expression. It depends on how you use these urges, desires, and aspirations. Your desire for food can be met without killing someone for a loaf of bread.

12. Resentment, hatred, ill will, and hostility are behind a host of maladies. Forgive yourself and everybody else by pouring out love, life, joy, and good will to all those who have hurt you. Continue until such time as you meet them in your mind and you are at peace with them.

13. To forgive is to *give something for*. Give love, peace, joy, wisdom, and all the blessings of life to the other, until there is no sting left in your mind. This is really the acid test of forgiveness.

14. Let us suppose you had an abscess in your jaw about a year ago. It was very painful. Ask yourself if it is painful now. The answer is negative. Likewise, if someone has hurt you, lied about and vilified you, and said all manner of evil about you, is your thought of that person negative? Do you sizzle when he or she comes into your mind? If so, the roots of hatred are still there, playing havoc with you and your good. The only way is to wither them with love by wishing for the person all the blessings of life, until you can meet the person in your mind, and you can sincerely react with a benediction of peace and good will. This is the meaning of "forgive until seventy times seven."

18

How Your Subconscious Removes Mental Blocks

The solution lies within the problem. The answer is in every question. If you are presented with a difficult situation and you cannot see your way clear, the best procedure is to assume that Infinite Intelligence within your subconscious mind knows all and sees all, has the answer, and is revealing it to you now. Your new mental attitude that the creative intelligence is bringing about a happy solution will enable you to find the answer. Rest assured that such an attitude of mind will bring order, peace, and meaning to all your undertakings.

How to Break or Build a Habit

You are a creature of habit. Habit is the function of your subconscious mind. You learned to swim, ride a bicycle, dance, and drive a car by consciously doing these things over and over again until they established tracks in your subconscious mind. Then, the automatic habit action of your subconscious mind took over. This is sometimes called second nature, which is a reaction of your subconscious mind to your thinking and acting. You are free to choose a good habit or a bad habit. If you repeat a negative thought or act over a period of time, you will be under the compulsion of a habit. The law of your subconscious is compulsion.

How He Broke a Bad Habit

Mr. Jones said to me, "An uncontrollable urge to drink seizes upon me, and I remain drunk for two weeks at a time. I can't give up this terrible habit."

Time and time again these experiences had occurred to this unfortunate man. He had grown into the habit of drinking to excess. Although he had started drinking of his own initiative, he also began to realize that he could change the habit and establish a new one. He said that while through his will power he was able to suppress his desires temporarily, his continued efforts to suppress the many urges only made matters worse. His repeated failures convinced him that he was hopeless and powerless to control his urge or obsession. This idea of being powerless operated as a powerful suggestion to his subconscious mind and aggravated his weakness, making his life a succession of failures.

I taught him to harmonize the functions of the conscious and subconscious mind. When these two cooperate, the idea or desire implanted in the subconscious mind is realized. His reasoning mind agreed that if the old habit path or track had carried him into trouble, he could consciously form a new path to freedom, sobriety, and peace of mind. He knew that his destructive habit was automatic, but since it was acquired through his conscious choice, he realized that if he had been conditioned negatively, he also could be conditioned positively. As a result, he ceased thinking of the fact that he was powerless to overcome the habit. Moreover, he understood clearly that there was no obstacle to his healing other than his own thought. Therefore, there was no occasion for great mental effort or mental coercion.

The Power of His Mental Picture

This man acquired a practice of relaxing his body and getting into a relaxed, drowsy, meditative state. Then he filled his mind with the picture of the desired end, knowing his subconscious mind could bring it about the easiest way. He imagined his daughter congratulating him on his freedom, and saying to him, "Daddy, it's wonderful to have you home!" He had lost his family through drink. He was not allowed to visit them, and his wife would not speak to him.

Regularly, systematically, he used to sit down and meditate in the way outlined. When his attention wandered, he made it a habit to immediately recall the mental picture of his daughter with her smile and the scene of his home enlivened by her cheerful voice. All this brought about a reconditioning of his mind. It was a gradual process. He kept it up. He persevered knowing that sooner or later he would establish a new habit pattern in his subconscious mind.

I told him that he could liken his conscious mind to a camera, that his subconscious mind was the sensitive plate on which he registered and impressed the picture. This made a profound impression on him, and his whole aim was to firmly impress the picture on his mind and develop it there. Films are developed in the dark; likewise, mental pictures are developed in the darkroom of the subconscious mind.

Focused Attention

Realizing that his conscious mind was simply a camera, he used no effort. There was no mental struggle. He quietly adjusted his thoughts and focused his attention on the scene before him until he gradually became identified with the picture. He became absorbed in the mental atmosphere, repeating the mental movie frequently.

There was no room for doubt that a healing would follow. When there was any temptation to drink, he would switch his imagination from any reveries of drinking bouts to the feeling of being at home with his family. He was successful because he confidently expected to experience the picture he was developing in his mind. Today he is president of a multimillion dollar concern and is radiantly happy.

He Said a Jinx Was Following Him

Mr. Block said that he had been making an annual income of twenty thousand dollars, but for the past three months all doors seemed to jam tightly. He brought clients up to the point where they were about to sign on the dotted line, and then at the eleventh hour the door closed. He added that perhaps a jinx was following him.

In discussing the matter with Mr. Block, I discovered that three months previously he had become very irritated, annoyed, and resentful toward a dentist who, after he had promised to sign a contract, had withdrawn at the last moment. He began to live in the unconscious fear that other clients would do the same, thereby setting up a history of frustration, hostility, and obstacles. He gradually built up in his mind a belief in obstruction and last minute cancelations until a vicious circle had been established. *What I fear most has come upon me.* Mr. Block realized that the trouble was in his own mind and that it was essential to change his mental attitude.

His run of so-called misfortune was broken in the following way: "I realize I am one with the Infinite Intelligence of my subconscious mind which knows no obstacle, difficulty, or delay. I live in the joyous expectancy of the best. My deeper mind responds to my thoughts. I know that the work of the infinite power of my subconscious cannot be hindered. Infinite Intelligence always finishes successfully whatever it begins. Creative wisdom works through me bringing all my plans and purposes to completion. Whatever I start, I bring to a successful conclusion. My aim in life is to give wonderful service, and all those whom I contact are blessed by what I have to offer. All my work comes to full fruition in divine order."

He repeated this prayer every morning before going to call on his customers, and he also prayed each night prior to sleep. In a short time he had established a new habit pattern in his subconscious mind, and he was back in his old accustomed stride as a successful salesman.

How Much Do You Want What You Want?

A young man asked Socrates how he could get wisdom. Socrates replied, "Come with me." He took the lad to a river, pushed the boy's head under the water, held it there until the boy was gasping for air, then relaxed and released his head. When the boy regained his composure, he asked him, "What did you desire most when you were under water?"

"I wanted air," said the boy.

Socrates said to him, "When you want wisdom as much as you wanted air when you were immersed in the water, you will receive it."

Likewise, when you really have an intense desire to overcome any block in your life, and you come to a clear-cut decision that there is a way out, and that is the course you wish to follow, then victory and triumph are assured.

If you really want peace of mind and inner calm, you will get it, regardless of how unjustly you have been treated, or how unfair the boss has been, or what a mean scoundrel someone has proved to be. All this makes no difference to you when you awaken to your mental and spiritual powers.

You know what you want, and you will definitely refuse to let the thieves (thoughts) of hatred, anger, hostility, and ill will rob you of peace, harmony, health, and happiness. You cease to become upset by people, conditions, news, and events by identifying your thoughts immediately with your aim in life. Your aim is peace, health, inspiration, harmony, and abundance. Feel a river of peace flowing through you now. Your thought is the immaterial and invisible power, and you choose to let it bless, inspire, and give you peace.

Why He Could Not Be Healed

This is a case history of a married man with four children who was supporting and secretly living with another woman during his business trips. He was ill, nervous, irritable, and cantankerous and he could not sleep without drugs. The doctor's medicine failed to bring down his high blood pressure of over two hundred. He had pains in numerous organs of his body which doctors could not diagnose or relieve. To make matters worse, he was drinking heavily.

The cause of all this was a deep unconscious sense of guilt. He had violated the marriage vows, and this troubled him. The religious creed he was brought up on was deeply lodged in his subconscious mind and he drank excessively to heal the wound of guilt. Some invalids take morphine and codeine for severe pains; he was taking alcohol for the pain or wound in his mind. It was the old story of adding fuel to the fire.

The Explanation and the Cure

He listened to the explanation of how his mind worked. He faced his problem, looked at it, and gave up his dual role. He knew that his drinking was an unconscious attempt to escape. The hidden cause lodged in his subconscious mind had to be eradicated, then the healing would follow.

He began to impress his subconscious mind three or four times a day by using the following prayer: "My mind is full of peace, poise, balance, and equilibrium. The infinite lies stretched in smiling repose within me. I am not afraid of anything in the past, the present, or the future. The Infinite Intelligence of my subconscious mind leads, guides, and directs me in all ways. I now meet every situation with faith, poise, calmness, and confidence. I am now completely free from the habit. My mind is full of inner peace, freedom, and joy. I forgive myself, then I am forgiven. Peace, sobriety, and confidence reign supreme in my mind."

He repeated this prayer frequently as outlined, being fully aware of what he was doing and why he was doing it. Knowing what he was doing gave him the necessary faith and confidence. I explained to him that as he spoke these statements out loud, slowly, lovingly, and meaningfully, they would gradually sink down into his subconscious mind. Like seeds, they would grow after their kind. These truths, on which he concentrated, went in through his eyes, his ears heard the sound and the healing vibrations of these words reached his subconscious mind and obliterated all the negative mental patterns which caused all the trouble. Light dispels darkness.

The constructive thought destroys the negative thought. He became a transformed man within a month.

Refusing to Admit It

If you are an alcoholic or drug addict, admit it. Do not dodge the issue. Many people remain alcoholics because they refuse to admit it.

Your disease is an instability, an inner fear. You are refusing to face life, and so you try to escape your responsibilities through the bottle. As an alcoholic you have no free will, although you think you have, and you may even boast about your will power. If you are a habitual drunkard and say bravely "I will not touch it anymore," you have no power to make this assertion come true, because you do not know where to locate the power.

You are living in a psychological prison of your own making, and you are bound by your beliefs, opinions, training, and environmental influences. Like most people, you are a creature of habit. You are conditioned to react the way you do.

Building In the Idea of Freedom

You can build the idea of freedom and peace of mind into your mentality so that it reaches your subconscious depths. The latter, being all-powerful, will free you from all desire for alcohol. Then you will have the new understanding of how your mind works, and you can truly back up your statement and prove the truth to yourself.

Fifty-One Percent Healed

If you have a keen desire to free yourself from any destructive habit, you are 51 percent healed already. When you have a greater desire to give up the bad habit than to continue it, you will not experience too much difficulty in gaining complete freedom.

Whatever thought you anchor the mind upon, the latter magnifies. If you engage the mind on the concept of freedom (freedom from the habit) and peace of mind, and if you keep it focused on this new direction of attention, you generate feelings and emotions which gradually emotionalize the concept of freedom and peace. Whatever idea you emotionalize is accepted by your subconscious and brought to pass.

The Law of Substitution

Realize that something good can come out of your suffering. You have not suffered in vain. However, it is foolish to continue to suffer.

If you continue as an alcoholic, it will bring about mental and physical deterioration and decay. Realize that the power in your subconscious is backing you up. Even though you may be seized with melancholia, you should begin to imagine the joy of freedom that is in store for you. This is the law of substitution. Your imagination took you to the bottle; let it take you now to freedom and peace of mind. You will suffer a little bit, but it is for a constructive purpose. You will bear it like a mother in the pangs of childbirth, and you will, likewise, bring forth a child of the mind. Your subconscious will give birth to sobriety.

Cause of Alcoholism

The real cause of alcoholism is negative and destructive thinking; for as a man thinketh, so is he. The alcoholic has a deep sense of inferiority, inadequacy, defeat, and frustration, usually accompanied by a deep inner hostility. He has countless alibis as to his reason for drinking, but the sole reason is in his thought-life.

Three Magic Steps

The First Step

Get still; quiet the wheels of the mind. Enter into a sleepy, drowsy state. In this relaxed, peaceful, receptive state, you are preparing for the second step.

The Second Step

Take a brief phrase which can readily be graven on the memory, and repeat it over and over as a lullaby. Use the phrase, "Sobriety and peace of mind are mine now, and I give thanks." To prevent the mind from wandering, repeat it aloud, or sketch its pronunciation with the lips and tongue as you say it mentally. This helps its entry into the subconscious mind. Do this for five minutes or more. You will find a deep emotional response.

The Third Step

Just before going to sleep, practice what Johann von Goethe, German author, used to do. Imagine a friend or loved one in front of you. Your eyes are closed, you are relaxed and at peace. The loved one or friend is subjectively present, and is saying to you, "Congratulations!" You see the smile; you hear the voice. You mentally touch the hand; it is all real and vivid. The word *congratulations* implies complete freedom. Hear it over and over again until you get the subconscious reaction which satisfies.

Keep On Keeping On

When fear knocks at the door of your mind, or when worry, anxiety, and doubt cross your mind, behold your vision, your goal. Think of the infinite power within your subconscious mind, which you can generate by your thinking and imagining, and this will give you confidence, power, and courage. Keep on, persevere, "until the day breaks and the shadows flee away."

Review Your Thought Power

1. The solution lies within the problem. The answer is in every question. Infinite Intelligence responds to you as you call upon it with faith and confidence.

2. Habit is the function of your subconscious mind. There is no greater evidence of the marvelous power of your subconscious than the force and sway habit holds in your life. You are a creature of habit.

3. You form habit patterns in your subconscious mind by repeating a thought and act over and over again until it establishes tracks in the subconscious mind and becomes automatic, such as swimming, dancing, typing, walking, driving your car, etc.

4. You have freedom to choose. You can choose a good habit or a bad habit. Prayer is a good habit.

5. Whatever mental picture, backed by faith, you behold in your conscious mind, your subconscious mind will bring to pass.

6. The only obstacle to your success and achievement is your own thought or mental image.

7. When your attention wanders, bring it back to the contemplation of your good or goal. Make a habit of this. This is called disciplining the mind.

8. Your conscious mind is the camera, and your subconscious mind is the sensitive plate on which you register or impress the picture.

9. The only jinx that follows anyone is a fear thought repeated over and over in the mind. Break the jinx by knowing that whatever you start you will bring to a conclusion in divine order. Picture the happy ending and sustain it with confidence.

10. To form a new habit, you must be convinced that it is desirable. When your desire to give up the bad habit is greater than your desire to continue, you are 51 percent healed already.

11. The statements of others cannot hurt you except through your own thoughts and mental participation. Identify yourself with your aim which is peace, harmony, and joy. You are the only thinker in your universe.

12. Excessive drinking is an unconscious desire to escape. The cause of alcoholism is negative and destructive thinking. The cure is to think of freedom, sobriety, and perfection and to feel the thrill of accomplishment.

13. Many people remain alcoholics because they refuse to admit it.

14. The law of your subconscious mind, which held you in bondage and inhibited your freedom of action, will give you freedom and happiness. It depends on how you use it.

15. Your imagination took you to the bottle; let it take you to freedom by imagining you are free.

16. The real cause of alcoholism is negative and destructive thinking. *As a man thinketh in his heart* [subconscious mind] *so is he.*

17. When fear knocks at the door of your mind, let faith in God and all things good open the door.

19

How to Use Your Subconscious Mind to Remove Fear

O ne of my students told me that he was invited to speak at a banquet. He said he was panic stricken at the thought of speaking before a thousand people. He overcame his fear this way. For several nights he sat down in an armchair for about five minutes and said to himself slowly, quietly, and positively, "I am going to master this fear. I am overcoming it now. I speak with poise and confidence. I am relaxed and at ease." He operated a definite law of mind and overcame his fear.

The subconscious mind is amenable to suggestion and is controlled by suggestion. When you still your mind and relax, the thoughts of your conscious mind sink down into the subconscious through a process similar to osmosis, whereby fluids separated by a porous membrane intermingle. As these positive seeds, or thoughts, sink into the subconscious area, more grow after their kind, and you become poised, serene, and calm.

Man's Greatest Enemy

Is is said that fear is man's greatest enemy. Fear is behind failure, sickness, and poor human relations. Millions of people are afraid of the past, the future, old age, insanity, and death. Fear is a thought in your mind and you are afraid of your own thoughts.

A little boy can be paralyzed with fear when he is told there is a boogeyman under his bed who is going to take him away. When his father turns on the light and shows him there is no boogeyman, he is freed from fear. The fear in the mind of the boy was as real as if there really was a boogeyman there. He was healed of a false thought in his mind. The thing he feared did not exist. Likewise, most of your fears have no reality. They are merely a conglomeration of sinister shadows, and shadows have no reality.

Do the Thing You Fear

Mark Twain, philosopher and writer, said, "Do the thing you fear most, and the death of fear is certain." There was a time when the writer of this chapter was filled with unutterable fear when standing before an audience. The way I overcame it was to stand before the audience, do the thing I was afraid to do, and the death of fear was certain.

When you affirm positively that you are going to master your fears, and you come to a definite decision in your conscious mind, you release the power of the subconscious which flows in response to the nature of your thought.

Banishing Stage Fright

A young lady was invited to an audition. She had been looking forward to the interview. However, on three previous occasions, she had failed miserably due to stage fright. She possessed a very good voice, but she was certain that when the time came for her to sing, she would be seized with stage fright. The subconscious mind takes your fears as a request, proceeds to manifest them, and then brings them into your experience. On three previous auditions she sang wrong notes, and she finally broke down and cried. The cause, as previously outlined, was an involuntary autosuggestion, i.e., a silent fear thought emotionalized and subjectified.

She overcame it by the following technique: Three times a day she isolated herself in a room. She sat down comfortably in an armchair, relaxed her body, and closed her eyes. She stilled her mind and body to the best of her ability. Physical inertia favors passivity and renders the mind more receptive to suggestion. She counteracted the fear suggestion by saying to herself, "I sing beautifully, I am poised, serene, confident, and calm."

She repeated this statement slowly, quietly, and with feeling from five to ten times at each sitting. She had three such "sittings" every day and one immediately prior to sleep. At the end of a week she was completely poised and confident, and gave an outstanding audition. Carry out the above procedure, and the death of fear is certain.

Fear of Failure

Occasionally young men from the local university come to see me, as well as school teachers, who often seem to suffer from suggestive amnesia at examinations. The complaint is always the same: "I know the answers after the examination is over, but I can't remember the answers during the examination."

The idea which realizes itself is the one to which we invariably give concentrated attention. I find that each one is obsessed with the idea of failure. Fear is behind the temporary amnesia, and it is the cause of the whole experience.

One young medical student was the most brilliant person in his class, yet he found himself failing to answer simple questions at the time of written or oral examinations. I explained to him that the reason was he had been worrying and was fearful for several days previous to the examination. These negative thoughts became charged with fear.

Thoughts enveloped in the powerful emotion of fear are realized in the subconscious mind. In other words, this young man was requesting his subconscious mind to see to it that he failed, and that is exactly what it did. On the day of the examination he found himself stricken with what is called, in psychological circles, suggestive amnesia.

How to Overcome Fear

He learned that his subconscious mind was the storehouse of memory, and that it had a perfect record of all he had heard and read during his medical training. Moreover, he learned the the subconscious mind was responsive and reciprocal. The way to be *en rapport* with it was to be relaxed, peaceful, and confident.

Every night and morning he began to imagine his mother congratulating him on his wonderful record. He would hold an imaginary letter from her in his hand. As he began to contemplate the happy result, he called forth a corresponding or reciprocal response or reaction in himself. The all-wise and omnipotent power of the subconscious took over, dictated, and directed his conscious mind accordingly. He imagined the end, thereby willing the means to the realization of the end. Following this procedure, he had no trouble passing subsequent examinations. In other words, the subjective wisdom took over, compelling him to give an excellent account of himself.

Fear of Water, Mountains, Closed Places, and So On

There are many people who are afraid to go into an elevator, climb mountains, or even swim in the water. It may well be that the individual had unpleasant experiences in the water in his youth, such as having been thrown forcibly into the water without being able to swim. He might have been forcibly detained in an elevator which failed to function properly, causing resultant fear of closed places.

I had an experience when I was about ten years of age. I accidentally fell into a pool and went down three times. I can still remember the dark water engulfing my head, and my gasping for air until another boy pulled me out at the last moment. This experience sank into my subconscious mind and for years I feared the water.

An elderly psychologist said to me, "Go down to the swimming pool, look at the water, and say out loud in strong tones, 'I am going to master you, I can dominate you.' Then go into the water, take lessons, and overcome it." This I did, and I mastered the water. Do not permit water to master you. Remember you are the master of the water.

When I assumed a new attitude of mind, the omnipotent power of the subconscious responded, giving me strength, faith, and confidence and enabling me to overcome my fear.

Master Technique for Overcoming Any Particular Fear

The following is a process and technique for overcoming fear which I teach from the platform. It works like a charm. Try it!

Suppose you are afraid of the water, a mountain, an interview, an audition, or you fear closed places. If you are afraid of swimming, begin now to sit still for five or ten minutes three or four times a day, and imagine you are swimming. Actually, you are swimming in your mind. It is a subjective experience. Mentally, you have projected yourself into the water. You feel the chill of the water and the moment of your arms and legs. It is all real, vivid, and a joyous activity of the mind. It is not idle daydreaming, for you know that what you are experiencing in your imagination will be developed in your subconscious mind. Then you will be compelled to express the image and likeness of the picture you impressed on your deeper mind. This is the law of the subconscious.

You could apply the same technique if you are afraid of mountains or high places. Imagine you are climbing the mountain, feel the reality of it all, enjoy the scenery, knowing that as you continue to do this mentally, you will do it physically with ease and comfort.

He Blessed the Elevator

I knew an executive of a large corporation who was terrified to ride in an elevator. He would walk up five flights of stairs to his office every morning. He said that he began to bless the elevator every night and several times a day. He finally overcame his fear. This was how he blessed the elevator: "The elevator in our building is a wonderful idea. It came out of the universal mind. It is a boon and a blessing to all our employees. It gives wonderful service. It operates in divine order. I ride in it in peace and joy. I remain silent now while the currents of life, love, and understanding flow through the patterns of my thought. In my imagination I am now in the elevator, and I step out into my office. The elevator is full of our employees. I talk to them and they are friendly, joyous, and free. It is a wonderful experience of freedom, faith, and confidence. I give thanks."

He continued this prayer for about ten days, and on the eleventh day, he walked into the elevator with other members of the organization and felt completely free.

Normal and Abnormal Fear

Man is born with two fears: the fear of falling and the fear of noise. These are a sort of alarm system given you by nature as a means of self-preservation. Normal fear is good. You hear an automobile coming down the road, and you step aside to survive. The momentary fear of being run over is overcome by your action. All other fears were given to you by parents, relatives, teachers, and all those who influenced your early years.

Abnormal Fear

Abnormal fear takes place when man lets his imagination run riot. I knew a woman who was invited to go on a trip around the world by plane. She began to cut out of the newspapers all reports of airplane catastrophes. She pictured herself going down in the ocean, being drowned, etc. This is abnormal fear. Had she persisted in this, she would undoubtedly have attracted what she feared most.

Another example of abnormal fear is that of a businessman in New York, who was very prosperous and successful. He had his own private mental motion picture of which he was the director. He would run this mental movie of failure, bankruptcy, empty shelves, and no bank balance until he sank into a deep depression. He refused to stop this morbid imagery and kept reminding his wife that "This can't last, there will be a recession," "I feel sure we will go bankrupt," etc. His wife told me that he finally did go into bankruptcy, and all the things he imagined and feared came to pass. The things he feared did not exist, but he brought them to pass by constantly fearing, believing, and experiencing financial disaster. Job said, *The thing I feared has come upon me.*

There are people who are afraid that something terrible will happen to their children, and that some dreadful catastrophe will befall them. When they read about an epidemic or rare disease, they live in fear that they will catch it and some imagine they have the disease already. All of this is abnormal fear.

The Answer to Abnormal Fear

Move mentally to the opposite. To stay at the extreme of fear is stagnation plus mental and physical deterioration. When fear arises, there immediately comes with it a desire for something opposite to the thing feared. Place your attention on the thing immediately desired. Get absorbed and engrossed in your desire, knowing that the subjective always overturns the objective. This attitude will give you confidence and lift your spirits. The infinite power of your subconscious mind is moving on your behalf and it cannot fail. Therefore, peace and assurance is yours.

Examine Your Fears

The president of a large organization told me that when he was a salesman he used to walk around the block five or six times before he called on a customer. The sales manager came along one day and said to him, "Don't be afraid of the boogeyman behind the door. There is no boogeyman. It is a false belief."

The manager told him that whenever he looked at his own fears he stared them in the face and stood up to them, looking them straight in the eye. Then they faded and shrank into insignificance.

He Landed in the Jungle

A chaplain told me of his experiences in the Second World War. He had to parachute from a damaged plane and land in the jungle. He said he was frightened, but he knew there were two kinds of fear, normal and abnormal, which we have previously pointed out.

He decided to do something about the fear immediately, and he began to talk to himself saying, "John, you can't surrender to your fear. Your fear is a desire for safety and security and a way out."

He began to claim, "Infinite Intelligence, which guides the planets in their courses, is now leading and guiding me out of the jungle."

He kept saying this out loud to himself for ten minutes or more. "Then," he added, "something began to stir inside me. A mood of confidence began to seize me, and I began to walk. After a few days, I miraculously came out of the jungle and was picked up by a rescue plane." His changed mental attitude saved him. His confidence and trust in the subjective wisdom and power within him was the solution to his problem.

He said, "Had I begun to bemoan my fate and indulge my fears, I would have succumbed to the monster fear and probably would have died of fear and starvation."

He Dismissed Himself

The general manager of an organization told me that for three years he feared he would lose his position. He was always imagining failure. The thing he feared did not exist, save as a morbid anxious thought in his own mind. His vivid imagination dramatized the loss of his job until he became nervous and neurotic. Finally, he was asked to resign.

Actually, he dismissed himself. His constant negative imagery and fear suggestions to his subconscious mind caused the latter to respond and react accordingly. It caused him to make mistakes and foolish decisions which resulted in his failure as a general manager. His dismissal would never have happened, if he had immediately moved to the opposite in his mind.

They Plotted against Him

During a recent world lecture tour, I had a two-hour conversation with a prominent government official. He had a deep sense of inner peace and serenity. He said that all the abuse he receives politically from newspapers and the opposition party never disturbs him. His practice is to sit still for fifteen minutes in the morning and realize that in the center of himself is a deep, still ocean of peace. Meditating in this way, he generates tremendous power which overcomes all manner of difficulties and fears.

Some time previously, a colleague called him at midnight and told him a group of people were plotting against him. This is what he said to his colleague, "I am going to sleep now in perfect peace. You can discuss it with me at 10:00 AM tomorrow."

He said to me, "I know that no negative thought can ever manifest except if I emotionalize the thought and accept it mentally. I refuse to entertain their suggestion of fear. Therefore, no harm can come to me."

Notice how calm he was, how cool, how peaceful! He did not start getting excited, tearing his hair, or wringing his hands. At his center he found the still water, an inner peace, and there was a great calm.

Deliver Yourself from All Your Fears

Use this perfect formula for casting out fear. *I sought the Lord, and He heard me, and delivered me from all my fears* (Psalms 34:4). The

Lord is an ancient word meaning law—the power of your sub-conscious mind.

Learn the wonders of your subconscious, and how it works and functions. Master the techniques given to you in this chapter. Put them into practice now, today! Your subconscious will respond, and you will be free of all fears. *I sought the Lord, and He heard me, and delivered me from all my fears.*

Step This Way to Freedom from Fear

1. Do the thing you are afraid to do, and the death of fear is certain. Say to yourself and mean it, "I am going to master this fear," and you will.

2. Fear is a negative thought in your mind. Supplant it with a con-structive thought. Fear has killed millions. Confidence is greater than fear. Nothing is more powerful than faith in God and the good.

3. Fear is man's greatest enemy. It is behind failure, sickness, and bad human relations. Love casts out fear. Love is an emotional attachment to the good things in life. Fall in love with honesty, integrity, justice, good will, and success. Live in the joyous expec-tancy of the best, and invariably the best will come to you.

4. Counteract the fear suggestions with the opposite, such as "I sing beautifully; I am poised, serene, and calm." It will pay fabulous dividends.

5. Fear is behind amnesia at oral and written examination time. You can overcome this by affirming frequently, "I have a perfect

memory for everything I need to know," or you can imagine a friend congratulating you on your brilliant success on the examination. Persevere and you will win.

6. If you are afraid of the water, in your imagination swim freely and joyously. Project yourself into the water mentally. Feel the chill and thrill of swimming across the pool. Make it vivid. As you do this subjectively, you will be compelled to go into the water and conquer it. This is the law of your mind.

7. If you are afraid of closed places, such as elevators, lecture halls, etc., mentally ride in an elevator blessing all its parts and functions. You will be amazed how quickly the fear will be dissipated.

8. You were born with only two fears: the fear of falling and the fear of noise. All your other fears were acquired. Get rid of them.

9. Normal fear is good. Abnormal fear is very bad and destructive. To constantly indulge in fear thoughts results in abnormal fear, obsessions, and complexes. To fear something persistently causes a sense of panic and terror.

10. You can overcome abnormal fear when you know the power of your subconscious mind can change conditions and bring to pass the cherished desires of your heart. Give your immediate attention and devotion to your desire which is the opposite of your fear. This is the love that casts out fear.

11. If you are afraid of failure, give your attention to success. If you are afraid of sickness, dwell on your perfect health. If you are afraid of an accident, dwell on the guidance and protection from

God. If you are afraid of death, dwell on eternal life. God is life, and that is your life now.

12. The great law of substitution is the answer to fear. Whatever you fear has its solution in the form of your desire. If you are sick, you desire health. If you are in the prison of fear, you desire freedom. Expect the good. Mentally concentrate on the good, and know that your subconscious mind answers you always. It never fails.

13. The things you fear do not really exist except as thoughts in your mind. Thoughts are creative. This is why Job said, *The thing I feared has come upon me.* Think good and good follows.

14. Look at your fears; hold them up to the light of reason. Learn to laugh at your fears. That is the best medicine.

15. Nothing can disturb you but your own thought. The suggestions, statements, or threats of other persons have no power. The power is within you, and when your thoughts are focused on that which is good, then God's power is with your thoughts of good. There is only one creative power, and it moves as harmony. There are no divisions or quarrels in it. Its source is love. This is why God's power is with your thoughts of good.

20

How to Stay Young in Spirit Forever

Your subconscious mind never grows old. It is timeless, ageless, and endless. It is a part of the universal mind of God which was never born and it will never die.

Fatigue or old age cannot be predicated on any spiritual quality or power. Patience, kindness, veracity, humility, good will, peace, harmony, and brotherly love are attributes and qualities which never grow old. If you continue to generate these qualities here on this plane of life, you will always remain young in spirit.

I remember reading an article in one of our magazines some years ago which stated that a group of eminent medical men at the Decourcy Clinic, in Cincinnati, Ohio, reported that years alone are not responsible for bringing about degenerative disorders. These same physicians stated that is is the fear of time, not time itself, that has a harmful aging effect on our minds and bodies, and that the neurotic fear of the effects of time may well be the cause of premature aging.

During the many years of my public life, I have had occasion to study the biographies of the famous men and women who have continued their productive activities into the years well beyond the normal span of life. Some of them achieve their greatness in old age. At the same time, it has been my privilege to meet and to know countless individuals of no prominence who, in their lesser sphere, belonged to those hardy mortals who have proved that old age of itself does not destroy the creative powers of the mind and body.

He Had Grown Old in His Thought-Life

A few years ago I called on an old friend in London, England. He was over eighty years of age, very ill, and obviously was yielding to his advancing years. Our conversation revealed his physical weakness, his sense of frustration, and a general deterioration almost approaching lifelessness. His cry was that he was useless and that no one wanted him. With an expression of hopelessness he betrayed his false philosophy, "We are born, grow up, become old, good for nothing, and that's the end."

This mental attitude of futility and worthlessness was the chief reason for his sickness. He was looking forward only to senescence and, after that, nothing. Indeed, he had grown old in his thought-life, and his subconscious mind brought about all the evidence of his habitual thinking.

Age Is the Dawn of Wisdom

Unfortunately, many people have the same attitude as this unhappy man. They are afraid of what they term "old age," the end, and extinction, which really means that they are afraid of life. Yet, life is endless. Age is not the flight of years, but the dawn of wisdom.

Wisdom is an awareness of the tremendous spiritual powers in your subconscious mind and the knowledge of how to apply these powers to lead a full and happy life. Get it out of your head once and for all that sixty-five, seventy-five, or eighty-five years of age is synonymous with the end for you or anybody else. It can be the beginning of a glorious, fruitful, active, and most productive life pattern, better than you have ever experienced. Believe this, expect it, and your subconscious will bring it to pass.

Welcome the Change

Old age is not a tragic occurrence. What we call the aging process is really change. It is to be welcomed joyfully and gladly as each phase of human life is a step forward on the path, which has no end. Man has powers, which transcend his bodily powers. He has senses, which transcend his five physical senses.

Scientists today are finding positive indisputable evidence that something conscious in man can leave his present body and travel thousands of miles to see, hear, touch, and speak to people even though his physical body never leaves the couch on which it reclines.

Man's life is spiritual and eternal. He need never grow old for life, or God, cannot grow old. The Bible says that God *is* life. Life is self renewing, eternal, indestructible, and is the reality of all men.

Evidence for Survival

The evidence gathered by the psychical research societies both in Great Britain and America is overwhelming. You may go into any large metropolitan library and get volumes on *The Proceedings of the Psychical Research Society* based on findings of distinguished scientists on survival following so-called death. You will find a startling report on scientific experiments establishing the reality of life after death in *The Case for Psychic Survival* by Hereward Carrington, Director of the American Psychical Institute.

Life Is

A woman asked Thomas Edison, the electrical wizard, "Mr. Edison, what is electricity?"

He replied, "Madame, electricity is. Use it."

Electricity is a name we give an invisible power which we do not fully comprehend, but we learn all we can about the principle of electricity and its uses. We use it in countless ways.

The scientist cannot see an electron with his eyes, yet he accepts it as a scientific fact, because it is the only valid conclusion, which coincides with his other experimental evidence. We cannot see life. However, we know we are alive. Life is, and we are here to express it in all its beauty and glory.

Mind and Spirit Do Not Grow Old

The Bible says, *And this is life eternal, that they might know thee the only true God* (John 17:3). The man who thinks or believes that the earthly cycle of birth, adolescence, youth, maturity, and old age is all there is to life is indeed to be pitied. Such a man has no anchor, no hope, no vision, and to him life has no meaning.

This type of belief brings frustration, stagnation, cynicism, and a sense of hopelessness resulting in neurosis and mental aberrations of all kinds. If you cannot play a fast game of tennis, or swim as fast as your son, or if your body has slowed down, or you walk with a slow step, remember life is always clothing itself anew. What men call death is but a journey to a new city in another dimension of life.

I say to men and women in my lectures that they should accept what we call old age gracefully. Age has its own glory, beauty, and wisdom, which belong to it. Peace, love, joy, beauty, happiness, wisdom, good will, and understanding are qualities which never grow old or die.

Ralph Waldo Emerson, poet and philosopher, said, "We do not count a man's years until he has nothing else to count." Your character, the quality of your mind, your faith, and your convictions are not subject to decay.

You Are as Young as You Think You Are

I give public lectures in Caxton Hall, London, England, every few years, and following one of these lectures, a surgeon said to me, "I am eighty-four years of age, I operate every morning, visit patients in the afternoons, and I write for medical and other scientific journals in the evening."

His attitude was that he was as useful as he believed himself to be, and that he was as young as his thoughts. He said to me, "It's true what you said, 'Man is as strong as he thinks he is, and as valuable as he thinks he is.'"

This surgeon has not surrendered to advancing years. He knows that he is immortal. His final comment to me was, "If I should pass on tomorrow, I would be operating on people in the next dimension, not with a surgeon's scalpel, but with mental and spiritual surgery."

Your Gray Hairs Are an Asset

Don't ever quit a job and say, "I am retired; I am old; I am finished." That would be stagnation, death, and you would be finished. Some men are old at thirty, while others are young at eighty. The mind is the master weaver, the architect, the designer, and the sculptor. George Bernard Shaw was active at ninety, and the artistic quality of his mind had not relaxed from active duty.

I meet men and women who tell me that some employers almost slam the door in their faces when they say they are over forty. This attitude on the part of the employers is to be considered cold, callous, evil, and completely void of compassion and understanding. The total emphasis seems to be on youth, i.e., you must be under thirty-five years of age to receive consideration. The reasoning behind this is certainly very shallow. If the employer would stop and think, he would realize that the man or woman was not selling his age or gray hair, rather, he was willing to give of his talents, his experience, and his wisdom gathered through years of experience in the market place of life.

Age Is an Asset

Your age should be a distinct asset to any organization, because of your practice and application through the years of the principles of the Golden Rule and the law of love and good will. Your gray hair, if you have any, should stand for greater wisdom, skill, and understanding. Your emotional and spiritual maturity should be a tremendous blessing to any organization.

A man should not be asked to resign when he is sixty-five years of age. That is the time of life when he could be most useful in handling personnel problems, making plans for the future, making decisions, and guiding others in the realm of creative ideas based on his experience and insight into the nature of the business.

Be Your Age

A motion picture writer in Hollywood told me that he had to write scripts which would cater to the twelve-year-old mind. This is a tragic state of affairs if the great masses of people are expected to become emotionally and spiritually mature. It means that the emphasis is placed on youth in spite of the fact that youth stands for inexperience, lack of discernment, and hasty judgment.

I Can Keep Up With the Best of Them

I am now thinking of a man sixty-five years of age who is trying frantically to keep young. He swims with young men every Sunday, goes on long hikes, plays tennis, and boasts of his prowess and physical powers, saying, "Look, I can keep up with the best of them."

He should remember the great truth: *As a man thinketh in his heart, so is he* (Proverbs 23:7). Diets, exercises, and games of all kinds will not keep this man young. It is necessary for him to observe that he grows old or remains young in accordance with his processes of thinking. Your subconscious mind is conditioned by your thoughts. If your thoughts are constantly on the beautiful, the noble, and the good, you will remain young regardless of the chronological years.

Fear of Old Age

Job said, *The thing which I greatly feared is come upon me.* There are many people who fear old age and are uncertain about the future because they anticipate mental and physical deterioration as the years advance. What they think and feel comes to pass.

You grow old when you lose interest in life, when you cease to dream, to hunger after new truths, and to search for new worlds to conquer. When your mind is open to new ideas, new interests, and when you raise the curtain and let in the sunshine and inspiration of new truths of life and the universe, you will be young and vital.

You Have Much to Give

If you are sixty-five or ninety-five years of age, realize you have much to give. You can help stabilize, advise, and direct the younger generation. You can give the benefit of your knowledge, your experience, and your wisdom. You can always look ahead for at all times you are gazing into infinite life. You will find that you can never cease to unveil the glories and wonders of life. Try to learn something new every moment of the day, and you will find your mind will always be young.

One Hundred and Ten Years Old

Some years ago while lecturing in Bombay, India, I was introduced to a man who said he was 110 years old. He had the most beautiful face I have ever seen. He seemed transfigured by the radiance of an inner light. There was a rare beauty in his eyes indicating he had grown old in years with gladness and with no indication that his mind had dimmed its lights.

Retirement—A New Venture

Be sure that your mind never retires. It must be a parachute which is no good unless it opens up. Be open and receptive to new ideas. I have seen men of sixty-five and seventy retire. They seemed to rot away, and in a few months passed on. They obviously felt that life was at an end.

Retirement can be a new venture, a new challenge, a new path, the beginning of the fulfillment of a long dream. It is inexpressibly depressing to hear a man say, "What shall I do now that I am retired?" He is saying in effect, "I am mentally and physically dead. My mind is bankrupt of ideas."

All this is a false picture. The real truth is that you can accomplish more at ninety than you did at sixty, because each day you are growing in wisdom and understanding of life and the universe through your new studies and interest.

He Graduated to a Better Job

An executive, who lives near me, was forced to retire a few months ago because he had reached the age of sixty-five. He said to me, "I look upon my retirement as promotion from kindergarten to the first grade." He philosophized in this manner: He said that when he left high school, he went up the ladder by going to college. He realized this was a step forward in his education and understanding of life in general. Likewise, he added, now he could do the things he had always wanted to do, and therefore, his retirement was still another step forward on the ladder of life and wisdom.

He came to the wise conclusion that he was no longer going to concentrate on making a living. Now he was going to give all his attention to living life. He is an amateur photographer, and he took additional courses on the subject. He took a trip around the world and took movies of famous places. He now lectures before various groups, lodges, and clubs and is in popular demand.

There are countless ways of taking an interest in something worthwhile outside yourself. Become enthusiastic over new creative ideas, make spiritual progress, and continue to learn and to grow. In this manner you remain young in heart, because you are hungering and thirsting after new truths, and your body will reflect your thinking at all times.

You Must Be a Producer and Not a Prisoner of Society

The newspapers are taking cognizance of the fact that the voting population of the elderly in California elections is increasing by leaps and bounds. This means that their voices will be heard in the legislature of the state and also in the halls of Congress. I believe there will be enacted a federal law prohibiting employers from discrimination against men and women because of age.

A man of sixty-five years may be younger mentally, physically, and psychologically than many men at thirty. It is stupid and ridiculous to tell a man he cannot be hired because he is over forty. It is like saying to him that he is ready for the scrap heap or the junk pile.

What is a man of forty or over to do? Must he bury his talents and hide his light under a bushel? Men who are deprived and prevented from working because of age must be sustained by government treasuries at county, state, and federal levels. The many organizations who refuse to hire them and benefit from their wisdom and experience will be taxed to support them. This is a form of financial suicide.

Man is here to enjoy the fruit of his labor, and he is here to be a producer and not a prisoner of society, which compels him to idleness. Man's body slows down gradually as he advances through the years, but his conscious mind can be made much more active, alert, alive, and quickened by the inspiration from his subconscious mind. His mind, in reality, never grows old. *Oh, that I were as in months past, as in the days when God preserved me; When his candle shined upon my head, and when by his light I walked through darkness; As I was in the days of my youth, when the secret of God was upon my tabernacle* (Job 29:2–4).

Secret of Youth

To recapture the days of your youth, feel the miraculous, healing, self-renewing power of your subconscious mind moving through your whole being. Know and feel that you are inspired, lifted up, rejuvenated, revitalized, and recharged spiritually. You can bubble over with enthusiasm and joy, as in the days of your youth, for the simple reason that you can always mentally and emotionally recapture the joyous state.

The candle, which shines upon your head, is divine intelligence and reveals to you everything you need to know; it enables you to affirm the presence of your good, regardless of appearances. You walk by the guidance of your subconscious mind because you know that the dawn appears and the shadows flee away.

Get a Vision

Instead of saying, "I am old," say, "I am wise in the way of the divine life." Don't let the corporation, newspapers, or statistics hold a picture before you of old age, declining years, decrepitude, senility, and uselessness. Reject it, for it is a lie. Refuse to be hypnotized by such propaganda. Affirm life, not death. Get a vision of yourself as happy, radiant, successful, serene, and powerful.

Your Mind Does Not Grow Old

Former President Herbert Hoover, now eighty-eight years old, is very active and is performing monumental work. I interviewed him a few years ago in his suite at the Waldorf-Astoria, New York City. I found him healthy, happy, vigorous, and full of life and enthusiasm. He was keeping several secretaries busy handling his correspondence and was himself writing books of a political and historical nature. Like all great men, I found him affable, genial, amiable, loving, and most understanding.

His mental acumen and sagacity gave me the thrill of a lifetime. He is a deeply religious man and is full of faith in God and in the triumph of the eternal truth of life. He was subjected to a barrage of criticism and condemnation in the years of the Great Depression, but he weathered the storm and did not grow old in hatred, resentment, ill will, and bitterness.

On the contrary, he went into the silence of his soul and communing with the divine presence within him, he found peace, which is the power at the heart of God.

His Mind Active at Ninety-Nine

My father learned the French language at sixty-five years of age, and became an authority on it at seventy. He made a study of Gaelic when he was over sixty, and became an acknowledged and famous teacher of the subject. He assisted my sister in a school of higher learning and continued to do so until he passed away at ninety-nine. His mind was as clear at ninety-nine as it was when he was twenty. Moreover, his handwriting and his reasoning powers had improved with age. Truly, you are as old as you think and feel.

We Need Our Senior Citizens

Marcus Porcius Cato, the Roman patriot, learned Greek at eighty. Madame Ernestine Schumann-Heink, the great German American contralto, reached the pinnacle of her musical success after she became a grandmother. It is wonderful to behold the accomplishments of the oldsters. General Douglas MacArthur, Harry S. Truman, General Dwight David Eisenhower, and American financier Bernard Baruch are interesting, active, and contributing their talents and wisdom to the world.

The Greek philosopher Socrates learned to play musical instruments when he was eighty years old. Michelangelo was painting his greatest canvases at eighty. At eighty, Ceos Simonides won the prize for poetry, Goethe finished *Faust*, and Leopold von Ranke commenced his *History of the World*, which he finished at ninety-two.

Alfred Tennyson wrote a magnificent poem, "Crossing the Bar," at eighty-three. Isaac Newton was hard at work close to eighty-five. At eighty-eight John Wesley was directing, preaching, and guiding Methodism. We have several men of ninety-five years who come to my lectures, and they tell me they are in better health now than they were at twenty.

Let us place our senior citizens in high places and give them every opportunity to bring forth the flowers of Paradise.

If you are retired, get interested in the laws of life and the wonders of your subconscious mind. Do something you have always wanted to do. Study new subjects and investigate new ideas.

Pray as follows: *As the hart panteth after the water brooks, so panteth my soul after thee, O God* (Psalms 42:1).

The Fruits of Old Age

His flesh shall be fresher than a child's; he shall return to the days of his youth (Job 33:25).

Old age really means the contemplation of the truths of God from the highest standpoint. Realize that you are on an endless journey, a series of important steps in the ceaseless, tireless, endless ocean of life. Then, with the Psalmist you will say, *They shall bring forth fruit in old age; they shall be fat and flourishing* (Psalms 92:14). *But the fruit of the spirit is love, joy, peace, patience, gentleness, goodness, faith, meekness, temperance; against such there is no law* (Galatians 5:22).

You are a child of infinite life, which knows no end, and you are a child of eternity.

Profitable Pointers

1. Patience, kindness, love, good will, joy, happiness, wisdom, and understanding are qualities which never grow old. Cultivate them and express them and remain young in mind and body.

2. Some research physicians say that the neurotic fear of the effects of time may well be the cause of premature aging.

3. Age is not the flight of years; it is the dawn of wisdom in the mind of man.

4. The most productive years of your life can be from sixty-five to ninety-five.

5. Welcome the advancing years. It means you are moving higher on the path of life which has no end.

6. God is life and that is your life now. Life is self renewing, eternal, and indestructible and is the reality of all men. You live forever because your life is God's life.

7. Evidence of survival after death is overwhelming. Study *Proceedings of the Psychical Research Society of Great Britain and America* in your library. The work is based on scientific research by outstanding scientists for over seventy-five years.

8. You cannot see your mind, but you know you have a mind. You cannot see spirit, but you know that the spirit of the game, the spirit of the artist, the spirit of the musician, and the spirit of the speaker is real. Likewise, the spirit of goodness, truth, and

beauty moving in your mind and heart are real. You cannot see life, but you know you are alive.

9. Old age may be called the contemplation of the truths of God from the highest standpoint. The joys of old age are greater than those of youth. Your mind is engaged in spiritual and mental athletics. Nature slows down your body so that you may have the opportunity to meditate on things divine.

10. We do not count a man's years until he has nothing else to count. Your faith and convictions are not subject to decay.

11. You are as young as you think you are. You are as strong as you think you are. You are as useful as you think you are. You are as young as your thoughts.

12. Your gray hairs are an asset. You are not selling your gray hairs. You are selling your talent, abilities, and wisdom which you have garnered through the years.

13. Diet and exercise won't keep you young. *As a man thinketh, so is he.*

14. Fear of old age can bring about physical and mental deterioration. *The thing I greatly feared has come upon me.*

15. You grow old when you cease to dream, and when you lose interest in life. You grow old if you are irritable, crotchety, petulant, and cantankerous. Fill your mind with the truths of God and radiate the sunshine of His love—this is youth.

16. Look ahead, for at all times you are gazing into infinite life.

17. Your retirement is a new venture. Take up new studies and new interests. You can now do the things you always wanted to do when you were so busy making a living. Give your attention to living life.

18. Become a producer and not a prisoner of society. Don't hide your light under a bushel.

19. The secret of youth is love, joy, inner peace, and laughter. *In Him there is fullness of joy. In Him there is no darkness at all.*

20. You are needed. Some of the great philosophers, artists, scientists, writers, and others accomplished their greatest work after they were eighty years old.

21. The fruits of old age are love, joy, peace, patience, gentleness, goodness, faith, meekness, and temperance.

22. You are a child of infinite life which knows no end. You are a child of eternity. You are wonderful!

Part II

COMMENTARY AND TEACHINGS

By

C. James Jensen

In the introduction, I described how I became acquainted with Dr. Joseph Murphy's teachings on the power of the incredible relationship between the conscious and subconscious mind, and ultimately taught four-day seminars of this material for eleven years.

Since Dr. Murphy's work was written over fifty years ago, there has been so much added to this field of study that further validates his creativity in introducing us to the power of the subconscious mind. As contemporary author Bruce H. Lipton, PhD, wrote in his remarkable book *Spontaneous Evolution*, "The subconscious mind controls 95 percent of our behavior and gene regulating cognitive activity through programs obtained primarily from the field of beliefs. . . . When we take command of our own subconscious beliefs and emotions, individually and collectively, we take back creative control over our lives."[2]

In this part, I will lead you through my lessons and experiences, expanding on Dr. Murphy's teachings about the subconscious and how it manifests in our everyday lives. First, we will look at the interrelationship between our subconscious and conscious mind. I will then introduce you to supraconscious and creative problem-solving using a specific technique to access the universal field of knowledge that transcends all data stored in our subconscious minds. In chapter 23, we will look at how our self-concept is developed by our self-talk, and how there is always a one-to-one relationship between our self-concept and our level of performance in every area of our lives.

The final chapters offer a tool kit of practices that have transformed and elevated my life beyond what I could have ever imagined, both professionally and personally. This tool kit includes affirmations, visualizations, communication, resiliency, meditation, and leadership. You will also read several testimonials from colleagues at companies I managed who were taught these same tools. They graciously shared with me how these daily practices—in particular, affirmations and meditation—have added greatly to the success and quality of their lives.

Mastering these tools yourself will improve every area of your life: your performance, your relationships, your level of happiness and well-being. Wherever you are starting from, you will be ever closer to creating and enjoying the life you truly desire!

21

Understanding the True Relationship between the Conscious and Subconscious Mind

> The reason there is so much chaos and misery in the world is because people do not understand the interaction of their conscious and subconscious minds. When these two principles work in accord, in concord, in peace, and synchronously together, you will have health, happiness, peace, and joy. There is no sickness or discord when the conscious and subconscious work together harmoniously and peacefully.
>
> —**Dr. Joseph Murphy**

Let's look more closely at the interaction between the conscious and subconscious that Dr. Murphy speaks of, and how the data stored in our subconscious largely determines the decisions we make and how we behave.

We have three areas of the mind that are the foundation for how we think, how we behave, how we create, and how we make decisions, both consciously and subconsciously. These are not three separate minds but three spheres of our one mind working together.

273

1. The conscious

2. The subconscious

3. The supraconscious

One of the primary functions of the subconscious is to store data. It is the area of our mind that records and stores memory. In computer terms, we could think of it as our hard drive. Everything we have seen, heard, and experienced—and how we have felt about those experiences since birth—are all stored in our subconscious or memory bank. Everything.

That which we have forgotten can be retrieved through chemicals or age-regression hypnosis. Many psychotherapists use hypnosis to rediscover early childhood traumas that may negatively impact a person's behavior as an adult. Powerful phobias and deep-rooted fears are often formulated as young children and when we become adults we forget where they came from; but we know that certain circumstances or situations trigger what often is irrational behavior.

Our negative habit patterns are stored in our subconscious. And as we learned from Dr. Murphy, the data stored in our subconscious largely determines our behavior. Since none of us have gone through life having had exactly the same experiences, or data input, no two of us can be expected to act exactly the same way. This is why when we see someone reacting completely differently than we would in the same situation, we think they are crazy or something is wrong with *them.*

All our behavior is conditioned by the data we have collected along the way that triggers our response. At the conscious level, four basic things occur:

1. We perceive incoming stimuli through our senses.

2. We go through a process of comparison or identification.

3. We analyze what we have identified.

4. We make a decision for directed action, reaction, or inaction.

So when we want to better understand our reactions, we can review the four functions of decision-making for some insight:

- **Perception:** We perceive incoming stimuli in the conscious mind through our senses. We see, hear, feel, smell, or taste something. I will also add that we have a sixth sense, which is our intuition.
- **Comparison:** We simultaneously go into our subconscious to identify what we are perceiving. A car? An airplane? A boat? A bird? An elephant? A kind of food? A friend? An enemy? Or something we have no data on whatsoever?
- **Analysis:** Once we have retrieved data telling us what we are perceiving, we ask ourselves, Is this a good thing? A bad thing? Something that will make me happy? Sad? Comfortable? Uncomfortable? And so on.
- **Decision:** Based on this internal self-analysis, we make a decision for action, inaction, or reaction.

The bottom line: we are all making decisions based largely on our past experiences or data we have received about something that may or may not be the truth. Our data also includes all beliefs, attitudes, and opinions we have formulated from birth right up to the present day, much of which may be completely out of date. Many of us become "prisoners" of our data. Our data, or subconscious, is like the software in a computer that literally runs us. We all operate on certain programs, but many people don't realize that they are operating old programs or belief systems that may no longer be relevant to their lives.

As Eric Hoffer, American author and recipient of the Presidential Medal of Freedom, so beautifully states, "In a time of change, learners inherit the earth, while the learned find themselves beautifully equipped to deal with a world that no longer exists."[3]

We all know people who allow very little gray in their lives. Almost everything is black or white. They have definite opinions about almost everything and very little interest in considering different viewpoints or new information that might change their old programs.

The learners who "inherit the earth" view education as a continuous lifelong process. They are constantly seeking new data, challenging their own assumptions, and willing to be introspective in analyzing their subconscious data bank to determine what programs may need to be updated and what old data may be erroneous and leading to decisions that no longer serve them well. Their egos are in check and the truth is more important than being right.

Let's examine how three different people may react differently to an identical situation, not based on the truth or reality of the situation, but rather based on their past experiences.

Imagine I am giving a lecture on this subject and I ask for three volunteers to come onto the stage. Jessica, Sarah, and Alex volunteer, and I seat them at a round table. I tell them we are going to have a discussion about snakes. We are going to talk about the garter snake. I tell them how the garter snake does not have fangs and eats insects, not people, so there is no rational reason why one should fear a garter snake. Intellectually they all agree. I then say, "Good, as long as we now know there is absolutely no reason to fear a garter snake, let me introduce you to Larry," and I pull out a live garter snake and place him on the table.

Before the snake even hits the table, Jessica is airborne, letting out a scream as she sprints offstage, down the aisle, and out the door never to be seen again. What just happened? Let's go through the four functions of decision-making.

1. **Perception:** Jessica perceives through her senses, in this case her eyes, an image of something alive, long and slender, that moves in a zigzag pattern.

2. **Comparison:** Jessica's subconscious memory bank finds some data that quickly tells her this is a "snake."

3. **Analysis:** While determining her reaction, it takes her only a nanosecond to bring up the subconscious recorded picture of that third-grade boy chasing her down the street with a garter snake. Jessica made a life decision at that time to never again get this close to a snake. In fact, if she is watching a movie and a snake appears on the screen, she will close her eyes or get up and leave the room. Just a picture of a snake can cause her anxiety and discomfort, not based on the reality of the situation but on past experience. Be assured, we all have "snakes" in our backgrounds that may still be causing irrational reactions to certain situations.

4. **Decision:** That's easy. Based on her analysis, Jessica makes a reactive decision and quickly exits.

Now, how does Sarah react to the same situation? She was raised on a farm and has been around animals her entire life. Some of her favorite creatures are snakes. In fact, Sarah lives with a pet boa constrictor in her condo.

Sarah goes through the same decision-making procedure as Jessica:

1. She **perceives** the object through her senses/eyes.

2. By **comparison** she identifies the object as a "snake."

3. A quick **analysis** stirs up warm feelings.

4. She makes a **decision** to move toward the snake and lovingly picks it up.

Now let's get to Alex, who is rather nonplussed over the whole situation. He is neither drawn toward snakes, nor does he fear them, so he remains inactive or neutral.

Our present decisions are based largely on our past experiences or information we have about something. We need to understand that we have also been conditioned to see certain things with a very subjective slant. This is where our prejudices come from.

Once we have the tools to bring about positive changes in our lives and we really learn how to use those tools, we have an enormous opportunity to examine our subconscious to determine what data is no longer relevant to our current life experience.

It's important to understand that when we perceive and identify something that strikes a negative habit pattern, the effect knocks out our analyzer, and we behave how we have been conditioned to respond: totally irrationally. By identifying our negative habit patterns, we can input new data into our subconscious that helps direct the reactions we desire, freeing us from the bonds of negative habit patterns.

The third area of the mind is the supraconscious. "Supra" means above or beyond consciousness. Most of the research in this area of the supraconscious has been done since Dr. Murphy wrote his book in 1963, so he does not reference it.

The supraconscious is our source of pure wisdom and creativity. As we will see in a subsequent chapter, it is in that area where we receive great inspiration and creative solutions, the area where the information needed to solve the situation transcends any data stored in our subconscious, or memory bank. The supraconscious is also our source of intuition, impetus, and free energy when we are constructively motivated. People considered to be real geniuses seem to tap into this vast reservoir at will.

To summarize, we have three areas of the mind that all interact with each other: the conscious, the subconscious, and the supraconscious. Unless we are aware of them and know how they interact, we are apt to drift through life on autopilot, always doing well in certain areas, poorly in others, and making the same mistakes over and over. Learning to understand the functions of each of these areas of the mind, plus the tools to revise old or outdated information and how to input new data, will help you achieve your goals with less effort, as you take true control of your life and direct it as you wish.

Reflection Practice

Take time today to reflect on a recent decision or reaction that was more negative than you would like. Examine what triggered it. Take the situation and break it down into the four steps of perception, comparison, analysis, and decision. Was the information behind your analysis accurate and up-to-date? Was your decision based on the reality of the situation? If not, you may learn that what drove your decision was an automatic response based on a past experience or memory—an old program or belief that may no longer be relevant.

22

The Supraconscious and Creative Problem-Solving

The solution lies within the problem. The answer is in every question. If you are presented with a difficult situation and you cannot see your way clear, the best procedure is to assume that Infinite Intelligence within your subconscious mind knows all and sees all, has the answer, and is revealing it to you now. Your new mental attitude that the creative intelligence is bringing about a happy solution will enable you to find the answer.

—Dr. Joseph Murphy

Although the concept of supraconscious came after Dr. Murphy's book was published, it is such an important part of our overall well-being that it must be included in any discussion of creative problem-solving.

As I wrote in the previous chapter, the conscious area of the mind, the subconscious, and the supraconscious are all spheres of our one mind, each with its own specific function. Let's now delve more deeply and provide you with a step-by-step procedure for engaging the transcendent and intuitive supraconscious in creative problem-solving.

First, let's examine the functions and characteristics of the supraconscious.

The supraconscious is the source of all pure creativity.

As we learned, the conscious area of the mind cannot create. It extrapolates data already stored in the subconscious, or accesses data and information from other sources, such as people (experts), books, computers, and so on. The conscious mind, through deductive reasoning, can solve problems when it accesses data that provides solutions to such problems.

On the other hand, the supraconscious has access to data not stored in the subconscious. It literally has access to universal knowledge, which leads to pure creativity beyond the normal reasoning of the conscious and subconscious. For example, artists who claim their creations (music, writing, and so forth) come to or through them, not from them. The idea(s) comes through on the level the conscious mind is working on and desires.

The supraconscious is capable of goal-oriented motivation.

There are two types of motivation:

1. **Constructive motivation:** This is when we are driven to achieve or attain something we really want to happen.

2. **Restrictive motivation:** This is doing something we have to do, which may often be the desire or need of someone else, such as our employer, parent, teacher, and so on. Our actions are not based on our desires; we do something because we have to.

The supraconscious provides free-flowing energy, but only when we are constructively motivated. We seldom get tired doing those things we are passionate about and love to do, while we are exhausted by doing things we have to do. To access this flow of energy, it is important that we align our goals with constructive motivation, and wherever possible reduce or eliminate our have-to-dos. Even changing our self-talk from "I have to" to "I choose to" reduces or eliminates the energy drain of restrictive motivation.

The supraconscious operates on a nonconscious level.
You can't watch it. There is no place to look for it.

The supraconscious has its own separate "computer system" that solves any problem assigned to it by the conscious mind, returning the best possible solution at that time.
"At that time" is important. If you choose not to use the supraconscious solution when you receive it, you may want to re-ask it for the solution to your problem if variables are added to the equation over time. The supraconscious may return to you the same solution you previously received, or a new solution more relevant to your problem or situation as it now stands. You don't need to use the supraconscious to work on every problem; 90 percent can be solved by the conscious mind once it has accessed the data for such a solution.

The supraconscious has instant access to all data stored in the subconscious and can discriminate between valid and invalid data in computing.
Remember, the data stored in our subconscious is the memory of prior experiences as well as the emotions associated with those experiences. It also contains "facts" that we learned earlier in our lives which may be completely erroneous or irrelevant to our present needs. Yet such erroneous data can often be a blockage to our perceiving the truth, or reality, of a given situation. The supraconscious can lead us to the truth.

The supraconscious cannot compute on any problem while the conscious mind is occupied with that problem.

When we "worry a problem to death" and can't seem to let go of it at the conscious level, we block the supraconscious from providing the answer we desire and need. In this chapter, I will show you how to constructively turn problems over to the supraconscious.

Worrying is a great waste of time! When we have repeatedly tried and failed to consciously solve a problem, we turn the problem over to the supraconscious knowing that we will receive the perfect answer or solution. This allows us to become detached from the problem at the conscious level, allowing great solutions to come to us from the supraconscious during moments of leisure and mental relaxation.

The supraconscious contains all monitor circuits.

Let me give you a simple and practical example. Let's say you normally wake up every morning around 6:00 AM. However, tomorrow morning you are going on vacation, and you have an early morning flight and need to wake up by 4:00 AM. You set the alarm and may even ask your traveling partner if she wouldn't mind calling you as an added precaution. As you crawl into bed that night, you are telling yourself how important it is to get up at four. The internal dialogue is a request from the conscious to the supraconscious to be awakened at four. You drift into a deep sleep and a few hours later you wake up with a start. You know it is much earlier than you normally wake up since it is still dark, and you roll over on your side to look at your digital clock, which reads 3:59 AM. You reach over to turn off the alarm just as the clock moves to 4:00 and simultaneously the clock starts to buzz just as your hand turns off the alarm. You turn on the light, sit on the edge of the bed thinking about the fun vacation you are about to begin, and the phone rings with your friend telling you it's time to get up. But who really woke you up? Your supraconscious woke you up because those were the instructions you gave it before you went to sleep. The supraconscious never sleeps.

The supraconscious makes all our actions and their effects fit into a pattern consistent with our self-concept.

If your self-concept about memory is, for example, "I can never remember names," the supraconscious will deliberately block our receiving the person's name in order "to make our effects fit into a pattern consistent with the level of our self-concept." Remember, our self-concept determines our level of performance in any area of our life (see chapter 23).

If we don't change the picture of our self that's recorded in our subconscious, we will continue to act in the same way, over and over. The key is to change the picture. And we do that with our own self-talk using affirmation processes and techniques (see chapter 24).

Five Steps to Creative Problem-Solving

Here is how we engage the supraconscious to help us solve problems, even when we seem to be at a dead end:

1. Define the problem.

2. Gather data.

3. Attempt to consciously solve the problem.

4. If unsuccessful, turn the problem over to the supraconscious.

5. Get your conscious mind busy elsewhere.

In Peter Drucker's wonderful book, *The Effective Executive*, he differentiates between efficiency and effectiveness. He writes, "Efficiency is the ability to do things right. Effectiveness is the ability to do the right things." He states if an executive has to make a hundred decisions, there may only be five of those that have any material outcome on the business.[4]

The point being, you don't need a supercomputer to count your change. Likewise, you don't need to engage the supraconscious to work on every problem. You will be able to solve most of your problems consciously. Engage the supraconscious only when the conscious approach fails.

1. Define the problem.
- Write the problem down.
- Make sure you clarify the problem and know exactly what needs resolution.

2. Gather data.
- This could be data from your own experience stored in your subconscious.
- You may engage a consultant or experts.
- Research written data from books, in reports, online, and so forth.

3. Attempt to consciously solve the problem.
- Work on the problem at the conscious level. Is it a black-and-white problem with only one correct solution, or one with multiple possible solutions for you to prioritize?
- In this step, speed is of the essence. Most problems will be solved in these first three steps, at the conscious level.

4. If unable to solve the problem at the conscious level, turn the problem over to the supraconscious.

- You have carefully followed the above three steps—clearly defined the problem, gathered information, and listed all the possible solutions you can think of—but nothing is working and find yourself repeating possible solutions.
- So turn it over to the supraconscious by mentally defining the problem and asking your supraconscious to take over and return the best possible solution (by a specified time, if there is a due date).

5. Get your conscious mind busy elsewhere.

- Detach from the problem at the conscious level. Creativity is a product of leisure. Go play golf, literally or figuratively.
- Don't take the problem back at the conscious level to see what progress is being made. Once you have turned it over to the supraconscious, have faith in its power.

How to Recognize a Supraconscious Solution

No church bells will ring. There will be no visions of angels or colored smoke. But you will know it came to you from the supraconscious because it will be a total solution. There will be no loose strings. You may feel a touch of chagrin, blinded by a flash of the obvious, while your own self-talk says, "Why didn't I think of that?"

Solutions will usually come to you when you are doing something passive. You might be driving, daydreaming, or having just awoken from a good night's sleep.

I have personally attended meetings where everyone was depending on me for an answer to a problem. I would arrive at the meeting without the solution, but still trusting that when it was my turn to speak, the answer would appear. And as I opened my mouth and words emerged, the perfect solution appeared. Even knowing how this material works, I am as amazed as everyone else. It works almost every time.

Where does the solution come from, you might ask. Carl Jung described the source of all knowledge as the collective unconscious, in which he theorizes that at some level of deeper consciousness we have potential contact with every person in the universe. This relates to theories of ESP (extrasensory perception) and mental telepathy. Just because we can't see something doesn't mean it doesn't exist.

More advanced science reveals how we are able to tap into the quantum field of information. Ralph Waldo Emerson refers to this as "the universal pool of all knowledge," which at some deeper level of consciousness we all have access to. Some may call it God or divine intervention, some might call it intuition or gut instinct. Regardless of one's beliefs, it all works the same way. The supraconscious has incredible, life-changing power for many.

Reflection Practice

This week, if you experience a problem at work or at home, practice working through the first three steps:

1. Define the problem.

2. Gather data.

3. Attempt to consciously solve the problem.

If you are unable to consciously find a solution, ask your supraconscious to help by following the last two steps:

4. Turn the problem over to the supraconscious.

5. Get your conscious mind busy elsewhere.

Remember, being able to relax the conscious mind allows the supraconscious to tap into a creative and universal source of wisdom. If you find it relaxing to garden, walk, jog, or meditate, do that as a way to calm your active mind so that a supraconscious solution can arise from within.

23

Self-Talk and Self-Concept

> The law of the mind is the law of belief. All your experiences,
> events, conditions, and acts are the reactions of your subconscious
> mind to your thoughts. Remember, it is not the thing believed in,
> but the belief in your own mind, which brings about the result.
>
> —**Dr. Joseph Murphy**

There may be *nothing* more powerful that affects our behavior and effectiveness than the beliefs and thoughts we create in our minds. The power of the law of belief largely determines the results of our endeavors, positively or negatively.

As small children we simply speak our thoughts out loud. I remember coming home from work one night and going up to my youngest son to see him before he went to bed. As I approached the door to his room I heard a bunch of chatter and commotion. I assumed he had friends or siblings in his room with him. But when I got to the doorway all I saw was BJ sitting on the floor with his back to me playing with several of his stuffed animals. He was having a grand time, engaged in an enthusiastic and animated conversation.

But the voice of each animal was that of my son. He was enjoying a real (to him) life experience with his animal friends.

As adults we often learn to keep these dialogues internal, though from time to time we may surprise ourselves by blurting thoughts out loud, even when we're alone. And we have all observed people (especially before cell phones) alone in their cars but apparently involved in expressive conversations with themselves.

When we talk with others we concurrently experience a streaming internal dialogue interpreting what the other person is saying and prepare our response while still "listening" to the person doing the talking. The most powerful dialogues, however, are those we have with ourselves when we are alone. This is the dialogue, or *self-talk*, of judgments and assessments, where we praise ourselves for something we did well or beat ourselves up for something we did poorly.

Remember, our conscious mind does all this self-talk, and it is important to become aware that it's also providing instructions to the subconscious, which in turn affects our actions, decisions, and beliefs—ultimately, our *self-concept*. As we become more knowing, more consciously aware that our present thoughts and self-talk determine our future, we can choose to more carefully monitor our minds to help us eliminate or change those thoughts that no longer serve us well.

How We Develop Self-Concept

We did not enter the world with a self-concept, nor did we have opinions or attitudes about anything. We may have inherited certain physical features, natural athleticism, a level of intelligence, but we did not inherit thoughts, opinions, or attitudes about anything, at least genetically.

As small children we are given an incredible amount of data by well-intentioned parents, siblings, teachers, coaches, and so on, about *everything*. "You are bad if you do this; you are good if you do that; this is right, this is wrong; these people are good, those people are bad; and be careful of those people, they don't share our religious/political/national beliefs."

By the time we are six years old we have a pretty good opinion of how the world (our world) looks. We have opinions and attitudes about a lot of things, and we have an early developed self-concept. And although they were not in our genes at birth, we typically "inherit" the views of our parents by simply living in their environment.

Let's say Logan does poorly on a math test. Maybe Logan was up late the night before watching television, didn't remember he had a math test the next day, didn't do his homework and, therefore, did poorly. The well-intentioned teacher mentions to Logan's mother that he is struggling in math (though not that Logan is poor at math). His mother tells Dad that Logan flunked the test. Dad gets mad and in frustration asks Logan why he is so lousy in math. Logan thinks of all the reasons why he must be lousy in math because Dad says he is.

From this point forward, when asked by his friends or siblings, Logan says, "I'm lousy at math." As he repeats this to himself with his own self-talk, he begins to form his self-concept: how he views himself relative to math. His self-talk forms his self-concept. His self-concept determines his effectiveness level or performance. As he performs consistent with his self-concept, his self-talk repeats the performance ("Gosh, I got another bad grade on my math test. I sure am terrible at math") further solidifying Logan's self-concept that he is "poor at math."

The *truth* is that Logan has all the capacity and natural intelligence in the world to do well in math. He may need some extra tutoring and encouragement, but once Logan begins to develop a negative opinion or attitude about his math skills, he will creatively sabotage any opportunities to get better. His newly formed attitude will cause him to say, "Why should I do my math homework? I'm awful at it anyway."

As small children we are very impressionable. We tend to accept at face value the strong opinions given to us by our authority figures. After all, we live in a land of giants. And when Mom, Dad, Ms. or Mr. Math Teacher, English Teacher, or Coach tells us firmly how we are good or bad at something, it strongly impacts our forming self-concepts. In some cases, one of these influencers even piles on with a comment like, "You know, Logan, you're just like your brother. He was lousy at math also!" exacerbating both Logan's negative self-concept and their own frustration. Pretty soon Logan is lying awake at night saying to himself, "I wish I wasn't so lousy at math, but I guess that's just the way I am."

By the time we reach adulthood we have pretty firm opinions about what we do well and do poorly, what we like and don't like, what kinds of people we prefer to be around and what kinds we try to avoid, and so on. We believe this is simply the way we are and are always going to be. In essence, we become prisoners of our own data, because we erroneously accept it as fact. Since most of us have never been taught how to make constructive changes in our behavior, we proceed with life as if on autopilot.

In my own life, understanding how the self-concept develops has made my wife and I better parents. We learned to catch our children doing things well, reinforcing behavior we were happy to see, rather than catching them doing things wrong. Scolding was no longer an option, but genuine praise was welcomed and appreciated. As Dr. Phil says, "It takes a thousand 'Atta-boys!' to erase one 'You're an idiot.'"

The Self-Esteem Cycle

Our self-talk forms our self-concept. Our self-concept determines our effectiveness level. This loop of self-talk to self-concept to how effectively we perform shapes our self-esteem, which influences our self-talk . . . and it can be a vicious cycle for many people, keeping them trapped for the balance of their lives. Generally, our performance is consistent with our self-concept, and weak performance *reinforces* an already-negative self-concept, ensuring we will continue to perform at the same level.

What happens in those rare cases where a person performs substantially better or substantially worse than their self-concept? In the case of superior performance, instead of saying, "Wow, look what I did! I am really good at _____," they say, "That never happens. I'm usually bad at that," increasing the probability that the next time their performance will match up their self-concept. Conversely, when the performance is lower than the self-concept, they will say something to themselves like, "That was really terrible. I am much better than that," and visualize a level of performance more in line with our self-concept. We become creative in order to get back in alignment with our core self-concept, not just when our performance is *worse* than our subconscious picture of reality, but to restore order any time our performance is *different*.

Why is it we sabotage our success when we start performing better than our self-concept? Because our self-concept is the regulating factor that determines our performance level. It is how we view ourselves in any area of our lives. And when we change the picture, positive or negative, we change the result of our performance, positive or negative.

If we want to truly improve our level of performance, we need to raise our core self-concepts. We have all developed conditioned responses that inhibit our ability to become all that we truly are. Most of us have been trained to believe that if we work hard on our performance, we can allow ourselves to think better of ourselves once we've attained a certain level of performance. Fortunately, it doesn't work that way. Instruction, training, and practice all have their place, but self-concept drives how we perform. Thinking better of yourself improves your performance, not the other way around.

By harnessing and expanding the power of our subconscious through conscious awareness and through the creative use of affirmations, we can break the chain of long-held beliefs, patterns, and self-concepts that no longer serve us well. We will learn how to do this in the next chapter.

Artie Buerk, a friend and colleague, shared with me his own realization of how self-talk and self-concept intertwine, and how empowering that knowledge can be if you want to break free of its negative hold:

> One of the most revealing factors to me was how we can go back in life and see the origins of our beliefs: how a person gets to be where they are in terms of strengths, weaknesses, things you think you're good at and things you think you're not good at. It gets down to understanding our self-talk and the power of the subconscious where many of these beliefs are stored, and no matter how much you try on a conscious basis to overcome them, they are very powerful. By understanding where I received some of my hang-ups, beliefs, and weaknesses, it is much easier to overcome them and develop new habits and beliefs that erase them. Understanding how this process of self-concept works allows you to move forward in life at your own pace without dragging anchors along with you.[5]

Reflection Practice

Consider these questions and write down your insights in a journal:

- What are your core self-concepts?
- How do your self-concepts affect your self-esteem?
- If your self-concept is hurting your self-esteem, identify possible sources for that belief or pattern. Examine if those sources may have created a negative habit of self-talk. More important, identify your positive self-concepts, how they were formed, and how your knowledge of that process can now assist in helping you erase what used to be a negative self-concept.

24

Affirmation and
Visualization Techniques

It is essential that you take charge of your thoughts so as to bring forth only desirable conditions. When your mind thinks correctly, when you understand the truth, when the thoughts deposited in your subconscious mind are constructive, harmonious, and peaceful, the magic working power of your subconscious will respond and bring about harmonious conditions, agreeable surroundings, and the best of everything.

—Dr. Joseph Murphy

Let's examine how the constructive use of affirmations can help reprogram our subconscious with updated, relevant, and truthful data that is consistent with who and what we want to be today, not who we used to be!

An affirmation is a statement of fact or belief, positive or negative, that tends to lead you toward the end result you expect. The statement of fact or belief may or may not be true, but we believe it to be true and act accordingly. Also, the expected end result may not be what you wanted. But by believing "I have never been good at

_____," you resign yourself to that limiting "truth" and program your subconscious with consistent data regarding your limitation, so that the subconscious ensures your behavior will consistently support your belief.

You and I have been using affirmations our entire lives. Any statement we make to ourselves or others that follows "I am" or "I" is an affirmation. The following are all affirmations:

I am a great spouse.

I am a lousy spouse.

I am a loving and patient parent.

I always lose my temper.

I am just not a good parent.

I am efficient and well organized.

I am sloppy and can never find a thing.

I am a great public speaker.

I always get nervous and screw up when I am in front of a group.

We were not born well organized or poorly organized. We were not born with poor or great public speaking skills. Our attitudes, opinions, and self-concept about any of these things, positive or negative, were developed. We were given factual data at very young ages by authority figures, which we interpreted to be true but which may or may not have been. Over many years, attitudes, opinions, beliefs, and self-talk were ingrained into us until we believe what we believe, which now feel like an unalterable truth in our personal reality. In fact, the beliefs have become so true that in extreme cases we are willing to die for them.

My first exposure to the formal teachings of affirmation techniques was when I attended the Omega Seminar, taught by its founder the late John Boyle. When I first started using affirmations, I was somewhat skeptical that by simply describing how I wanted to be or become, I could achieve such a change. Others attending Omega, who had been through the seminar previously and who had already been using affirmations for a period of time, raved about their successes. There seemed to be no limits to the areas of their lives that were affected (positively) through the deliberate use of affirmations. Relationships, parenting, health, business, and financial issues—all seemed to enjoy positive benefits or improvements in the lives of the people giving testimony to their own use of affirmations.

I thought, "If it can work for them, why couldn't it work for me?"

Fifty years later, I am still using affirmations. This is not to suggest I have not experienced setbacks or failures along the way. I once heard, "We teach that which we need to learn the most," and I certainly have lots of room for further growth and development, which I enthusiastically embrace. But the quality of my thinking has been positively affected, which has resulted in a greatly improved quality of how I have chosen to live my life.

One of our former employees, Linda Creswell, also attests to how affirmations not only benefit a company or organization, but also carry over into our personal lives:

Affirmations have been part of my life since Jim [Jensen] first introduced me to the concept many years ago. I was fortunate enough to have the job of presenting motivational/goal-setting seminars to the employees of our company. The employees benefitted greatly, thus benefitting the company. I believe, however, that I was the greatest recipient of the value of what I was teaching.

In the beginning, there was a huge chunk of new information I needed to absorb and become comfortable with enough to present to an audience, with the ability to field questions and facilitate conversations. Along the way, I still had a life, and it took a while to incorporate this new information into my daily habits. Those habits had to change in many ways, one of which was being away from home for a very large amount of time.

I was at that time living with my best friend and her fiancé. We always joked that we were the original *Three's Company*, and we got along very well.

A short time after I began my new venture, I started feeling an uncomfortable presence when I was interacting with my roommates. I stewed about it for a time and then thought to myself, well, if you are preaching this stuff in your seminars, you might want to put it to the test in your own life! That's an example of an "aha!" moment. So, following all the guidelines of writing good affirmations, I designed one addressing my situation and began affirming it daily. In a matter of just a few weeks, my roommates changed! The negative feelings lifted and the situation changed for good! So, you see, by affirming a positive statement of the situation I felt was negative, somehow my subconscious set about to propel me into actions that brought about the desired end result.

This is only one of the many things I was able to bring about in my life with positive affirmations. The value is tremendous, but it doesn't simply happen because you want it to happen. It takes work and careful attention to the details of creating your affirmations. Then, of course, you must do them. They are mental exercises and, just like physical exercises, if you don't do them nothing changes.[6]

The Affirmation Process

Presuming you have a list of goals or needs, use affirmations as a supplemental technique to assist you in attaining them. Through daily repetition, combined with visualization and strong emotional feelings, you condition—or recondition—your subconscious to help you achieve your goals.

To write an affirmation, construct a sentence in first person, present tense, describing the end result you desire as if it were already true today. In other words, you don't say, "My relationship with _____ will get better," or "My business will improve" (i.e., hope for something better in the future). Rather, you write the affirmation, "I enjoy an excellent relationship with _____, and it gets stronger every day," or "I am a very successful businessperson and find ways to improve my business each day."

Let's say you want to use affirmations to achieve a health goal. Let's use losing weight as an example. If getting on the scale today reports that your "current reality" is that you weigh 225 pounds and you develop a new goal to weigh 195 pounds, you would develop an affirmation that reads, "I look good and feel good at 195 pounds." This is written in the first person, present tense as though it were true today. You would not write the affirmation, "I am not overweight." The emphasis there is on being overweight, which is exactly the picture you don't want to create.

You may also develop a couple of supportive affirmations such as, "I eat only enough to maintain my perfect weight of 195 pounds," or "I enjoy exercising every day and never miss a day." Remember, our affirmations are intended to bring about a change in our behavior. The affirmation "I look good and feel good at 195 pounds" does not give us permission to move our bed next to the refrigerator!

Your affirmation should support visualizations that form the picture of success in your mind as you would like it to be. For example, when you say to yourself, "I enjoy an excellent relationship with _____," you picture yourself and that person together in a setting where you are enjoying each other's company and truly having "an excellent relationship." It can be a mental picture from a past experience you enjoyed together or an imaginary picture you simply create. Either picture, actual or imaginary, is recorded in the subconscious mind as though it actually happened—provided that you reinforce the picture with the last step: strong, positive emotional support.

The purpose of language (words) is to create or access an image. It is this visualization of an image (not the words) that records in the subconscious along with the feelings and emotions associated with that image. This is why the visualization that supports the words, accompanied by feelings and emotions, is such a necessary step to the affirmation process.

Now let me share with you six affirmations that have brought about substantial improvements in the lives of many. If this is your first use of affirmations, I recommend for the sake of simplicity and accessibility that you use just these for the first thirty days before adding additional affirmations.

I like (love) myself unconditionally.

This is a link to all other goals. It is an affirmation you should fully expect to use for the rest of your life. It is an affirmation that continues to build high self-esteem. We cannot give more love to another than that which we have for our self. With small children it is good to teach them to say, "I like myself." Over time this transforms to, "I love myself," which then transforms to, "Now that I love myself, I find that I love everyone."

I never devalue myself or others with destructive self-criticism.
It makes no sense to use the affirmation "I like myself" if we keep beating ourselves up with demeaning and destructive self-criticism. Some people with low self-esteem simply find it easier to accept a criticism than a compliment. To them I might say, "What if your best friend talked all day long about you the way you talk about yourself all day? Would you like to hang out with that person? Of course not." Immediately cease all destructive self-criticism. Make that the "old you." Return to the first affirmation, "I like (love) myself unconditionally."

I have unconditional warm regards for all people at all times.
The use of the word "all" is for emphasis. Certainly we cannot have warm regards for one who inflicts physical harm on their spouse, children, or others. We are simply seeking doors of opportunity to "have unconditional warm regards for all people at all times."

I am calm, peaceful, and healthy in both mind and body.
A growing body of scientific evidence shows us that so many health problems are related to tension, stress, and our inability to relax. In a rapidly growing technology and information world, it seems like someone keeps turning up the speed on the treadmill. We run faster but don't seem to run farther. We need to proactively manage the stress in our lives. If we let stress accumulate and don't have healthy outlets to allow it to siphon off, such as exercise or meditation, we may subject ourselves to physical dis-ease-ness.

I am self-determined and allow others the same right.
Most of us don't have a problem with the first half of this affirmation but may put up a little resistance when our business partner, spouse, or others exert their right to do the same.

This resistance usually comes from our need to control what is deemed to be important to ourselves. Those who have strong opinions or views that differ from our own are often falsely perceived as "against" us, leading to sayings like, "My way or the highway."

In a more enlightened environment, the need to control evolves to the desire to influence. And those with contrary views are respected and free to share their opinions with no fear of unjust reprisal. All discussions are open and valued, and the affirmation "I am completely self-determined and allow others the same right" is a strong value within the organization and family when contrary views are acknowledged and respected.

I am accountable for all my responses to other people and situations.

This means simply assuming accountability for all of our actions and reactions to the data input we receive through reading and conversations with others and ourselves. People who don't assume this accountability tend to blame others. Anything that is not perfect or happens to go wrong is never their fault but always the fault of the incoming data that may be contrary to their own personal views. So we need to understand and be respectful that everyone is entitled to his or her own perceptions. And if their views are contrary to our own, we have no need to blame them for the differences.

● ● ●

Begin using these six affirmations now, and only these affirmations, for the next thirty days. You may find people start saying positive, constructive things to you, like "What have you been doing? You're different!"

The Hidden Power within
Directed Visualization

Highly effective people have a very clear picture of what they want and where they are going. Their pictures are laser sharp. If it's a better home, they have a clear image of what that home looks like: the number of bedrooms and stories, pool, choice of neighborhoods, price range, and so on. Those who often fall short of their goals lack the intensity of a clearly defined picture. The affirmation "I want a better home," unsupported by the clarity of what that home looks like, dissipates the energy required to bring the goal to fruition.

We all know that when we take a magnifying glass on a hot summer day and hold it steady over a piece of paper it will erupt in flames. Think about this. The source of the energy, the sun, is constant. But the magnifying glass, when properly focused, harnesses that energy and magnifies its power manyfold. The same thing happens when we are crystal clear on what we want and continue to relentlessly hold that thought (picture) and the emotional intensity associated with that picture. We then both harness and magnify the power of the subconscious to manifest this picture and bring it into reality in our lives.

Now let me share with you an actual life experience that further documents the power of directed visualization. While flying home to Portland, Oregon, from Los Angeles, I read *The Inner Game of Tennis* by W. Timothy Gallwey. I was so impressed with Tim's writing that upon my arrival home, I picked up the telephone and began calling names or institutions mentioned in his book in an attempt to locate Tim.

After probably ten phone calls, I finally reached Tim at his home in Malibu, California. My first words were, "Tim, you don't know me, but I know you because I just read your book. I would like to invite you to come to Portland as my guest (and for a fee) to speak with our employees." And he did.

Tim came up to Portland to talk with our company's management team as well as the Oregon chapter of the Young Presidents' Organization, and as a result of that encounter, we developed a friendship and association. To this day I consider him one of the greatest mentors/teachers in my life. He really taught me the inner game of performance in any area of my life, by which he simply used tennis as a metaphor.

Tim invited my wife, Jeri, and me to join him and a group at Copper Mountain, Colorado. With coauthor Bob Kriegel, the Copper Mountain ski experience was to become the basis for Tim's next book, *Inner Skiing*. My wife and I have both been skiing since early childhood. I was on our high school ski team and raced competitively in pro-amateur events until age fifty. Even as I write these words, my wife and I are enjoying the month skiing in Sun Valley, Idaho. My point being that I am not a stranger to skiing or conventional ski instruction. Approximately thirty of us gathered together at Copper Mountain to experience a week of "inner skiing." As those of you who are skiers know, conventional ski instruction is very linear where the instructor observes you for a couple of ski turns and then says, "Bend knees" or "Put more weight on the downhill ski." The whole process is very mechanical.

None of this occurred at Copper Mountain, and yet our skiing proficiency increased dramatically. We began each day by grouping together after breakfast in one of the hotel's ballrooms where we were staying. We were in our ski attire and were invited to lie down on the carpet of the ballroom. We experienced a group deep relaxation exercise, and then with our eyes closed we were asked to visualize ourselves skiing. We were given several different visual scenarios such as different terrains, moguls, smooth slopes, steep slopes, and gentle slopes. In each scenario we were instructed to visualize ourselves skiing in that situation. We did this exercise for thirty to forty-five minutes. We then adjourned and gathered with our respective groups, put on our skis, and hit the slopes.

Once on the mountain, our instructor (really more a facilitator) would tell us he was going to go down the mountain making ten to fifteen turns, and then we were to follow and ski to him, one at a time. As each of us arrived, he only asked one question, "How was that compared to your visualization this morning?" The skier would respond, "I think I was bent over too far at the waist," or "I was using too much upper body movement," and so on. The instructor would simply say, "Good, just become more aware of your picture this morning."

There was no agreeing or disagreeing with our own assessment. There was no correctional instruction—simply, "Be aware of your mental picture this morning."

When you internally visualize yourself performing, you don't see yourself making mistakes. In skiing you don't visualize yourself falling, you see yourself skiing flawlessly. If you are visualizing your golf swing, you don't see yourself hitting the ball out of bounds, you see yourself hitting the ball down the center of the fairway or hitting the ball on the green next to the pin. If you are visualizing yourself playing the piano, you don't see yourself hitting the wrong keys. You see yourself playing the piece perfectly. This is a very important fact associated with visualizing performance, as it becomes the recorded subconscious picture and instructs how you are to perform.

As we skied our next ten to fifteen turns, once again the instructor would ask, "How was that?" We might answer by saying, "I wasn't as bent over at the waist and my upper body movement was more centered." The instructor wouldn't say good or bad, he would simply say, "Great, just continue to focus on your image during our visualization this morning." Throughout the day and the week our performance continued to improve with no instruction. We were our own "instructors."

One very impressive exercise occurred one day when we stood at the top of a double diamond run. These are the most difficult and challenging of all the ski runs on the mountain. Our instructor completely unbuckled his boots, and then asked each of us to do the same. He said, "When I get to the bottom, each of you ski down to me one at a time." He then took off skiing the terrain masterfully, and when he got to the bottom of the hill, he came to a sudden stop, planted his poles in the snow, and leapt completely out of his boots landing softly with his stocking feet in the snow. We were all flabbergasted.

When it came my turn to ski the run, I pushed off from the top, made a few awkward turns and heard my inner voice screaming, "I'm going to kill myself!" At another level, however, I was aware that our whole week was about turning off that voice of fear and doubt (what Tim calls "Self One") and trusting that my inner self ("Self Two") knows exactly what to do, if I can keep Self One out of the way.

So, I gently told Self One to shut up and surrendered to the trust that Self Two would know perfectly what to do. I skied the rest of that run as well as I have ever skied an expert run, and with my boots completely unbuckled, which is the complete antithesis of any conventional teachings or instruction. (And not something for anyone to try on his or her own.)

Self One is always clamoring for attention and is the little voice that loves to judge everything. Since I have become aware of how distracting and destructive Self One can be, when he comes knocking on my door now, I gently (not too gently) tell him to buzz off, and I re-center myself in the present. Whatever you clearly visualize and imprint into your subconscious mind will actualize into your present reality.

● ● ●

A colleague, Bob Sherwin, shared with me a testimonial extolling the virtues and power of visualization in manifesting his dream home. His first step was to write down in detail what his dream home was going to look and feel like—from how many bedrooms it would have to the size of the yard to the specific neighborhood he wanted to live in. Once he created his dream home visualization, he fueled that vision by tapping into his desire, imagination, and expectancy—turning his vision over to a higher source.

With daily practice and focus, Bob's visualization became a reality. When he walked into his dream house for the first time, he was amazed to find that it was exactly as he'd imagined. "I was so happy and in awe of what I was seeing. Everything I had written down and more was staring right back at me." The experience left a deep imprint on him, empowering him to realize that with focused attention, practice, and belief anything is possible:

Thoughts, feelings, attitudes, beliefs, choices, and decisions are all the seeds that we plant every day. Our desires, fears, and imagination are the fuel to our creations. Life, God, Source, or whatever you are comfortable with calling it is the soil, water, and sunshine that germinates, sprouts, and grows our seeds. It is our job to choose what seeds we want to plant.

What you sow, so shall ye reap! These are two-thousand-year-old spiritual laws that are just as valid as the physical laws we live with such as gravity. For best results . . . align with your Creator and your Creations and Choose wisely.[7]

Reflection Practice

Create your own affirmation with these four basic steps:

1. Write and repeat the affirmation to yourself in the first-person present tense as though you have already achieved the goal. For example: "I look good and feel good at (goal) pounds." "I like (person) unconditionally and enjoy a very good relationship with him/her."

2. Create a visual image of yourself having achieved the affirmation.

3. Notice how good you feel having accomplished the affirmation; savor the emotion.

4. Say the affirmation to yourself several times daily.

Each affirmation should last several seconds and should be repeated three to five times daily. Like goals, it is usually best to not have more than fifteen affirmations at a given time.

Our minds are most receptive to receiving affirmations when we first awake in the morning and at night as we go to bed. I know many people who keep their affirmations next to their bed on three-by-five cards or handheld devices.

Daily practice can bring about almost miraculous changes in one's life; but like anything else, knowing how to do them and doing them are two separate issues. Daily repetition, practicing your affirmations, will transform it into a habit. And like all other habits, you will feel cheated on the days you don't do them. I personally affirm to do my affirmations daily. I have a written statement, which precedes my affirmations: "I enjoy reading my affirmations the first thing each morning and the last thing in the evening. My daily practice of affirmations, combined with supportive visualization and strong emotional feelings, imprints into my subconscious mind the values, goals, and attitudes I deem important in the enrichment of my life."

25

The Power within Communication

> Begin *now* to sow thoughts of peace, happiness, right action, good
> will, and prosperity. Think quietly and with interest on these qual-
> ities and accept them fully in your conscious, reasoning mind.
>
> **—Dr. Joseph Murphy**

We have all had the experience of being in an audience listening
to someone and thinking, "Wow, *this* is really powerful! What
is *this*?" Let me share with you the mystery of the power that lies
within communication.

If asked where the power comes from, people may point to the
presenter's words, content, public speaking skills, personality, and so
on. These are various components that influence the success and value
of a presentation, but they are not the power.

Words, for example, are just words. In the English language,
we are restricted by the use or combination of twenty-six symbols,
our alphabet, which we must construct in an orderly sequence to
have meaning with the person, or people, hearing them. Often, the
same word may stimulate totally different images and feelings from

315

different people. Like in the example we saw earlier, when three people had a different reaction to the idea of a snake. They may likewise have similar responses to just the word "snake": the animal lover's favorite pet boa may conjure totally different emotions and responses for them than for the person whose memory of snakes is filled with horror from an early experience.

Knowing your audience and aligning word selection and content accordingly is a great skill, but it is not what creates the power within the communicator. The same could be said of the other presentation components used by the presenter. What, then, is the power?

Those who have mastered the art of communication know either intuitively or intellectually that the power lies within their ability to *imprint energy* within the minds, hearts, and souls of their audience. The imprinting of energy is a real phenomenon. It can't be specifically measured or quantified, but its impact is observable. Let me provide an example.

I used to do a lot of public speaking. I literally gave speeches around the world: Australia, New Zealand, Brazil, South Africa, England, Russia, Canada, and the United States. Most of the subject matter dealt with goal-setting, motivation, and our own unlimited potential. I knew the information I presented very well. Often, the content from one speech to another was identically the same. However, the speech itself and the audiences' response might be totally different. I learned early on (in my late twenties) that what I said wasn't nearly as important as *how* I said it. And, like all presenters, I had some off days mixed in with my on days. On one of my off days, my flight arrived late, I was rushed to the meeting place, and was thrust on the stage to make my appointed time slot. I covered the information well, received an ovation along with the customary enthusiastic audience members who remained behind to tell me how great my speech was. But I felt flat. I felt I had cheated the audience.

What was missing? The usual strong imprinting of my energy field with the audience.

I learned that to truly be of greatest value and service to my audience, I had to not only prepare my content but prepare my energy field and align it with the group consciousness and energy field of those people I was addressing.

Here is how I did that. An hour or so before my speech, I would find a room where I could be alone. I would go into a deep meditation, perhaps saying a prayer, such as, "Please give me the understanding and information that will provide the greatest benefit to the people I am meeting with today." I made a *conscious* effort to align my energy field as it was *that day* with the energy field of that day's physical environment.

For many years, I knew I had this power to communicate effectively, but I didn't know what the power was. After much contemplation, I realized that the power is the ability to create a lasting imprint of one's energy with the person, or people, with whom one is communicating. This makes so much sense.

Have you noticed, for example, how certain people can consistently tell jokes that bring people to their knees, while another person telling the same joke barely elicits a laugh? Let's say you are giving a speech and you know you are in the zone. At the end, you receive a standing ovation. You know you are on. We could take the videotape of your speech and give it to a professional presenter and ask him or her to memorize it, learn your delivery style, your gestures, anecdotes, jokes, and so on. Then have this same presenter address the theoretically same audience. Although the content is the same, the audience response may be completely different. What's missing is your energy imprint.

The purpose of language is to create or access an image, which in turn evokes feelings or emotions. What records in our subconscious are not the words, but rather the pictures the words trigger, as well as how we feel about those images. Therefore, when preparing your next speech or presentation, once you have completed the content, make sure that on the day of the presentation you allow sufficient time to develop your energy for that specific presentation. Visit the meeting room, visualize where you will be standing, where the audience will be, etc.

Our own energy field and vibrations change from day to day. That's why on days where my subject matter was the same as I had presented elsewhere I learned to not simply rely on my old notes but to sit down and rewrite the notes for that day's presentation. Although the words might be the same, how I *felt* would be different. My mental rehearsal was not so I would memorize the words, but rather to align my energy field and how I was *feeling* about those words that day. By following this practice, each of my presentations was unique even though the content may have appeared to be the same.

Sometimes a person who had attended my presentation the previous day might comment on how much more they got from the speech the second day. Ironically, the content was identical. What they noticed was a difference in my energy imprint between the two days, or in theirs. The audience brings their own energy and moods along, with a varying degree of receptivity. Often it seems that a great presenter *transcends* this variety to reach or imprint members of the audience.

Our energy imprint is as unique to us as our fingerprint. Unlike our fingerprint, which is static, our energy imprint fluctuates—but it is still uniquely ours. Additionally, it provides the context for a field of information. This combination is what is recorded in the memory of the recipient. It is like an actor or screenwriter portraying a strong emotional scene.

I remember when Alfred Hitchcock's classic movie *Psycho* was in theaters, and many women reported psychological problems and fears associated with taking a shower. The emotional impact of the murder scene where the actress is stabbed repeatedly in the shower affected the behavior of some viewers. In reality, what was happening in the theater was simply light reflecting off the screen. Emotionally, for the audience, this was really happening and the *imagined* horror and the associated disturbance was recorded in the memory bank of the viewers.

This analogy illustrates how the audience of a speech or, say, a Broadway play is affected by the presentation. Likewise, great authors transmit their energy imprint to the mind and emotional body of the reader through the written page. What the reader is getting is not just the words and their meaning, but the emotional surge and the energy imprint of the author at the precise moment he was writing those words. Authors will tell you the quality of their writing varies from sitting to sitting, based on how they are feeling and their level of energy when writing. And yet great authors create a consistency of energy.

The combination of your prepared content *together* with preparing and aligning your energy field to the audience will determine the effectiveness and impact of your message. Most people place their emphasis on the first half of this equation (content) and assume the second half (energy) will be what it will be. Deliberate preparation of your energy field is the equally, if not more, important discipline. Combined, this is what creates the power within communication.

The Gift of Silence

On the other side of communication, but equally valuable, is the practice of silence and the ability to listen. In many ways this falls under developing mastery in the art of communication. The people I learn the most from are those who talk the least and listen the most. When they do speak, they talk slowly, methodically, and efficiently. I hang on every word, spellbound. They are such great listeners and observers that they seem to acquire a knowledge and understanding of a person or a situation that simply transcends the spoken word. I am sure you have met such people, who hold you in their thrall, even as you are doing most of the talking. They have the capacity to draw out your innermost thoughts, feelings, and emotions by just *listening* to you. It's almost like standing naked in front of them. Their power truly lies in their silence.

When I am giving speeches to large audiences, I often ask people to raise their hand if they have ever had a class on speaking. Nearly everyone raises their hand. I then ask to see the hands of those who have had a class on listening. Seldom do I ever see a hand raised from that question.

Most people's skill in listening is just keeping their mouth shut as the other person is talking while they, themselves, are rehearsing what they are going to say when the other person stops. But listening isn't just striving to hear the other person talk. It's actively delving into the words being spoken and silently asking oneself, "What is this person really saying?" We have all had the experience of the person talking trying to make a point, and through our active listening process, often with questions, we find the person's words mean something different than what's actually coming out of his mouth. Being an active listener can often mean being a creative one as well.

In group settings, I pay more attention to those talking less than those dominating the conversation. I am drawn toward the quiet ones. Many years of observation and having graduated from the school of "teller sellers" have taught me to listen most to the quiet ones.

The outdated "teller seller" sales training is a "one size fits all" sales presentation to *every* sales prospect. Sales practitioners today are taught to listen more and talk less. They determine what they are going to say by asking the prospect what their spouse's interests are in the product or service and let those answers guide the salesperson in their response.

Listening to the quiet ones seems paradoxical but actually, it's not. Here's a story I'd like to share about how even in the world of sales, effective listening is a win-win.

In the past, a salesperson trained in direct selling and related sales was told to memorize a canned sales pitch with a large sign in the training center that read, "NO DEVIATION!" It was a one-size-fits-all practice of how the company's products and services were to be presented to prospective buyers.

I know this to be true because, as I described in the introduction, my first career, starting my senior year in college, was a wonderful eleven-year run with Encyclopædia Britannica. As I made progress to division manager, national sales manager of Australia and New Zealand, and eventually director of international sales, the sales process above was exactly how our salespeople were trained: the top salespeople learned how to *control* (and dominate) the sales environment with their prospective buyers.

Fortunately, today's consumers are much better informed and educated. Today's top salespeople are much more *creative* listeners who *enable* the prospective buyer, through a disciplined questioning process, to better assist the salesperson in focusing on how the benefits of the product or service might best fit the needs of that particular buyer. It is no longer the antiquated "one-size-fits-all" sales communication process, at least not for those salespeople who lead the company's sales results. Their genius is not how well they talk, but rather how well they *listen*.

Although the preceding parable is about the world of sales, its principles are just as applicable in other positions of leadership, parenting, relationships, coaching, and so on. The noise that drones out of the mouth of another often has little or nothing to do with what the talker is really feeling or trying to convey. There are so many other ways to "hear" what a person is thinking or feeling than just relying on what they say, for example, trusting your feelings, instincts, and observations.

Reflection Practice

Remember, to master the art of communication is to know that the power lies within your ability to *imprint energy* within the minds, hearts, and souls of your audience. Make it a point to mindfully practice this technique—especially if you have an important presentation or meeting—by speaking and listening with your full presence and attention, with honesty and empathy. After your presentation or conversation, take time to reflect and note what the experience was like and how you can improve the next time. As with all things, practice is mastery.

26

Resiliency: Bouncing Back from Setbacks

> When fear knocks at the door of your mind, or when worry, anxiety, and doubt cross your mind, behold your vision, your goal. Think of the infinite power within your subconscious mind, which you can generate by your thinking and imagining, and this will give you confidence, power, and courage. Keep on, persevere, "until the day breaks and the shadows flee away."
>
> —Dr. Joseph Murphy

We all experience setbacks. Whether in business, relationships, health, or finances, life will continue to provide us with challenges. However, it is often not the setback that immobilizes us but our own inability to deal with it. For our intentions, *Merriam-Webster* defines resilience as "an ability to recover from or adjust easily to misfortune or change."

High-performance people tend to also be highly resilient. When they get knocked down, they bounce back rapidly. In this chapter we will learn and discuss what gets in the way of most people bouncing back quickly from setbacks, such as:

- reluctance to let go of the past and forgive,
- distorted perception of the truth, and
- their inability or resistance to dissolve anger.

The information in this chapter is not intended to prevent future setbacks, which are simply part of the human condition, but rather enable you to handle them differently than you may have in the past. My goal is to provide you with tools and techniques that may increase your resiliency and more efficiently deal with future setbacks as you experience them.

As stated, one key factor affecting resilience is reluctance to let go of the past. The only time there is, is Now! There is no past, there is no future, and there never will be. And the only time we can be happy is now. Can you be happy yesterday? Go ahead, I'll wait. No, you can only be happy, or unhappy, now. You might be reflecting on something you did yesterday, but that happiness, or lack of it, you feel is now. Can you be happy tomorrow? No, you can't be happy tomorrow. Again, you can be happy now thinking about something you plan to do tomorrow, but again, that happiness is right now.

Since the only time we can be happy is now, how much of our nowness is being cheated of experiencing happiness by thoughts lamenting an unhappy experience yesterday? Or worrying (now) about something that may (or may not) happen in the future? That's why I love the acronym for FEAR: False Expectations Appearing Real.

So, if we truly desire to be happy and we understand the only time we can *be* happy is now, then we need to develop the discipline to *let go of the past*. Mistakes are part of the human condition. Often one of the funniest parts of a movie is at the end where they show the outtakes that occurred in the production of the film. And often those who laugh the hardest at their mistakes are the actors themselves.

A question to ask yourself: "What percentage of my now time is spent dwelling on events of the past or worrying about things that may or may not happen in the future?" Unhappy people are truly only present a small percentage of their time. For example, let's say 20 percent of their nowness time is being happy, but 40 percent of their nowness is being sad, because they're holding on to the previous nows (the past) that they lament, and the other 40 percent of their nowness is spent experiencing feelings of dread, worrying about the possible outcomes of some future nows.

Resilient and happy people live in the present and don't waste their precious nowness dwelling on the past or worrying about the future. They are individuals we might describe as having a positive attitude about life. Yes, they are human, and may still have moments where they reflect on a poor choice made in the past, or feel anxiety over an upcoming event, but those feelings don't dominate their waking time.

● ● ●

I was blessed early in my adult life to have Howard Behar as a partner and senior executive in two companies that I served as president. Later, Howard joined Starbucks, and when he retired he was president of Starbucks International.

In the two companies where we worked together, we had optional Human Development Programs where employees could learn affirmation techniques and meditation practices. Recently, as I was talking with Howard about his use of affirmations, he shared that at an early age affirmations helped him stay resilient and deal with personal setbacks. The following is what he said:

When I was in my twenties and thirties, I was constantly dissatisfied with where I was in life. I suffered a lot of depression and anxiety.

I started affirming daily, "I am enough, I have enough, I do enough." It took a while, but within a five-year period I was more satisfied with where I was in life. That affirmation allowed me to take a lot of pressure off myself and accomplish a lot more. The depression and anxiety disappeared, and I was a lot happier.

The most difficult thing I had to learn was to love myself. I would beat myself up if I made a mistake or didn't do the right thing for myself or someone else. I started affirming, "I love myself unconditionally." I kept that affirmation in my bathroom ensuring I would be reminded more than once to affirm my love and acceptance of myself. I thought if I could love myself in the bathroom I could love myself anywhere. And I do.[8]

Reflection Practice

Like Howard, when faced with a setback, I have also found affirmations are a helpful practice that can turn around my attitude and circumstances for the better. The practice will definitely help us react to setbacks with resilience and courage. For example, this is my personal affirmation: *I treat all setbacks as temporary. I am resilient and bounce back quickly from setbacks or misfortune.* (To create your own affirmation for a setback, take a look at chapter 24.)

Focusing attention on the present is another helpful practice. Ask yourself, Am I replaying a past setback over and over again? If so, use the time to constructively reflect on how you want to do things differently the next time: What is the positive learning experience I can glean from this setback? Afterward, guide yourself back to the present by sitting quietly, bringing your attention back to the Now with gentle, deep breaths.

27

Meditation

> He closes the door of his mind to all outside distractions as well
> as appearances, and then he quietly and knowingly turns over his
> request or desire to his subconscious mind, realizing that the intel-
> ligence of his mind will answer him according to his specific needs.
>
> —Dr. Joseph Murphy

For some time now I've been puzzled at how few people in our Western culture regularly practice some form of daily medita-tion, despite abundant data on its benefits. The scientific research on the physiological effects of meditation on the body, mind, and emotions is hard to refute. This is quantifiable, hard data developed in rigid laboratory conditions by quantum physicists. Add to this the countless testimonials from meditation practitioners who describe enhancements in the overall quality of their lives.

I was blessed to serve on the board of directors of the Institute of Noetic Sciences (IONS) for over a decade. During that time I developed a relationship with Dean Radin, PhD, chief scientist at IONS and coeditor-in-chief of the medical journal *Explore*, which publishes many research papers on meditation. I asked Dr. Radin his view on meditation, and he provided this response:

> Meditation, once considered an exotic import from the East, introduced to the West mainly by stoned-out hippies, was not a topic that most respectable scientists considered worthy of investigation. That dismissive attitude began to change in the 1970s, when a few articles about the benefits of meditation appeared in the scientific literature. The pace of publications slowly began to increase as investigators repeatedly observed other benefits of meditation, and over the course of the next five decades the literature increased from a handful of studies to thousands of controlled experiments.
>
> Today, based on laboratory data, there is no longer any question that meditation promotes physical and mental health. Many top-tier journals regularly publish studies investigating the use of meditation for improving sleep, treating depression, reducing anxiety, improving blood pressure, down-regulating inflammatory genes, up-regulating immune system genes, improving insulin and glucose genes, and even increasing telomerase, which indicates a slowing of the aging process. There is also some evidence that meditation increases prosocial behavior, like improved compassion and empathy.
>
> As a result, most meditation research today is no longer focused on whether it is beneficial, but on the underlying mechanisms for how it works, on comparisons of different kinds of contemplative practice, and on advanced mental capacities associated with long-term meditation practice.[9]

I believe a growing and evolving individual cannot help but become more than a little intrigued about meditation if they examine its practice with an open mind. Other reported results of regular meditation practice include

- improved brain functioning,
- increased creativity and intelligence,
- faster reaction time,
- reduction of high blood pressure, and
- reduced anxiety and depression.

More and more leaders in the corporate world have been taking note of the benefits of meditation, including Rupert Murdoch, Bill Ford, Oprah Winfrey, Robert Stiller, and Arianna Huffington. A number of Fortune 500 companies, including Google, AOL, Apple, and Aetna, offer meditation and mindfulness classes for employees. Corporate America is beginning to understand that meditation can help employees and top executives achieve and sustain a high level of success.

In the remaining pages of this chapter, I share my own experience with meditation and outline the benefits of regular meditation on physical, mental, emotional, and spiritual aspects of being.

● ● ●

My wife and I were first introduced to Transcendental Meditation (TM) over forty-five years ago, and we have practiced TM, and other forms of meditation, ever since.

I do not endorse TM over any other means of meditation; in fact, Qigong is the most powerful meditation I have experienced in moving energy through the body for better healing and immune enhancement. Whether learning TM, Qigong, or any other form of meditation, I have never been told that one meditation is necessarily better than another. I have never been asked for money (beyond an instructor's fees) or asked to introduce others to a particular following. Consequently, there are no dogmas or belief systems taught in my own experience with meditation. When I exercise my body, I don't necessarily believe in one form of exercise over another. One day I may jog, on another day lift weights, and then the following day participate in a yoga class. Exercise is exercise just as meditation is meditation.

I have benefitted immensely from the regular practice of meditation. I have a great deal of energy and fit the description of a typical type A personality. I can be intense, determined, and easily motivated. When I meditate regularly, I feel more calm, quieter, and balanced. I simply feel better.

Now to the physical. Interestingly, the founder of TM, Maharishi Mahesh Yogi, was a physicist. He and his organization conducted research on the physical benefits of meditation (specifically, TM), which showed that while in a meditative state pulse rate slowed, blood pressure decreased, metabolism increased, and brain wave activity shifted from beta to alpha, and even theta (our most creative and serene state of mind). Other physiological measurements indicating well-being and general health were also noted.

When I feel run-down, fatigued, or concerned I might become ill, I direct energy to the particular area of my body that I think needs a boost, or healing, and most often ward off the physical manifestation of my dis-ease-ness. Knock on wood, but I can't remember having had a common cold or the flu in over twenty years.

I'd like to share one story for which I have no scientific explanation.

Years ago, when my family was living in Sun Valley, Idaho, I was under the weather with a sore throat and didn't seem to be getting any better (unusual for me). I saw a doctor friend of mine who examined me and told me I had an acute case of mononucleosis. At his insistence, I was admitted to the hospital overnight for intravenous feedings and whatever else. I was told it could take as long as a month to fully recover, which was unacceptable to me as I was moving to Seattle the following week to begin a new career. My physician friend smiled empathetically and said, "Jim, I appreciate your positive attitude, but your red cells and white cells . . ." and proceeded to tell me, medically, why it would take so many weeks to restore my system to its normal health.

Well, he had his schedule and I had mine. I was very determined to heal my body *that* night.

I put myself into a deep meditative state and visualized a white-light energy healing and restoring my blood cells to normal. I don't think I ever fell asleep, but I was in the deepest state of rest (theta), and for the longest time that I had ever (or have since) experienced. It was quite something.

In the morning I felt very energized and called my wife, asking her to please bring my jogging shoes, shorts, and a T-shirt to the hospital. I asked the nurses to remove the tubes in my arms and told the on-duty doctor I was going for a run. He didn't want me to leave the hospital and told me I wouldn't be able to run a hundred feet. He was right. Instead, I ran eight miles around what Sun Valley residents call "The Loop." I felt great!

When I returned to the hospital, my physician friend kindly told me I was crazy. I asked him to draw blood from my arm and call me at home when he had the test results. He called me a couple of hours later and asked me to return to the hospital because they had to do another blood test. I said, "You didn't find any mono, did you?" I returned to the hospital for a second blood test, which also returned negative.

He had never seen anything like this before, nor had I. There was no scientific explanation for it, but at a deeper level I knew I had experienced a healing, which I believe to have been facilitated through my deep meditation. I didn't make any fanfare about it, but simply said, "Thank you, God," and went about my work.

Mentally, some of my greatest ideas and inspirations come to me in meditation. Meditation quiets the mind. When you quiet your mind, you are able to listen or better hear those thoughts that may come from your higher consciousness or the creative center of your mind.

●　●　●

I had the good fortune to become the president of Grantree Furniture Rental headquartered in Portland, Oregon. We were a young, highly energetic company experiencing rapid growth and soon became the leader within our industry. We worked hard and played hard.

I can remember time after time having to address a group of managers or employees, not sure of what I was going to say. Approximately forty-five minutes before I was to speak, I would find a quiet room and begin to meditate. Prior to going into the meditation, I would ask my higher self (my supraconscious) to please provide me with the most appropriate thoughts for that particular occasion. As I entered a meditative state, I would not think about my speech, the audience, or how "I" (the ego) was going to perform. I would simply quiet my mind, go into a deep meditative state, and *trust* the best information would be given to me when I came out of it.

Twenty minutes later, I would return to Earth, refreshed and relaxed; I would jot down a couple of thoughts and proceed to meet my audience. Several times, as I was walking to the podium or front of the room, I still wouldn't know what I was going to say, until my lips opened and the right words came out.

Emotionally, I think of meditation as the great soother, like certain adages, such as "Things are never as good or as bad as they seem" or "There are no stressful situations, only stressful responses."

But I, like you, experience stress and anxiety. Usually because of an overload of incoming thoughts and what-if scenarios, played over and over in my mind. As meditation quiets the mind, it shuts down the excessive chatter and takes us within, to that sanctuary of peace and stillness. It is also the pathway to the domain of the supraconscious. When the meditation is over, the problem isn't necessarily gone, but the anxiety and tension are, and our perspective is clear. We are able to see the truth about the situation without anxiety and fear, allowing us to more clearly sort out options and possible solutions. Meditation would certainly benefit those who experience excessive anxiety or depression.

A former employee, Barbara Basile, wrote to me how meditation and affirmations changed the path of her life:

> In my early twenties I worked for a mega-corporation. I was surprised when I was laid off along with 4,999 other employees, two weeks before Christmas. In the summer of the next year I began to work for a smaller corporation. I was pleased to feel valued, even as a new employee. There was an attitude of respect, and well-thought-out training. This corporation made available a myriad of tools for my success, which of course translated to the company's success. There were seminars on achieving, managing stress, even meditations available to any employee.

Daily meditation was key to managing my stress and translated into a consistent, positive management style, fostered by the company. The affirmations were essential to maintaining an awareness of supportive behaviors, encompassing everyone concerned regarding company goals and philosophy of each employee's self-worth.

Affirmations, meditations, and visualizations have been tools that have helped me realize who *I am*. It inspired me to go back to school to study psychology. I work with domestic violence offenders, and I teach these tools to troubled children and families I work with. I know from the feedback I receive from my clients that these practices have a huge positive impact. Now thirty-eight years later, each tool remains an integral part of my life, and I have had the privilege of teaching the same to many others.[10]

Reflection Practice

If you already meditate, keep practicing, and make it a daily ritual. If you haven't tried, this is a great opportunity to start. Start slow and easy, maybe five or ten minutes a day for a couple of weeks. If you feel like you need to schedule that time, then do it, or you can use one of the many available meditation apps. Guided meditations are also a good option.

Here's a simple 10-to-15-minute meditation for beginners:

1. Sit or lie comfortably.

2. Close your eyes.

3. Breathe naturally.

4. Focus your attention on the breath as it flows in and out. Feel how your body moves with each inhalation and exhalation.

28

From Me to We: Principles of Enlightened Leadership

A successful person loves his work and expresses himself fully. Success is contingent upon a higher ideal than the mere accumulation of riches. The man of success is the man who possesses great psychological and spiritual understanding. Many of the great industrialists today depend upon the correct use of the subconscious minds for their success.

—Dr. Joseph Murphy

Have you ever wondered how some people seem to like almost everyone while others are often grouchy and constantly critical of every little thing? In the world of business, much has been written about corporate cultures and the impact they can have—positive or negative—on a company's success.

I have been blessed to have been part of the management of companies where the leadership was trained to catch an employee doing something right (rather than wrong) and reinforce behavior with praise and positive reinforcement. These are great companies to work with: where management constantly acknowledges the members in their work unit for all their positive, successful results. I find joy, happiness, and success in supporting a corporate culture based in abundance consciousness rather than scarcity consciousness. I once said to my personal attorney of more than forty years, "Gerry, I am simply the kind of person who always sees the glass as half full." He laughed and replied, "Jensen, you don't see the glass as half full, you see it as overflowing!" This is how I have chosen to live my life.

Here's how to distinguish between these two opposing management environments:

Abundance Consciousness	Scarcity Consciousness
Centered in love	Centered in fear
Trusts most everyone	Distrusts everyone
It's all about the team	It's all about me
Great place to work	Just a job
Purpose driven	Ego driven
Loyal to team	Primary loyalty to self
Learner: lifelong learning	Learned: already knows it all
The glass is half full	The glass is half empty
Produces energy	Produces exhaustion
Inclusive of all	Exclusive of most
Creative listener	Teller seller

It doesn't mean that management and employees in abundance-consciousness environments don't make mistakes or that they don't sometimes need constructive criticism. As anywhere, some employees aren't a good fit and may need to be replaced. It simply means the workplace atmosphere is generally very positive and not fear-based. In these environments, work becomes fun.

Companies that place high value on the quality of their employees, and on building a workplace that fosters personal growth in addition to employee training, earn reputations for being good companies and also attract employees with high self-esteem. People much prefer being valued and appreciated as opposed to being criticized and denigrated. The same is true outside the workplace.

Some managers just seem to get up on the wrong side of the bed every morning and come to work with an attitude of trying to catch people doing things wrong, almost taking pleasure in reprimanding employees and putting transgressors in their place. Managers with such attitudes usually have a low self-concept, and their modus operandi is to try to make themselves look important by putting others down. Then they wonder why they just can't find good people to work for their company. Only people with low self-concepts subject themselves to working in such a negative environment. For them, it's only about receiving a paycheck. "Fun" is what happens away from work. Unfortunately, the same people who manage their companies with such negative attitudes often manage their families and personal friendships with the same arrogance and disrespect.

The best leaders I know have excellent human relations skills. They genuinely like people. They have a great attitude, and attitudes are a matter of personal choice. So, why wouldn't we choose to value high human relations skills? Life is so much more fun and things come together more effortlessly with good teams working toward a shared vision, each team member embracing both their individual goals and the goals of their fellow teammates.

I recommend these two excellent affirmations to help develop a high sense of human relations (the second one was first introduced in chapter 24): "I have unconditional warm regards for all people at all times," and "I am self-determined and allow others the same right!"

In the first affirmation, the word "all" is used for emphasis. The most important words in the second affirmation are, "and allow others the same right!" Many people are self-determined but don't allow others the same right. These people tend to be consistently disagreeable. When we "allow others the same right," we can agree to disagree without becoming disagreeable.

Working to develop great human relations is a worthy goal and adds greatly to the value of those who do. Leaders who have great human relations skills truly value and like their employees. Not just as employees but as people.

I haven't met Tony Hsieh, the CEO of Zappos, but I was inspired reading his book, *Delivering Happiness*. Although conceived as a customer experience, Tony and his team extended delivering happiness to the employees, their families, vendors, shareholders, and everyone Zappos has the opportunity to touch. Tony really gets it! (I highly recommend his book.)

These kinds of new-age management styles and corporate cultures were not a subject of much discussion within companies fifty years ago. Most management was traditional, top-down, with little interest or patience in hearing ideas or receiving input from the workforce. The organizational hierarchy was sacrosanct and most employees lived in fear of upsetting the boss. This attitude fostered the growth of labor unions.

In today's successful organizations that have transcended the old management paradigm, there is an almost inverted pyramid where enlightened leaders understand the value and importance of working *for* those who report to them. They are constantly receiving input and feedback from their employees to better understand the root causes of production challenges. The leader's role is to help to eliminate barriers and obstacles to heightened performance.

Many books have been written about organizational development and management structure and style. Consider that, in the year 1900, over 90 percent of the workforce in the United States was in agriculture, mostly male farmers. The industrial revolution was just beginning to birth. Within fifteen years the young men of that same class were enlisting or being drafted into the armed services to serve in World War I. For many, military service was their first "model" of management.

By necessity, this was a top-down model. For things to work there had to be clear understanding of rank. One was taught to respect the uniform (title) as much as the person who wore it. Again, completely understandable (and appreciated). When under enemy fire, no one is taking time to build consensus or survey employees for input. We won the war largely because of strong leadership, great strategic planning at the top, and a military who followed orders as directed. So, what is the relevance here to organizational development?

When our soldiers returned home, there was a great migration of families moving from the farmlands to the big cities. It was easy for these young men to slide into companies and corporations that had similar management structures. Even language learned in the military became common within the workplace:

"We're under the gun to get this done."

"We're on the firing line to achieve our quota."

"Make sure you're well armed when you attend that meeting."

"We need to attack our competition with full force. They are the enemy!"

"This is not the time to retreat."

"You're fired!"

The primary motivation for people to become leaders in the old management paradigm was to have personal power, to control others, and to be served by the workforce. In the strictly top-down environment, titles were very important and you never dared question a person of higher authority.

"Jensen, you don't talk to vice presidents that way!" It was not uncommon for bosses to strut their power by loudly dressing down an underling in front of fellow workers. Human Resource departments and notions of workers' rights and harassment didn't exist. The primary mood within the company was fear-based. Fear that you might do or say the wrong thing that could lead to you getting fired. The environment was suppressive. And beneath the external veneer of the macho boss was a person also driven by fear and doubt. Fear of failure and fear of others learning of his own insecurities and doubts as to whether he really had the right stuff to succeed.

These kinds of environments attracted workers with a predominantly low self-concept. They literally felt "worthless" and since their primary motivation was survival, they just kept their mouths shut and did what they were told to do. As time progressed, more and more people were able to attend college and the general education level increased. In the 1950s seminars, books, and teachings emerged that dealt with the subject of self-discovery and the importance of developing our self-concept and self-esteem. We began to see more enlightened leaders: leaders who truly recognized the ingenuity of the human spirit in all people, and leaders whose self-concepts were well intact and who appreciated and valued creative ideas and solutions from anywhere within the organization. They created environments that fostered openness and developed reward and recognition systems for such valued contributions.

Enlightened leaders perceive themselves as teachers and mentors. Instead of seeking personal power, they recognize the value of empowering others. Rather than controlling their employees, they are inspired to influence them. They realize when you control someone you no longer influence them. As a parent, for example, would you rather control your children or influence them? I hope the answer is obvious. Lastly, an enlightened leader is not into being served by others but rather being of service to his or her fellow workers.

Which work environment would you choose to work in?

Reflection Practice

List the attributes of the leader you admire and want to emulate. Consider how you can show up as that kind of leader in your life, whether in the home, workplace, or community. Take this week to start practicing one of the traits you listed. For example, I admire the skill of listening, so as a parent and grandparent, I practice deep listening in my relationships by showing up for my family, fully present and without judgment.

Conclusion:
Expanding on Enlightenment

In the pursuit of knowledge, something is added every day. In the pursuit of enlightenment, something is dropped every day.

—Lao-tzu

So, what have we learned? We should have an understanding of the three areas of the mind—conscious, subconscious, and supraconscious—and how they interact with each other.

Remember, the subconscious is our hard drive, where we store learning and other experiences, and the feelings we associate with them. It is constantly at work, carrying out the instructions given to it by the conscious mind, for better or for worse. It is nonjudgmental and proceeds to help facilitate the wishes and commands from the conscious mind. It also monitors and manages our bodily functions.

The conscious mind determines what is good or bad, right or wrong: not always the Truth but rather its perception of the truth based on prior data and experiences stored in the subconscious. It directs us to move toward comforting, good-feeling events and situations and to avoid uncomfortable, painful situations (that is, moving toward pleasure and away from discomfort).

The supraconscious is our higher source of all pure creativity and provides the conscious mind access to all data or information not stored in our subconscious memory bank. It also provides generous, free-flowing energy when we are constructively motivated.

It is important to understand that consciousness creates matter and form. Matter does not create consciousness. This book—in print, as an ebook, or however you are reading these pages—was created by conscious thought, just as were the words written. The chair you are sitting in or the bed you are lying on was created through consciousness. Look around the room you are in right now and realize that everything you see was created through conscious intent.

So, we have been given this incredible gift of creativity. We truly create our own reality through our conscious intent. Now that you know how this works and have the tools to create whatever you want, you can begin to eliminate the false beliefs and erroneous data you have carried for too long and that no longer serve you well.

To close this book, I will leave with you a personal experience that expanded my concept of enlightenment. Remember my story in the introduction, about meeting my friend Tim Gallwey after reading his book and immediately tracking him down to come speak at my work?

Tim is one of the clearest thinkers I have ever met. He always seems to have a profound answer for any question I ask, regardless of the subject. I used to think that no human being could have possibly learned that much and that somehow Tim had opened certain channels to receive knowledge beyond what he personally "knew."

After some time, I asked Tim this question on one of our many get-togethers: "Tim, what is enlightenment?"

I don't remember his exact words, but I do believe I remember his meaning. (Forgive me, Tim, if I take a little editorial license here.) The essence of what I heard, which has stayed with me for many years, was this: **Enlightenment becomes a process where we begin to discover that everything we have always thought we wanted to be, we already are.** Wrapped up in this piece of skin we call "me" already exists total love, truth, wisdom, knowledge, intelligence, beauty, and so on. But to become more of that, which in truth we already are, requires an ability to become less of that which we *think* we are.

For the truly enlightened individual, therefore, growth becomes a process of subtraction. Most of us have been trained to believe that growth is a process of addition. We become addicted to adding on. Better car, bigger house, more toys, and so forth.

Tim implied that real growth occurs when we begin to unlearn or take away those things that are interfering with our ability to express that which in truth we already are. I took Tim to mean we should eliminate beliefs, attitudes, and outdated ways of viewing the world that simply no longer serve us.

When we first arrived in this world, we were like an empty vessel. We had no opinions, attitudes, beliefs, or prejudices about anything. I think this is part of the fascination that attracts us to infants and small children. We are almost reverent of their innocence and belief that nothing is impossible. Parents, teachers, coaches, and others we admire as small children also have significant impact and influence on shaping us to become who we think we are. It is the "who we think we are," our persona, how we describe ourselves to others, that causes us to become that description, filtered through our perceptions of others' expectations of us. Most of us go through life not understanding or realizing that this description (or self-image) is no different than a costume. But, we mistakenly come to believe the costume is the real us.

When we come to realize our true self is often radically different than our self-perception, we can begin to grow. And once again growth becomes the process of subtracting the myths and false beliefs that have hindered our growth and development. Finally, we are liberated and empowered when we come to see the difference between the Truth and our perception of the "truth." We become fully accountable for our actions and no longer play the role of the victim of destiny. This is enlightenment.

Lastly, knowing this Truth and being this Truth are not always the same. Having information about a subject, in this case enlightenment, doesn't prove that the person speaking or writing on enlightenment is necessarily enlightened. As I say about myself, "God is always with me, but I may not always be with God." (It has been said we teach that which we need to learn the most.) We put a lot of time and effort into the making of our costume, and old habits are sometimes hard to change. But it gets easier once we learn how that costume was created and we clearly see it for what it is.

● ● ●

Thank you for joining Dr. Murphy and me on this journey. You really are terrific just the way you are. Accept your magnificence.

Visualize yourself as a tugboat plowing through the water with great effort towing a barge full of garbage. Think of the barge as your excess baggage. Think of the barge housing all the garbage you have collected along the way that is no longer relevant to how you choose to live your life today. In our homes we throw out the garbage daily. Why not do the same thing with your own mind?

And now you know how. Cut the line towing the garbage so your tugboat can now joyfully cruise through the waters of life relieved of the burden of towing unnecessary weight.

Much love to you all and to the better world we all have the capacity to cocreate as our own legacy and gift to our children's and grandchildren's generations.

> The artist does not identify with the colors he uses. He knows he chooses them, and applies them with a brush. So you paint your reality with your ideas in the same manner. You are not your ideas, nor even your thoughts. You are the self who experiences them. If a painter finds his hands stained with pigment at the end of a day, he can wash the stain off easily, knowing its nature. If you think that limiting thoughts are a portion of you, permanently attached therefore, you will not think of washing them off.[11]
>
> —**Jane Roberts,** *The Nature of Personal Reality*

EXPAND
the
POWER
of Your
SUBCONSCIOUS
MIND

Acknowledgments

My first acknowledgment is to you, the reader. The fact that the title of this book would be of interest to you speaks volumes of where you are in your own evolution. Thank you. I welcome you as a fellow change agent to assist in the transformation of the quality of life on our planet.

Next, I would like to thank the more than five thousand employees I have had the privilege to work with in three companies over a period of thirty years. Each company became the leading company within its respective industry. Many of the principles taught in this book were made widely available to our workforce(s). For those who chose to drink the "Kool-Aid," I have witnessed many, many significant transformational changes both personally and professionally. I love you (all) unconditionally.

To my life partner, Jeri, who has read the multiple drafts of my manuscript many times and provided her constructive input to help make this a better book.

And to my executive assistant of twenty-three years, Mary Fabish, who has typed every word in this book many, many times and made valuable editorial contributions. Thank you so much, Mary.

To our daughter Julie and son-in-law Ted Kalmus, who surprised me on my birthday by gifting four hours of review time on the latest draft of my book (it having been clandestinely procured for them by Mary). Their observations and input led to many changes in the final draft of the book.

Thanks to our daughter Jill and her husband, Jason Anderson, for their input as well as assistance in graphic design. And to our sons, Brian and JJ, and our beautiful daughter-in-law, Wendy, for their continuing support. Special kudos to JJ and Wendy for their technical assistance.

And to the people who made it possible for you to be reading this now. Thank you, Richard and Michele Cohn, for your leadership, and to all the people at Beyond Words Publishing—Emily Einolander, Lindsay Brown, Emmalisa Sparrow Wood, Jenefer Angell, Ashley Van Winkle, Devon Smith, Bill Brunson, Corinne Kalasky, and Brennah Hale. You are creative and a delight to work with. And a special thank you to our editor, Emily Han, who has worked tirelessly for several months with my executive assistant, Mary, and myself. And thank you Devra Jacobs for your marketing creativity and the development of my new website. Breanne Reeves, I look forward to your leadership in the creation of our speaking engagements.

My heartfelt thanks to my longtime friend, Dr. Lee Pulos, who so generously gave of his time and professional expertise in making relevant and insightful contributions to this book. Your friendship has enriched my life through many fun-filled and intriguing journeys of adventure and discovery.

Lastly, a special thank you to the Trifilm Productions team led by its CEO, Mike Morrisroe, and the late founder and CEO, Mark Dickison. Thank you for your vision in creating the runway to help ensure the readership we believe this book deserves.

Thank you all so much.

Special Recognition

I would like to recognize an organization that has special meaning to me. I invite you to explore how its teachings may be of value to your life as well.

Institute of Noetic Sciences

Our Vision

The Institute of Noetic Sciences (IONS) serves an emerging movement of globally conscious citizens dedicated to manifesting our highest capacities. We believe that consciousness is essential to a paradigm shift that will lead to a more sustainable world. We encourage open-minded explorations of consciousness through the meeting of science and spirit. We take inspiration from the great discoveries of human history that have been sourced from insight and intuition and that have harnessed reason and logic for their outer expression. It is our conviction that systematic inquiries into consciousness will catalyze positive concrete transformations in the world. In this process, our vision is to help birth a new worldview that recognizes our basic interconnectedness and interdependence and promotes the flourishing of life in all its magnificent forms.

Our Mission

Broadening our knowledge of the nature and potentials of mind and consciousness and applying that knowledge to enhancing human well-being and the quality of life on the planet.

EarthRise Retreat Center is located on two hundred acres of rolling hills about ten minutes from downtown Petaluma, California.

101 San Antonio Road

Petaluma, CA 94952

Tel: 707-775-3500

Fax: 707-781-7420

www.noetic.org

Notes

1. Joseph Murphy, *The Power of Your Subconscious Mind* (San Francisco: Reward Books/Open Library and Internet Archive, 200), 10–11.

2. Bruce H. Lipton and Steve Bhaerman, *Spontaneous Evolution: Our Positive Future (and a Way to Get There from Here)* (Carlsbad, CA: Hay House, 2009), 343.

3. Eric Hoffer, *Reflections on the Human Condition* (Titusville, NJ: Hopewell Publications, 2006), 26.

4. Peter F. Drucker, *The Effective Executive: The Definitive Guide to Getting the Right Things Done*, rev. ed. (New York: HarperCollins, 2006), 2.

5. Artie Buerk, in discussion with author, March 11, 2019.

6. Linda Creswell, in discussion with author, March 14, 2019.

7. Bob Sherwin, in discussion with author, March 20, 2019.

8. Howard Behar, in discussion with author, March 10, 2019.

9. Dean Radin, in discussion with author, March 9, 2019.

10. Barbara Basile, in discussion with author, March 11, 2019.

11. Jane Roberts, *The Nature of Personal Reality: Specific, Practical Techniques for Solving Everyday Problems and Enriching the Life You Know* (Novato, CA: New World Library, 1994), 34.